ROME

THE MINI ROUGH GUIDE

There are more than one hundred and fifty
Rough Guide travel, phrasebook, and music titles,
covering destinations from Amsterdam to Zimbabwe,
languages from Czech to Vietnamese, and music
from World to Opera and Jazz

Forthcoming titles include

Beijing • Cape Town • Croatia • Ecuador

Rough Guides on the Internet

www.roughguides.com

Rough Guide Credits

Text editor: Martin Dunford
Series editor: Mark Ellingham
Typesetting: Helen Ostick
Cartography: Maxine Repath,
Nichola Goodliffe, Ed Wright

Publishing Information

This first edition published April 2000 by
Rough Guides Ltd, 62–70 Shorts Gardens, London, WC2H 9AB

Distributed by the Penguin Group:
Penguin Books Ltd, 27 Wrights Lane, London W8 5TZ
Penguin Books USA Inc., 375 Hudson Street, New York 10014, USA
Penguin Books Australia Ltd, 487 Maroondah Highway,
PO Box 257, Ringwood, Victoria 3134, Australia
Penguin Books Canada Ltd, 10 Alcorn Avenue,
Toronto, Ontario, Canada M4V 1E4
Penguin Books (NZ) Ltd, 182–190 Wairau Road,
Auckland 10, New Zealand

Typeset in Bembo and Helvetica to an original design by Henry Iles.
Printed in Spain by Graphy Cems.

ISBN 1-85828-599-2

ROME

THE MINI ROUGH GUIDE

Written and researched by
**Martin Dunford, Kate Davies,
Jeffrey Kennedy
and Norman Roberson**

edited by
Martin Dunford

We set out to do something different when the first Rough Guide was published in 1982. Mark Ellingham, just out of university, was travelling in Greece. He brought along the popular guides of the day, but found they were all lacking in some way. They were either strong on ruins and museums but went on for pages without mentioning a beach or taverna. Or they were so conscious of the need to save money that they lost sight of Greece's cultural and historical significance. Also, none of the books told him anything about Greece's contemporary life – its politics, its culture, its people, and how they lived.

So with no job in prospect, Mark decided to write his own guidebook, one which aimed to provide practical information that was second to none, detailing the best beaches and the hottest clubs and restaurants, while also giving hard-hitting accounts of every sight, both famous and obscure, and providing up-to-the-minute information on contemporary culture. It was a guide that encouraged independent travellers to find the best of Greece, and was a great success, getting shortlisted for the Thomas Cook travel guide award, and encouraging Mark, along with three friends, to expand the series.

The Rough Guide list grew rapidly and the letters flooded in, indicating a much broader readership than had been anticipated, but one which uniformly appreciated the Rough Guide mix of practical detail and humour, irreverence and enthusiasm. Things haven't changed. The same four friends who began the series are still the caretakers of the Rough Guide mission today: to provide the most reliable, up-to-date and entertaining information to independent-minded travellers of all ages, on all budgets.

We now publish more than 150 titles and have offices in London and New York. The travel guides are written and researched by a dedicated team of more than 100 authors, based in Britain, Europe, the USA and Australia. We have also created a unique series of phrasebooks to accompany the travel series, along with an acclaimed series of music guides, and a best-selling pocket guide to the Internet and World Wide Web. We also publish comprehensive travel information on our Web site: **www.roughguides.com**

Help Us Update

We've gone to a lot of effort to ensure that this first edition of *The Rough Guide to Rome* is as up to date and accurate as possible. However, if you feel there are places we've underrated or over-praised, or find we've missed something good or covered something which has now gone, then please write: suggestions, comments or corrections are much appreciated.

We'll credit all contributions, and send a copy of the next edition (or any other Rough Guide if you prefer) for the best letters. Please mark letters: "Rough Guide Rome Update" and send to:

Rough Guides, 62–70 Shorts Gardens, London, WC2H 9AB,
or Rough Guides, 375 Hudson St, New York NY 10014.
Or send email to: mail@roughguides.co.uk
Online updates about this book can be found on
Rough Guides' Web site (see opposite)

The Author

Martin Dunford was born and bred in southeast London, where he still lives. He first visited Rome, to research this guide, in 1986. As Rough Guides' Travel Publisher, he is the only Rough Guide author to take fourteen years to complete a book.

Acknowledgements

The biggest **thanks** are due to Kate, Jeffrey and Norm, without whom this book would never have seen the light of day. Thanks are also due to David Price for proofreading, Max, Helen and Susanne for their patience, and Ed Wright for some seriously close work on the maps; to Jonathan Buckley for sound advice, not least spotting a cover image howler; to Jeremy and Kate for putting me up all those years ago; to Caroline, Russell and Sarah for the good company; and to Paddy and Mr Claws for their Zen-like calm.

Thanks from Norm go to Linda Bettman; to Kathleen Weil Garris-Brandt, Joe Connors, Marcia Hall, Darby Scott, Mac Bell, Lisa Fentress, Larissa Bonfante and Ili Nagy, for art history advice; and to Oscar Hijuleos for encouragement over the years. Thanks from Jeffrey go to Suzanne Hartley and Max Delgado for joining in with the restaurant research. Kate especially thanks her parents and mentors, Charles and Patty, and her twin sister Clarissa, as well as the Trinciarellis Charles, George, John, Erin, Shanna, and everyone at Enjoy Rome.

CONTENTS

Colour map section (back of book)

Introduction

O f all Italy's historic cities, it's perhaps **Rome** which exerts the most compelling fascination. There's more to see here than in any other city in the world, with the relics of over two thousand years of inhabitation packed into its sprawling urban area. You could spend a month here and still only scratch the surface. As a historic place, it is special enough; as a contemporary European capital, it is utterly unique.

Perfectly placed between Italy's North and South, and heartily despised by both, Rome is perhaps the perfect **capital** for a country like Italy. Once the seat of a great empire, and later the home of the papacy, which ruled its dominions from here with a distant and autocratic hand, it's still seen as a place somewhat apart from the rest of Italy, spending money made elsewhere on the corrupt and bloated government machine that runs the country. Romans, the thinking seems to go, are a lazy lot, not to be trusted and living very nicely off the fat of the rest of the land. Even Romans find it hard to disagree with this analysis: in a city of around four million, there are around 600,000 office-workers, compared to an industrial workforce of one sixth of that.

For the traveller, all of this is much less evident than the sheer weight of **history** that the city supports. There are of course the city's classical features, most visibly the Colosseum, and the Forum and Palatine Hill; but from here there's an almost uninterrupted sequence of monuments – from early Christian basilicas, Romanesque churches, Renaissance palaces, right up to the fountains and churches of the Baroque period, which perhaps more than any other era has determined the look of the city today. There is the modern epoch too, from the ponderous Neoclassical architecture of the post-Unification period to the self-publicizing edifices of the Mussolini years. All these various eras crowd in on one other to an almost overwhelming degree: there are medieval churches atop ancient basilicas above Roman palaces; houses and apartment blocks incorporate fragments of eroded Roman columns, carvings and inscriptions; roads and piazzas follow the lines of ancient amphitheatres and stadiums.

All of which is to say that Rome is not an easy place to absorb on one visit, and you need to approach things slowly, even if you only have a few days here. You can't see everything on your first visit to Rome, and there's no point in even trying. Most of the city's sights can be approached from a variety of directions, and it's part of the city's allure to stumble across things by accident, gradually piecing together the whole, rather than marching around to a timetable on a predetermined route. In any case, it's hard to get anywhere very fast. Despite regular pledges to ban motor vehicles from the city centre, the congestion can be awful. On foot, it's easy to lose a sense of direction winding about in the twisting old streets. In any case, you're so likely to come upon something interesting it hardly makes any difference.

Rome doesn't have the **nightlife** of, say, Paris or London, or even of its Italian counterparts to the north – culturally it's rather provincial – and its **food**, while delicious, is earthy rather than haute cuisine. But its atmosphere is like no other city – a monumental, busy capital and yet an appealingly relaxed place, with a centre that has yet to be taken over by chainstores and big multinational hotels. Above all, there has perhaps never been a better time to visit the city, whose notoriously crumbling infrastructure is looking and functioning better than it has done for some time – the result of the feverish activity that took place in the last months of 1999 to have the city centre looking its best for the Church's jubilee, which they expect to attract several million extra visitors. On the surface the city still looks much as it has done for years. But there are museums, churches and other buildings that have been "in restoration" as long as anyone can remember that have reopened, and some of the city's historic collections have been rehoused, making it all the more easy to get the most out of Rome.

Opening Hours

Most **shops and businesses** don't open until lunchtime or late afternoon on a Monday; during the rest of the week, opening times are generally Tuesday to Saturday, 9am to around 1pm, and then 4pm until around 7.30pm – although there are a few places in the city centre that are open right through. Most places are closed on Sundays. All but the most popular or touristed **churches** keep to fairly predictable hours, most opening early each morning, at 7am or 8am, and closing up around noon, and opening again from 4pm until around 7pm. **Archeological sites** keep longer hours, usually open from dawn until dusk. Most **museums** are closed Mondays, and then open from around 10am to 6pm, Tuesday to Saturday, and for half the day on Sunday.

Climate, clothes, currency

Rome is a year-round city, and you can really visit at any **time of year**. Some times, however, are better than others. If you can, you should avoid visiting Rome in **July and August**, when the weather is hot and sticky, and those Romans that don't make their living exclusively from the tourist industry have left town; many businesses are closed, and in those places that are open most of the patrons will be fellow-tourists. The weather is more comfortable in **May, June and September**, when most days will be warm but not unbearably so, and less humid, though you'll still find the city busy during these times; **April**, outside of Easter, and **October**, are quieter and the weather can still be clement – making this in many ways the ideal time to come. The **winter months** can be nice, with many of the city's more popular sights pleasantly uncrowded: the weather can be rainy but the temperatures are usually mild. Whenever you visit, you'd be well advised to book your **accommodation** in advance.

What to wear is almost as important as when to come. Sturdy comfortable shoes are essential – you're going to be doing a lot of walking – and, if you're here during the summer, you should wear loose, cool clothes, and a sunhat. Bear in mind that some sights – the catacombs, the Domus Aurea, even some churches – can be unlit and cold, even when it's warm outside, so dress in layers; bear in mind also that even on the hottest days women are required to cover up to enter many churches. Be frugal with your possessions when sightseeing, and only take out as much money, or jewellery, as you can bear to lose; pickpockets can be rife during the high season.

Finally **money**. The Italian national currency is the **lira**, and at time of writing there were around L3000 to the pound sterling, and L2000 to the US dollar. However, Italy is one of eleven European countries that have decided to adopt the European single currency – the **euro**. At the moment you can only make paper transactions in the new currency, but you will notice shops, restaurants and other businesses list prices in euros as well as lira. Euro notes will be in circulation from January 1, 2002, and are scheduled to replace the lira six months later.

Rome's average temperature (°C)

January	7.4	July	25.7
February	8.0	August	25.5
March	11.5	September	22.4
April	14.4	October	17.7
May	18.4	November	13.4
June	22.9	December	8.9

$$°C = (°F - 32) \text{ multiplied by } 5/9$$

THE GUIDE

Introducing the City

ome's **city centre** is divided neatly into distinct blocks. The warren of streets that makes up the **centro storico** occupies the hook of land on the left bank of the River Tiber, bordered to the east by Via del Corso and to the north and south by water. From here Rome's central core spreads east: across Via del Corso to the major shopping streets and alleys around the **Spanish Steps** down to the main artery of **Via Nazionale**; to the major sites of the **ancient city** to the south; and to the huge expanse of the **Villa Borghese** park to the north. The left bank of the river is oddly distanced from the main hum of this part of the city, home to the **Vatican** and **Saint Peter's**, and, to the south of these, **Trastevere** – even in ancient times a distinct entity from the city proper and still with a reputation for separatism, as well as the focus of much of the city centre's nightlife.

To see most of this, you'd be mad to risk your blood pressure in any kind of vehicle, and really the best way to **get around** the city centre and points east to Termini is to walk. The same goes for the ancient sites, and probably the Vatican and Trastevere too – although for these last two you might want to jump on a bus going across the river. Keep public transport for the longer hops, down to Testaccio, EUR or the catacombs, or other more scattered attractions.

ARRIVAL

By air

Rome has two **airports**: Leonardo da Vinci, better known simply as Fiumicino, which handles most scheduled flights, and Ciampino, where you'll arrive if you're travelling on a charter, or with Go or one of the other low-cost European airlines. **Taxis** in from either airport cost around L80,000, more at night, and take 30–45 minutes; they're worth considering if you are in a group but otherwise the public transport connections are reasonable.

Fiumicino is connected to the centre of Rome by direct trains, which make the thirty-minute ride to Termini for L16,000; services begin at 7.37am, and then leave hourly from 8.07am until 10.07pm. Alternatively, there are more frequent trains to Trastevere, Ostiense and Tiburtina stations, each on the edge of the city centre, roughly every twenty minutes from 6.27am to 11.27pm; tickets to these stations cost L8000, and Tiburtina and Ostiense are just a short metro ride from Termini, making it a much cheaper (and not necessarily slower) journey; or you can catch city bus #175 from Ostiense, or city bus #492 or #649 from Tiburtina, to the centre of town. These cheaper alternatives do inevitably, however, involve a certain amount more bag-hauling.

There are no direct connections between the city centre and **Ciampino**. Hourly buses run from the airport to the Anagnina metro station, at the end of line A – a thirty-

**The telephone code for Rome is 06; for Italy it is 39.
You must dial 06 before any Roman number, even if
you are in Rome.**

minute journey (L2000), from where it's a twenty-minute ride into the centre. Failing that, you can take a bus from the airport to Ciampino overground train station, a ten-minute journey, and then take a train into Termini, which is a further twenty minutes. The BA budget off-shoot, Go, incidentally, lay on their own bus to Piazza Santa Maria Maggiore, half an hour after the arrival of each of their flights, but it's no quicker and they charge L18,000 for it.

By train

Travelling by **train** from most places in Italy, or indeed from other parts of Europe, you arrive at **Stazione Termini**, centrally placed for all parts of the city and meeting-point of the two metro lines and many city bus routes. There's a **left-luggage** facility here (daily 5:15am–midnight; L5000 per piece every 12hr), but bear in mind that they won't accept plastic bags; note that the Enjoy Rome office (see below) will also look after its customers' luggage.

Among **other rail stations** in Rome, Tiburtina, is a stop for some north–south intercity trains; selected routes around Lazio are handled by the Regionali platforms of Stazione Termini (a further five-minute walk from the regular platforms); and there's also the COTRAL urban train station on Piazzale Flaminio, which runs to La Giustiniana – the so-called Roma-Nord line.

By bus

Arriving by **bus** can leave you in any one of a number of places around the city. The main stations include Ponte Mammolo (trains from Tivoli and Subiaco); Lepanto (Cerveteri, Civitavecchia, Bracciano area); EUR Fermi (Nettuno, Anzio, southern Lazio coast); Anagnina (Castelli

Romani); Saxa Rubra (Viterbo and around). All of these stations are on a metro line, except Saxa Rubra, which is on the Roma-Nord line and connected by trains every fifteen minutes with the station at Piazzale Flaminio, on metro line A. Eurolines buses from outside Italy terminate on Piazza della Repubblica.

By road

Coming into the city by **road** can be quite confusing. If you are on the A1 highway coming from the north take the exit "Roma Nord"; from the south, follow exit "Roma Est". Both lead you to the Grande Raccordo Anulare, which circles the city and is connected with all of the major arteries into the city centre – the Via Cassia from the north, Via Salaria from the northeast, Via Tiburtina or Via Nomentana from the east, Via Appia Nuova and the Pontina from the south, Via Prenestina and Via Casilina or Via Cristoforo Colombo from the southeast, and Via Aurelia from the northwest.

INFORMATION

There are **tourist information booths** on arrival at Fiumicino (daily 8.15am–7.15pm; ℂ06.6595.6074), and at Termini (daily 8.15am–7.15pm; ℂ06.487.1270 or ℂ06.482.5078), although the long queues that often develop at both of these mean you're usually better off heading straight for the main **tourist office** at Via Parigi 5 (Mon–Fri 8.15am–7.15pm, Sat 8.15am–1.45pm; ℂ06.4889.9253 or ℂ06.4889.9255), ten minutes' walk from Termini. They have free maps that should – together with our own – be ample for finding your way around, although the rest of their information can be uneven and out of date. There are also **information kiosks** in key locations around

Information Kiosk locations

Spanish Steps, Largo Goldoni (✆06.6813.6061)
San Giovani, Piazza San Giovani in Laterno (✆06.7720.3535)
Via Nazionale, Palazzo delle Esposizioni (✆06.4782.4525)
Piazza Navona, Piazza delle Cinque Lune (✆06.6880.9240)
Castel Sant'Angelo, Piazza Pia (✆06.6880.9707)
Forum, Piazza del Tempio della Pace (✆06.6992.4307)
Trastevere, Piazza Sonnino (✆06.5833.3457)
Santa Maria Maggiore, Via dell'Olmata (✆06.4788.0294)

the city centre (daily 9am–6pm). They too often have out-
dated general information but the staff usually speak
English, and they are useful for free maps, directions and
new information (opening times, for example) about nearby sights.

You might be better off bypassing the official tourist
offices altogether and going to **Enjoy Rome**, Via Varese 39
(Mon–Fri 8.30am–2pm & 3.30–6pm, Sat 8.30am–2pm;
✆06.445.1843), whose friendly, English-speaking staff run a
free room-finding service; they also organize tours (see
below), and have a left-luggage service for those who take
them. Their information is often more up to date and reliable than that handed out by the various tourist offices, and
they will also advise on where to eat, drink, and party, if
you so wish.

For what's-on information, the city's best source of **listings** is perhaps *Romae'è* (L2000, Thursdays), which has a
helpful section in English giving information on tours,
clubs, restaurants, services and weekly events. The ex-pat
bi-weekly, *Wanted in Rome* (L1500, every other
Wednesday), which is entirely in English, is also a useful
source of information, especially if you're looking for an
apartment or work. If you understand a bit of Italian, there's

7

Rome on the Web

www.capitolium.org
The official Web site of the Roman forums, with pictorial reconstructions of how the ruins would have looked in their day, as well as how they look now; material on life in ancient Rome; and even a live Web view of the forum.

www.catacombe.roma.it
Official site of Rome's Christian catacombs, with visuals, historical descriptions, and explanations of ancient symbols – a good supplement to our own accounts if you're extra keen.

www.comune.roma.it
Italian-language Web site of the Rome city authorities.

www.enjoyrome.com
Helpful site of the helpful Rome tourist organization, with information on accommodation and tours – and links to other popular Rome Web sites.

www.gamberorosse.it/e/romausa
Nice site in English, detailing walks around Rome that take in Gambero Rosso's speciality – restaurants and bars.

www.initaly.com/regions/latium
A quirky site that gives links, and subjective rundowns, on everything Italian – and in this case Roman.

www.roma2000.it
Everything about Rome in the Millennium, with comprehensive, if irregularly updated, information on all aspects of the city.

www.romeguide.it
The place to go whether you're after a bus or walking tour of the city centre, a guide to a particular monument or gallery, even the chance to go on a "ghost tour" of Rome.

www.vatican.va
Slick, multilingual Web site of the Holy See, with material – some still under construction – on the Vatican Museums, the institutions of the city state, its newspaper online, and a calendar of the whole of the Holy Year's events.

www.venere.it/home/lazio/roma
Probably the best site for accessing the Web pages of those hotels that have them – and booking rooms online.

Time Out Roma (L2000, Thursdays), a weekly review full of listings as well as articles on the trendiest everything in Rome, and the daily arts pages of the Rome **newspaper**, *Il Messaggero*, which can be found in most bars for the customers to read, and lists movies, plays and major musical events. The newspaper *La Repubblica* also includes the "*Trova Roma*" section in its Thursday edition, another handy guide to current offerings.

CITY TRANSPORT

Like most Italian cities, even the larger ones, the best way to get around Rome is to **walk** – you'll see more and will better appreciate the city. The city wasn't built for motor traffic, and it shows in the traffic jams, the pollution, and the bad tempers of its drivers. That said, its **bus service**, run by ATAC, is, on the whole, a good one – cheap, reliable and as quick as the clogged streets allow. Remember to

Travellers with Disabilities

Only two stops on Line A have accessibility for **disabled persons** (Cipro-Musei Vaticani and Valle Aurelia) but bus #591 does the same route and can accommodate those with disabilities. Also, be advised that on Line B, Circo Massimo, Colosseo and Cavour do not have accessibility but bus #75 stops at those sights and has new buses that can accommodate those with disabilities (although you may have to wait for a few of the older buses to go by).

board through the rear doors and punch your ticket as you enter.

To sidestep the traffic, Rome also has a **metro**, which runs from 5.30am to 11.30pm, though it's not as useful as you might think, since its two lines are more directed at ferrying commuters out to the suburbs than transporting tourists around the city centre. Nonetheless, there are a few useful city-centre stations: Termini is the hub of both lines, and there are stations at the Colosseum, Piazza Barberini and the Spanish Steps.

When the buses and the metro stop around midnight, a network of **nightbuses** clicks into service, accessing most parts of the city through to about 5am; they normally have conductors so you can buy a ticket on board (but keep spare tickets handy just in case); they are easily identified by the owl symbol above the "bus notturno" schedule. During the day there are also a few **tram** routes in operation, one of which – the #8, connecting Viale Trastevere with Largo Argentina – is brand new and very quick.

Maps, tickets, passes

Metro **maps** are posted up in every station, and we've

printed one at the end of this book. If you're going to use the system a lot, especially the buses, it may be worth investing in the excellent detailed **Lozzi transport map** (L8000), available from most newsstands, or getting hold of the official **ATAC map** – free from tourist information offices, and from the **ATAC information office** in the centre of Piazza dei Cinquecento – although this can be out-of-date and somewhat unreliable. There is a toll-free **enquiries line** (Mon–Fri 9am–1pm & 2–5pm; ℂ167.431.784) for information on COTRAL services in Rome and Lazio.

Flat-fare **tickets** cost L1500 each and are good for any number of bus rides and one metro ride within 75 minutes of validating them. Buy them from tobacconists, news-stands and ticket machines located in all metro stations and at major bus stops. You can also get a **day pass**, valid on all city transport until midnight of the day purchased, for L6000, or a **seven-day pass** for L24,000. Finally, it's worth knowing that there's a L100,000 spot fine for fare-dodging, and pleading a foreigner's ignorance will get you nowhere. **BIRG tickets** (regional transport passes) for COTRAL and ATAC services, available from machines in the metro, tabacchi and newsstands, are well worth buying if you are going out of Rome for the day; prices range from L3500 to L15,500, depending on the distance you intend to travel.

Taxis

The easiest way to get a **taxi** is to find the nearest taxi stand (*fermata dei taxi*) – central ones include Termini, Piazza Venezia, Piazza San Silvestro, Piazza di Spagna and Piazza Barberini. Alternatively, taxis can be radio paged (ℂ06.3570, ℂ06.4994, ℂ06.4157 or ℂ06.5551), but remember that you'll pay for the time it takes to get to you. Only take licensed yellow or white cabs, and make sure the meter is switched on; a card in every official taxi explains – in English – the extra charges for luggage, late-night, Sundays and holidays, and airport journeys. To give you a rough idea of how much taxis cost, you can reckon on a journey from one side of the centre to cost around L10,000, if the traffic isn't too bad, though the supplement after 10pm is L5000, L2000 on a Sunday.

Car and bike rental

Car rental is only worthwhile for trips out of the city, but renting a **bike** or **scooter** can be a nippy way to negotiate Rome's clogged streets (see Chapter 21, "Directory" for outlets).

Tours

A number of companies run **organized trips** around the city centre, though these are, for the most part, quite pricey and not really worth the money. Probably the best value, for general orientation and a glance at the main sights, is the ATAC-run **#110 bus tour**, which in summer leaves Termini Station at 10.30am, 2pm, 3pm, 5pm, 6pm and costs L15,000 for a three-hour jaunt, with twenty-minute stops at the Vatican, in Via dei Fori Imperiali and in Piazza Venezia. The air-conditioned grey coach, with pictures of Rome's monuments on the sides, stands out against the ocean of orange buses.

Of several companies that organize all kinds of tours, one of the best is **Enjoy Rome**, Via Varese 39 (06.445.1843), which runs inexpensive walking and cycling tours of Rome given by native English speakers, as well as day trips to

Useful bus routes

#23-Piazza Clodio-Piazza Risorgimento-Ponte Vittorio Emanuele II-Ponte Garibaldi-Via Marmorata-Piazzale Ostiense-Basilica di S. Paolo.

#64 Termini: Piazza della Repubblica–Via Nazionale–Piazza Venezia–Corso Vittorio Emanuele II–St Peter's.

#492 Stazione Tiburtina–Termini–Piazza Barberini–Via del Corso–Piazza Venezia–Largo Argentina–Corso del Rinascimento–Piazza Cavour–Piazza Risorgimento.

#660 Largo Colli Albani-Via Appia Nuova–Via Appia Antica.

#714 Termini–Santa Maria Maggiore–San Giovanni in Laterano–Baths of Caracalla–EUR.

#590 Same route as Metro Line A but with accessibility for disabled; runs every 90 minutes.

#910 Termini-Piazza della Repubblica-Via Piedmonte-Via Pinciana (Villa Borghese)-Piazza Euclide-Palazetto dello Sport-Piazza Mancini.

Night Buses
#29N Piazzale Ostiense-Lungotevere Aventino-Lungotevere De'Cenci-Via Crescenzio-Via Barletta-Piazza Marina-Via Belle Arte-Viale Liegi-Viale Regina Margherita-Via dei Marruccini-Via Labicana-Viale Aventino.

#40N Same route as Metro line B.

#55N Same route as Metro line A.

#78N Piazza Clodio-Piazzale Flaminio-Piazza Cavour-Largo di Torre Argentina-Piazza Venezia-Via Nazionale-Termini.

Pompeii. **Il Sogno**, Viale Regina Margherita 192 (℡06.8530.1758, fax 06.8530.1756), runs all kinds of tours,

Useful Tram Routes

Trams

#8 Viale Trastevere–Largo Argentina.

#19 Porto Maggiore–Viale Regina Margherita–Viale Belle Arti–Ottaviano–Piazza Risorgimento.

#30 Piramide–Viale Aventino–Colosseum–San Giovanni–Viale Regina Margherita–Villa Giulia.

and is perhaps the best one-stop place to go if you're not sure what you want. Finally, for the ultra-personal touch, **Norman Roberson** (℅06. 5820.3105), one of the contributors to this guide, specializes in tours of the ancient sights and some of the larger galleries, as well as the Etruscan sites north of the city; contact him by phone, or get details from *www.agora.stm.it/n.roberson/home.htm*

The Centro Storico

The real city centre of Rome is the **centro storico**, or historic centre, which makes up the greater part of the roughly triangular knob of land that bulges into a bend in the Tiber, above and below Corso Vittorio Emanuele, to the west of Via del Corso, Rome's main street. This area, known in Roman times as the *Campus Martius*, was outside the ancient city centre, a low-lying area that was mostly given over to barracks and sporting arenas, together with several temples, including the Pantheon. Later it became the heart of the Renaissance city, and nowadays it's the part of the town that is densest in interest, an unruly knot of narrow streets and alleys that holds some of the best of Rome's classical and Baroque heritage and its most vivacious street- and nightlife.

The main square and transport hub of **Piazza Venezia** is a good orientation point: to its north lies the main body of the old centre of Rome, with the graceful oval of **Piazza Navona** and the great dome of the **Pantheon** at the heart of its tangle of streets and churches; to its west is more of the same, focusing on the busy squares of **Campo de' Fiori** and **Largo Argentina**, and fading as you move towards the river into Rome's ancient **Jewish Ghetto**. To the south is the **Capitoline Hill** and its museums, on the edge of Rome's ancient centre – covered in Chapter 4.

Piazza Venezia and South

Piazza Venezia is not so much a square as a road junction, and a busy one at that. But it's a good central place to start your wanderings, close to both the medieval and Renaissance centre of Rome and the bulk of the ruins of the ancient city. Flanked on all sides by imposing buildings, it's a dignified focal point for the city in spite of the traffic, and a spot you'll find yourself returning to time and again.

PALAZZO VENEZIA

Map 3, J6. Via del Plebiscito 118. Tues–Sat 9am–1.30pm, Sun 9am–1pm; L8000.

Forming the western side of the piazza, **Palazzo Venezia** was the first large Renaissance palace in the city, built for the Venetian Pope Paul II in the mid-fifteenth century and for a long time the embassy of the Venetian Republic. More famously, Mussolini moved in here while in power, occupying the vast *Sala del Mappamondo* and making his declamatory speeches to the huge crowds below from the small balcony facing on to the piazza proper. In those days the palace lights would be left on to give the impression of constant activity in what was the centre of the Fascist government and war effort; now it's a much more peripheral building, a venue for great temporary exhibitions and home to a museum of Renaissance arts and crafts made up of the magpie-ish collection of Paul II (times and prices above).

SAN MARCO

Map 3, J6. Daily except Mon morning and Wed afternoon 8.30am–12.30pm & 4–7pm.

Adjacent to the palace on its southern side, the church of **San Marco**, accessible from Piazza San Marco, is a tidy basilica rebuilt in 833 and added to by various Renaissance and eighteenth-century popes. Currently under restoration, it's a warm, cosy church, restored by Paul II – who added the graceful portico and gilded ceiling – with an apse mosaic dating from the ninth century showing Pope Gregory offering his church to Christ.

VITTORIO EMANUELE MONUMENT

Map 3, K7.

Everything pales into insignificance beside the marble monstrosity rearing up across the street – the **Vittorio Emanuele Monument** or "Vittoriano", erected at the turn of the century as the "Altar of the Nation" to commemorate Italian Unification. Variously likened in the past to a typewriter (because of its shape), and, by American GIs, to a wedding cake (the marble used will never mellow with age), King Vittorio Emanuele II, who it's in part supposed to honour, probably wouldn't have thought much of it – he was by all accounts a modest man; indeed, the only person who seems to have benefited from the building is the prime minister at the time, who was (perhaps not entirely coincidentally) a deputy for Brescia, from where the marble was supplied. At the top of the stairs is the Tomb of the Unknown Soldier, flanked by eternal flames and a permanent guard of honour. Incidentally, the equestrian statue of the king here is claimed to be the world's largest (its moustache is apparently 3m long) – though perhaps the greatest irony is that all this memorializes a royal dynasty that produced just four monarchs.

THE CAPITOLINE HILL

The real pity about the Vittorio Emanuele Monument is that it obscures views of the **Capitoline Hill** behind – once, in the days of Imperial Rome, the spiritual and political centre of the Roman Empire. Apart from anything else, this hill has contributed key words to the English language, including, of course, "capitol", and "money", which comes from the temple to Juno Moneta that once stood up here and housed the Roman mint. The Capitoline also played a significant role in medieval and Renaissance times: the flamboyant fourteenth-century dictator Cola di Rienzo, stood here in triumph in 1347, and was murdered here by an angry mob seven years later – a humble nineteenth-century statue marks the spot where he is said to have died. Michelangelo gave the piazza its present form, redesigning it as a symbol of Rome's regeneration after the city was sacked in 1527.

SANTA MARIA IN ARACOELI

Map 3, K7. Daily: summer 7am–noon & 4–6.30pm; winter closes 5.30pm.

The church of **Santa Maria in Aracoeli** crowns the highest point on the Capitoline Hill, built on the site of a temple to Jupiter where, according to legend, the Tiburtine Sybil foretold the birth of Christ. Reached by a flight of steps erected by Cola di Rienzo in 1348, it's a steep climb to the top, but the church is worth it, one of Rome's most ancient basilicas. Inside, in the first chapel on the right, there are some fine, humane frescoes by Pinturicchio recording the life of San Bernardino – realistic tableaux of landscapes and bustling town scenes. The church is also known for its role as keeper of the so-called "Bambino", a small statue of the child Christ, carved from the wood of a Gethsemane olive tree, that is said to have healing powers and was traditionally called out to the sickbeds of the ill and dying all over the city, its coach commanding instant right of way through the heavy Rome traffic. The Bambino was stolen in 1994, however, and a copy now stands in its place, in a small chapel to the left of the high altar.

THE CAPITOLINE MUSEUMS

Map 3, K8. Tues–Sun 9am–7pm; L10,000, free last Sun of month.
Next door to the steps up to Santa Maria, the **cordonata** is an elegant, gently rising ramp, topped with two Roman statues of Castor and Pollux, which leads to the **Campidoglio** one of Rome's most elegant squares. Designed by Michelangelo in the last years of his life for Pope Paul III, who was determined to hammer Rome back into shape for a visit by Charles V, the square wasn't in fact completed until the late seventeenth century. Michelangelo balanced the piazza, redesigning the facade of what is now Palazzo dei Conservatori and projecting an identical building across the way, known as Palazzo Nuovo.

These buildings, which should now be open again after a lengthy restoration, are home to the **Capitoline Museums** and feature some of the city's most important ancient sculpture. Both are angled slightly to focus on **Palazzo Senatorio**, Rome's town hall. In the centre of the square Michelangelo placed an equestrian statue of Emperor Marcus Aurelius, which had previously stood unharmed for years outside San Giovanni in Laterano; early Christians had refrained from melting it down because they believed it to be of the Emperor Constantine. After careful restoration, the original is behind a glass wall in the Palazzo Nuovo, and a copy has taken its place at the centre of the piazza.

THE CAPITOLINE MUSEUMS

Palazzo Nuovo

Of the two museum buildings, it's the **Palazzo Nuovo** (on the left) that really steals the show. Just inside the entrance is the original Marcus Aurelius statue, and the first floor concentrates some of the best of the city's Roman copies of Greek sculpture into half a dozen or so rooms and a long gallery crammed with elegant statuary. There's a remarkable, controlled statue of the *Dying Gaul*, a Roman copy of a Hellenistic original; a naturalistic *Boy with Goose* – another copy; an original grappling depiction of *Eros and Psyche*; a *Satyr Resting*, after a piece by Praxiteles, that was the inspiration for Hawthorne's book the *Marble Faun*; and the red marble *Laughing Silenus*, another Roman copy of a Greek original. Walk through, too, to the so-called *Sala degli Imperatori*, with its busts of Roman emperors and other famous names, including a young Augustus, a cruel Caracalla, and a portrait of Helena, the mother of Constantine, reclining gracefully. And don't miss the *Capitoline Venus*, housed in a room on its own – a coy, delicate piece, again based on a work by Praxiteles.

Palazzo dei Conservatori

The same ticket will get you into the **Palazzo dei Conservatori** across the square (though it must be on the same day) – a larger, more varied collection, with more ancient sculpture but also later pieces. Littered around the courtyard are the feet and other fragments of a gigantic statue of Constantine. Inside, in various first-floor wings, there are friezes and murals showing events from Roman history, a couple of enormous statues of popes Innocent X (by Algardi) and Urban VIII (by Bernini), the exquisite *Spinario* – a Hellenistic work from the first century BC showing a boy plucking a thorn from his foot – and the sacred symbol of Rome, the Etruscan bronze she-wolf nursing the mythic founders of the city; the twins themselves are not Etruscan but were added by Pollaiuolo in the late fifteenth century. Look, too, for the so-called *Esquiline Venus* and *Capitoline Tensa*, the latter a reconstructed chariot in bronze; and the soft *Muse Polymnia* and a gargantuan Roman copy of *Athena*.

The second floor pinacoteca holds Renaissance painting from the fourteenth century to the late seventeenth century – well-labelled, with descriptions of each painting in Italian and English. The paintings fill half a dozen rooms or so, and highlights include a couple of portraits by Van Dyck and a penetrating *Portrait of a Crossbowman* by Lorenzo Lotto, a pair of paintings from 1590 by Tintoretto – a *Flagellation* and *Christ Crowned with Thorns* – some nice small-scale work by Annibale Carracci, and a very fine early work by Lodovico Carracci, *Head of a Boy*. There are also several sugary works by Guido Reni, done at the end of his life. In one of two large main galleries, there's a vast picture by Guercino, depicting the *Burial of Santa Petronilla* (the legendary daughter of St Peter, who died young), which used to hang in St Peter's and arrived here via the Quirinale palace and the Louvre, to hang alongside several other works by the same artist, notably a lovely, contemplative Persian Sybil and a wonderful picture of Cleopatra cowed before a young and victorious Octavius. In the same room, there are also two paintings by Caravaggio, one a replica of the young *John the Baptist* which hangs in the Palazzo Doria-Pamphili, the other a famous canvas known as the *Fortune-Teller* – an early work that's an adept study in deception.

SAN PIETRO IN CARCERE

Map 3, L8. Daily: summer 9am–noon & 2.30–6pm; winter 9am–noon & 2–5pm; donation expected.

After seeing the museums, walk around behind the Palazzo

Senatorio for a great view down onto the Forum, with the Colosseum in the background. On the right, Via del Monte Tarpeio follows, as its name suggests, the brink of the old **Tarpeian Rock**, from which traitors would be thrown in ancient times – so-called after Tarpeia, who betrayed the city to the Sabines. Steps lead down from here to the little church of **San Pietro in Carcere**, built above the ancient Mamertine Prison, where spies, vanquished soldiers and other enemies of the Roman state were incarcerated, and where St Peter himself was held. Steps lead down into the murky depths of the jail, where you can see the bars to which he was chained, along with the spring the saint is said to have created to baptize the other prisoners down here. At the top of the staircase, hollowed out of the honeycomb of stone, is an imprint claimed to be of St Peter's head as he tumbled down the stairs (though when the prison was in use, the only access was through a hole in the ceiling). It's an unappealing place even now, and you won't be sorry to leave – through an exit cunningly placed to lead you through the gift shop.

North of Piazza Venezia

Immediately **north of Piazza Venezia** is the *centro storico* proper. It's here that most people find the Rome they have been looking for – the Rome of small crumbling piazzas, Renaissance churches and fountains, blind alleys and streets humming with scooters and foot-traffic. Whichever direction you wander in there's something to see; indeed it's part of the appeal of Rome that even the most aimless ambling leads you past some breathlessly beautiful and historic spots.

VIA DEL CORSO

Map 2, E9–E7

The boundary of the historic centre to the east, **Via del Corso** is Rome's main thoroughfare, leading all the way from Piazza Venezia at its southern end up to the Piazza del Popolo to the north. On its eastern side, it gives onto the swish shopping streets that lead up to Piazza di Spagna, on the western side the web of streets that tangles its way right down to the Tiber. So named for races that used to take place along here during Renaissance times, the street has had its fair share of famous residents during the years: Goethe lived for two years at no.18, close to the Piazza del Popolo end; the Shelleys – Percy and Mary – lived for several years in the Palazzo Vesporio, at 375 Via del Corso (now a bank), during which time they lost their son William to a fever. More recently, it has become Rome's principal shopping street, home to a mixture of upmarket boutiques and chain stores that make it a busy stretch during the day, full of hurrying pedestrians and crammed buses, but a relatively dead one come the evening.

GALLERIA DORIA PAMPHILI

Map 3, J5. Via del Collegio Romano 2. Jan–Aug 15 & Sept–Dec Mon–Wed & Fri–Sun 10am–5pm; L13,000; private apartments tours every 30min 10.30am–12.30pm; L5000.

Walking north from Piazza Venezia, the first building on the left of Via Del Corso, the Palazzo Doria Pamphili, is among the city's finest Rococo palaces. Inside, through an entrance on Piazza di Collegio Romano, the **Galleria Doria Pamphili** constitutes one of Rome's best private late-Renaissance art collections.

The private apartments

The Doria Pamphili family still lives in part of the building, and the first part of the gallery is made up of a series of **private apartments**, furnished in the style of the original palace, through which you're guided by way of a free audio-tour narrated by the urbane Jonathan Pamphili. On view is the large and elegant reception hall of the original palace, off which there is a room where Innocent X used to receive guests, complete with a portrait of the Pamphili pope. There's also a couple of side salons filled with busts and portraits of the rest of the family; a late – and probably by Rococo standards, rather pokey – ballroom, complete with a corner terrace from which the band played; and a private chapel, which astonishingly contains the incorruptible body of St Theodora, swathed in robes, and the relics of St Justin under the altar.

The picture gallery

Beyond here, the **picture gallery** extends around a courtyard, the paintings mounted in the style of the time, crammed in frame-to-frame, floor-to-ceiling. The labelling is better than it once was, with sporadic paintings labelled, and selected others numbered and described on the audiotour, but it's still deliberately old-fashioned, and perhaps all the better for it. Just inside, at the corner of the courtyard, there's a badly cracked bust of Innocent X by Bernini, which the sculptor apparently replaced in a week with the more famous version down the hall, in a room off to the left, where Bernini appears to have captured the pope about to erupt into laughter. In the same room, Velazquez's famous painting of the same man is quite different, depicting a rather irritable character regarding the viewer with impatience.

The rest of the collection is just as rich in interest, and there are many paintings and pieces of sculpture worth lingering over. There is perhaps Rome's best concentration of Dutch and Flemish paintings, including a rare Italian work by Bruegel the Elder, showing a naval battle being fought outside Naples, complete with Vesuvius, Castel Nuovo and other familiar landmarks, along with a highly realistic portrait of two old men, by Quentin Metsys, and a Hans Memling *Deposition*, in the furthest rooms, as well as a further Metsys painting – the fabulously ugly *Moneylenders and their Clients* – in the main gallery. There is also a *St Jerome*, by the Spanish painter Giuseppe Ribera, one of 44 he is supposed to have painted of the saint; Carracci's bucolic *Flight into Egypt*, painted shortly before the artist's death; two paintings by Caravaggio – *Mary Magdalene* and *John the Baptist*; and *Salome with the head of St John*, by Titian. Spare some time, also, for the marvellous classical statuary, busts, sarcophagi and figurines, displayed in the Aldobrandini room and on the Via del Corso side of the main gallery. All in all, it's a marvellous collection of work, displayed in a wonderfully appropriate setting.

SANT'IGNAZIO

Map 3, I4. Daily 7.30am–12.30pm & 4–7.15pm.

The next left off Via del Corso after the palace leads into **Piazza Sant'Ignazio**, a lovely little square, laid out like a theatre set and dominated by the facade of the Jesuit church of **Sant'Ignazio**. The saint isn't actually buried here; appropriately, for the founder of the Jesuit order, he's in the Gesù church a little way south. But it's a spacious structure, worth visiting for its marvellous Baroque ceiling by Andrea del Pozzo showing the entry of St Ignatius into paradise, a spectacular work that employs sledgehammer trompe l'oeil effects, notably in the mock cupola painted into the dome of the crossing. Stand on the disc in the centre of the nave, the focal point for the ingenious rendering of perspective: figures in various states of action and repose, conversation and silence, fix you with stares from their classical pediment.

THE PANTHEON

Map 3, G4. Mon–Sat 9am–6.30pm, Sun 9am–1pm; free

Via del Seminario leads down to **Piazza della Rotonda**, one of the city's most picturesque squares, and perhaps suffering because of it, invariably thronged with sight-weary tourists, hawkers and street musicians, besieging the café tables that fringe the edge. The waters of the fountains in the middle are a soothing influence, an eighteenth-century construction topped by yet another obelisk, but the main focus of interest is of course the **Pantheon**, which forms the square's southern edge, easily the most complete ancient Roman structure in the city, and along with the Colosseum, visually the most impressive. Though originally a temple that formed part of Marcus Agrippa's redesign of the Campus Martius in around 27 BC – hence the inscription – it's since been proved that the building was entirely rebuilt by the emperor Hadrian and finished around the year 125 AD. It's a formidable architectural achievement even now, although like the city's other Roman monuments, it would have been much more sumptuous in its day. It was consecrated as a Christian site in 609 AD and dedicated to Santa Maria ai Martiri in allusion to the Christian bones that were found here; a thousand years later, the bronze roof was stripped from the ceiling of the portico by Pope Urban VIII, to be melted down for the baldacchino in St Peter's and the cannons of the Castel Sant'Angelo. (Interestingly, some of the "stolen" bronze later found its way back here when, after Unification, the cannons were in turn melted down to provide materials for the tombs of two Italian kings, which are housed in the right and left chapels.)

Inside, you get the best impression of the engineering expertise of Hadrian: the diameter is precisely equal to its height (43m), the hole in the centre of the dome – from which shafts of sunlight descend to illuminate the musty interior – a full 9m across. Most impressively, there are no visible arches or vaults to hold the whole thing up; instead they're sunk into the concrete of the walls of the building. Again, it would have been richly decorated, the coffered ceiling heavily stuccoed and the niches filled with the statues of gods. Now, apart from the sheer size of the place, the main thing of interest is the tomb of Raphael, between the second and third chapel on the left, with an inscription by the humanist bishop Pietro Bembo: "Living, great Nature feared he might outvie Her works, and dying, fears herself may die." The same kind of sentiments might well have been reserved for the Pantheon itself.

SANTA MARIA SOPRA MINERVA

Map 3, H5. Mon–Sat 7am–7pm, Sun 8am–7pm

There's more artistic splendour on view behind the Pantheon, though Bernini's **Elephant Statue** doesn't really prepare you for the church of Santa Maria sopra Minerva beyond. The statue is Bernini's most endearing piece of work, if not his most characteristic: a cheery elephant trumpeting under the weight of the obelisk he carries on his back – a reference to Pope Alexander VII's reign and supposed to illustrate the fact that strength should support wisdom. **Santa Maria sopra Minerva** is Rome's only Gothic church, and worth a look just for that, though its soaring lines have since been overburdened by marble and frescoes. Built in the late thirteenth century on the ruins of a temple to Minerva, it is also one of Rome's art-treasure churches, crammed with the tombs and self-indulgences of wealthy Roman families. Of these, the Carafa chapel, in the south transept, is the best known, holding Filippino Lippi's fresco of *The Assumption*, a bright, effervescent piece of work, below which one painting shows a hopeful Carafa (the religious zealot, Pope Paul IV) being presented to the Virgin Mary by Thomas Aquinas; another depicts Aquinas confounding the heretics in the sight of two beautiful young boys – the future Medici popes Leo X and Clement VII (the equestrian statue of Marcus Aurelius, destined for the Capitoline Hill, is just visible in the background). You should look too at the figure of *Christ Bearing the Cross*, on the left-hand side of the main altar, a serene work that Michelangelo completed for the church in 1521.

SANT'IVO

Map 3, F5. Sun 10am–1pm.

A few steps west of the Pantheon, on Corso del Rinascimento, the rather blank facade of the **Palazzo della Sapienza** cradles the church of **Sant'Ivo** – from the outside at least, one of Rome's most impressive churches, with a playful facade designed by Borromini. Though originally built for the most Barberini pope, Urban VIII, the building actually spans the reign of three pontiffs. Each of the two small towers is topped with the weird, blancmange-like groupings that are the symbol of the Chigi family (representing the hills of Monti Paschi), and the central cupola spirals helter-skelter-fashion to its zenith, crowned with flames that are supposed to represent the sting of the Barberini bee, their family symbol. Inside, too, is very cleverly designed, very light and spacious given the small space the church is squeezed into, rising to the tall parabolic cupola.

SAN LUIGI DEI FRANCESI

Map 3, F4. Daily except Thurs afternoon 7.30am–12.30pm & 3.30–7pm.

A short walk from here, at the bottom of Via della Scrofa, the French national church of **San Luigi dei Francesi** is another church in the vicinity of the Pantheon that is worth a look, mainly for the works by Caravaggio that it numbers amongst its collection. In the last chapel on the left are three paintings: the *Calling of St Matthew*, in which Christ points to Matthew, who is illuminated by a shaft of sunlight; Matthew visited by an angel as he writes the Gospel; and the saint's martyrdom. Caravaggio's first public commission, these paintings were actually rejected at first, partly on grounds of indecorum, and it took considerable reworking by the artist before they were finally accepted.

PIAZZA NAVONA

Map 3, E4–E5.

Piazza Navona is Rome's most famous square. Lined with cafés and restaurants, pedestrianized and often thronged with tourists, street artists and pigeons, it is as picturesque as any piazza in Italy. The best time to come is at night, when the inevitably tourist-geared flavour of the place is at its most vibrant, crowds hanging out around the fountains or clocking the scene while nursing a pricey drink at a table outside one of the bars, or watching the buskers and street artists entertain the merry throng.

The piazza takes its shape from the first century AD Stadium of Domitian, the principal venue of the athletic events and later chariot races that took place in the Campus Martius. Until the mid-fifteenth century the ruins of the arena were still here, overgrown and disused, but the square was given a facelift in the mid-seventeenth century by Pope Innocent X, who built most of the grandiose palaces that surround it and commissioned Borromini to design the facade of the church of **Sant'Agnese in Agone** on the piazza's western side. The story goes that the thirteen-year-old St Agnes was stripped naked before the crowds in the stadium as punishment for refusing to marry, whereupon she miraculously grew hair to cover herself. This church, typically squeezed into the tightest of spaces by Borromini, is supposedly built on the spot where it all happened.

Opposite, the **Fontana dei Quattro Fiumi**, one of three that punctuate the square, is a masterpiece by Bernini, Borromini's arch-rival. Each figure represents one of the four great rivers of the world – the Nile, Danube, Ganges and Plate – though only the horse, symbolizing the Danube, was actually carved by Bernini himself. It's said that all the figures are shielding their eyes in horror from Borromini's church facade (Bernini was an arrogant man who never had time for the work of the less successful Borromini), but the fountain had actually been completed before the facade was begun. The grand complexity of rock is topped with an Egyptian obelisk, brought here by Pope Innocent X from the Circus of Maxentius.

Bernini also had a hand in the fountain at the southern end of the square, the so-called **Fontana del Moro**, designing the central figure of the Moor in what is another fantastically playful piece of work, surrounded by toothsome dolphins and other marine figures. The fountain at the opposite end of the square, the **Fontana del Nettuno**, is equally fanciful, depicting Neptune struggling with a sea monster, surrounded by other briny creatures in a riot of fishing nets and nymphets, beards and breasts, scales and suckers.

STADIUM OF DOMITIAN

Map 3, E4. Sat & Sun 10am–12.30pm; L10,000.

Just off the north side of Piazza Navona there are some visible remains of the **Stadium of Domitian**. You can visit these on a short, half-hour guided tour, in English or Italian, and in doing so you can learn a little more about the stadium and its relationship with present-day Piazza Navona. But to be honest there's not a lot more to see than you can view from the street.

VIA DEI CORONARI

Map 3, E4–E5.

You might be better off spending any money you save on the Stadium in the antique dealers of narrow **Via dei Coronari**, almost opposite. This street, and some of the streets around, are the fulcrum of Rome's antiques trade, and, although the prices are as high as you might expect in such a location, there is a huge number of shops (Via dei Coronari consists of virtually nothing else), selling a tremendous variety of stuff, and a browse along here makes for one of the city's absorbing bits of sightseeing.

SANTA MARIA DELL'ANIMA

Map 3, E4. Daily 8am–1pm & 4–7.30pm.

A few steps left from the start of Via dei Coronari takes you down Via dell'Anima, where the church of **Santa Maria dell'Anima** is another darkly cosy Roman church, crammed into a seemingly impossibly small space. Nowadays it's the German national church in Rome, and a richly decorated affair, almost square in shape, with a protruding main sanctuary flanked by Renaissance tombs. The one on the right, a beautiful, rather sad concoction, is that of the last non-Italian pope before John Paul II, the Dutchman Hadrian VI, who died in 1523, while at the far end, above the altar there is a dark and glowing *Virgin with Saints* by Giulio Romano.

SANTA MARIA DELLA PACE

Map 3, E4.

Just off to the left of Via dei Coronari, the church of **Santa Maria della Pace** dates originally from the late fifteenth century but has a facade and portico that were added a couple of hundred years later by Pietro da Cortona. Inside, if you're lucky enough to find the church open, you can see Raphael's frescoes of various sibyls above the Chigi chapel (first on the right), executed in the early sixteenth century. But perhaps the most impressive part of the church is the one you're most likely to be able to get into – the attached **chiostro del Bramante**, done in 1504, a beautifully proportioned two-tiered cloister that is nowadays given over to fairly decent temporary art exhibitions.

PALAZZO ALTEMPS

Map 3, E3. Piazza Sant'Apollinare 44. Tues–Sat 9am–7pm, Sun 9am–6pm; L10,000; L20,000 for Palazzo Massimo, Colosseum and Palatine

Just across the street from the north end of Piazza Navona, **Piazza Sant'Apollinare** is home of the beautifully restored **Palazzo Altemps** built between 1477 and completed just under a hundred years later, which houses a branch of the Museo Nazionale Romano. This is a relatively new – and major – addition to the sights around Piazza Navona, and you'd be well advised to make some time for it, housing as it does the cream of Museo Nazionale's aristocratic collections of Roman statuary. Divided between two storeys of the

palace, in rooms which open off its elegant courtyard, most of
what is on display derives from the collection of the seventeenth century Roman cardinal, Ludovico Ludovisi – pieces
he either purchased elsewhere to adorn his villa on the
Quirinal Hill, or found in the grounds of the villa itself,
which occupied the site of a former residence of Julius Caesar.

The ground floor

First up, at the far end of the courtyard's loggia, is a statue
of the emperor Antoninus Pius, who ruled from 138 to 161
AD, and, around the corner, a couple of marvellous heads
of Zeus and Pluto, a bust of Julia, the daughter of the
emperor Augustus, and a grave-looking likeness of the
philosopher Demosthenes, from the second century AD.
Further rooms hold more statuary. There are two, almost
identical statues of *Apollo the Lyrist*, a magnificent statue of
Athena taming a serpent, pieced together from fragments
found near the church of Santa Maria sopra Minerva, an
Aphrodite from an original by Praxiteles, and, in the far corner of the courtyard, a shameless *Dionysus* with a satyr and
panther, found on the Quirinal Hill.

The first floor

Upstairs you get a slightly better sense of the original sump-
tuousness of the building – some of the frescoes remain and
the north loggia retains its original, late-sixteenth century
decoration, simulating a vine-laden pergola, heavy with
fruit, leaves and gambolling putti. Also, the objects on display are if anything even finer. The Painted Views room,
so-called for the bucolic scenes on its walls, has a fine statue
of Hermes, restored in the seventeenth century in an ora-
torical pose according to the fashion of the time; the
Cupboard Room, next door, named for its fresco of a dis-

play of wedding gifts, against a floral background, has a wonderful statue of a warrior at rest, something called the *Ludovisi Ares*, which is perhaps an image of Achilles, restored by Bernini in 1622, and, most engagingly, a charmingly sensitive portrayal of *Orestes and Electra*, from the first century AD by a sculptor called Menelaus – his name is carved at the base of one of the figures,

Beyond are even more treasures, and it is hard to know where to look first. One room retains a frieze telling the story of Moses as a cartoon strip, with each scene displayed by nude figures as if on an unfurled tapestry, while in the room itself there is a colossal head of Hera, and – what some consider the highlight of the entire collection – the famous *Ludovisi throne*: an original fifth-century-BC Greek work embellished with a delicate relief portraying the birth of Aphrodite. She is shown being hauled from the sea, where she was legendarily formed from the genitals of Uranus, while on the other side reliefs show a flute player and a woman sprinkling incense over a flame – rituals associated with the worship of Aphrodite.

Further on, the Fireplace Salon, whose huge fireplace is embellished with caryatids and lurking ibex – the symbol of the Altemps family – has the so-called *Suicide of Galatian*, apparently commissioned by Julius Caesar to adorn his Quirinal estate; at the other end if the room, an incredible sarcophagus depicts a battle between the Romans and barbarians in graphic, almost viscerally sculptural detail, while in the small room next door there are some quieter, more erotic pieces – a lovely *Pan and Daphne*, a *Satyr and Nymph*, and the muses *Calliope* and *Urania*. Once you've made it to here, you'll be ready for a quick peek at the Altemps chapel, off the opposite end of the fireplace room, and a skim back through your favourite pieces, before leaving what is without question one of Rome's best collections of classical art.

PALAZZO PRIMOLI

Map 3, E3.

Around the corner from Palazzo Altemps, at the end of Via Zanardelli, the sixteenth-century **Palazzo Primoli** was the home of a descendant of Napoleon, Joseph Primoli, and now houses two minor museums that may command your attention on the way to the Vatican, just across the Tiber from here. The first, the **Museo Mario Praz** (Tues–Sun 9am–1pm & 2.30–6.30pm, Mon 2.30–6.30pm; L4000), on the first floor, was the home of one Mario Praz, an art historian and writer who lived here for twenty or so years until his death in the 1980s, and it is kept pretty much as the elegant and cultured Praz left it.

Next door, the second museum, the **Museo Napoleonico** (Tues–Sat 9am–7pm, Sun 9am–1.30pm; L3750), is less interesting if you're anything but an enthusiast for the great Frenchman and in particular his dynasty. Rome was home for the Bonapartes in the 1820s – Pauline married Camillo Borghese, and Napoleon's mother, Letizia, lived nearby – and this is a rather weighty assortment of their personal effects. There's a letter from Napoleon himself from his exile in St Helena, a bad portrait of Pauline, a stirring depiction of Napoleon III, portraits of Count Primoli's mother, Carlotta Bonaparte, sketchbook in hand, hung amongst a number of her own quite adept drawings, even a Napoleonic bike. All things considered, though, it takes a pretty gritty determination, or a peculiar fascination with the family, to get through it all.

SANT'AGOSTINO

Map 3, F3. Daily 7.45am–noon & 4–7.30pm.

To the northeast of Piazza Navona, across **Piazza delle Cinque Lune** and through an arch, is the Renaissance facade of the church of **Sant'Agostino**, which takes up one side of a drab piazza of the same name. It's not much to look at from the outside, but a handful of art treasures might draw you in. Just inside the door, the serene statue of the *Madonna del Parto*, by Sansovino, is traditionally invoked during pregnancy, and is accordingly surrounded by photos of newborn babes and their blissful parents. Further into the church, take a look also at Raphael's vibrant fresco of *Isaiah*, on the third pillar on the left, beneath which is another work by Sansovino, a craggy *St Anne, Virgin and Child*. But the biggest crowds gather around the first chapel on the left, where the *Madonna and Pilgrims* by Caravaggio (L500 to switch on the lights) is a characteristic work of what was at the time almost revolutionary realism, showing two peasants with dirty limbs and clothes praying at the feet of a sensuous Mary and Child.

TORRE DELLA SCIMMIA

Map 3, F3.

Just beyond Sant'Agostino on Via dell'Orso, take a look at the **Torre della Scimmia** – literally the "Tower of the Monkey" – which grows almost organically out of a fork in the road above an ivy-covered palazzo. The story goes that in the seventeenth century a pet monkey kidnapped a child and carried it to the top of the tower; the father of the child called upon the Virgin for help and the monkey promptly clambered down, delivering the child to safety. By way of thanks, the man erected a shrine to the Virgin, which you can still see at the top of the tower, accompanied by a glowing lamp that is to this day kept constantly burning.

PALAZZO DI MONTECITORIO AND AROUND

Map 3, H3.

A couple of minutes' walk from the Monkey Tower,

Piazza Montecitorio takes its name from the bulky **Palazzo di Montecitorio** on its northern side, home since 1871 to the Italian parliament – though the building itself is a Bernini creation from 1650. The obelisk in the centre of the square was brought to Rome by Augustus and set up in the Campus Martius, where it formed the hand of a giant sundial.

Just beyond, off Via del Corso, the **Palazzo Chigi** flanks the north side of **Piazza Colonna**, official residence of the prime minister. The **Column of Marcus Aurelius**, which gives the square its name, was erected between 180 and 190 AD to commemorate military victories in northern Europe, and, like the column of Trajan which inspired it, is decorated with reliefs depicting scenes from the campaigns. As for the square, it used to be the site of the city's principal coffee-roasters market, so was always a busy spot, and it still has an elegant backdrop in the **Palazza Wedekind**, home to *Il Tempo* newspaper, whose dozen or so Ionic columns, originally Roman, support a gracious balustraded terrace. Across the way, the **Galleria Colonna** – not to be confused with the collection of paintings just off Piazza Venezia (see p.65) – is a classic, Y-shaped nineteenth-century shopping arcade, these days used for temporary art installations.

SAN LORENZO IN LUCINA

Map 3, H2.

A little further up Via del Corso, on the left, the wedge-shaped **Largo San Lorenzo** is a surprisingly spacious and relatively peaceful escape from the bustle of the Corso. On its left side, the church of **San Lorenzo in Lucina** stands out among the largely undistinguished buildings, due to its manifestly ancient campanile and columned portico; the church originally dates from the fifth century but was rebuilt in the twelfth century. Inside, like so many Roman churches, it doesn't look or feel nearly so old, indeed much of it dates from the seventeenth century, but there are several features of interest, not least a section of the griddle on which St Lawrence was roasted, in a reliquary in the first chapel on the right – though this is almost impossible to see. A little further down on the same side, the tomb of Nicholas Poussin is a delicate nineteenth-century marble affair by the French sculptor Chateaubriand; Poussin spent much of his life in Rome, and died here in 1665. Beyond, take a look also at Bernini's bust of the doctor of Innocent X, Fonseca, in the next chapel but one, and the *Crucifixion* by Guido Reni in the apse.

MAUSOLEUM OF AUGUSTUS

Map 5, F6–F7. Guided tours Sat & Sun 11am; L10,000.

A little further up Via del Corso, off to the left, cut through to **Piazza del Augusta Imperatore**, an odd square of largely Mussolini-era buildings surrounding the massive **Mausoleum of Augustus**, the burial place of the emperor and his family – these days not much more than a peaceful ring of cypresses, circled by paths, flowering shrubs and the debris of tramps. Augustus died in 14 AD, giving way to his son Tiberius, who ruled mostly from his notoriously decadent court in Capri until 37 AD, when Caligula took over and effectively signalled the end of the Augustan age.

The mausoleum has been transformed into many buildings over the years, not least a fortress, like Hadrian's mausoleum across the river, and only recently has been opened to the public. If you can time your visit with a guided tour, it is worth going inside, although the passageways and central crypt, where the ashes of the members of the Augustan dynasty were kept, don't add much to the picture you get from the outside.

ARA PACIS AUGUSTAE

Map 5, E6. Summer Tues–Sat 9am–7pm, Sun 9am–1pm; winter Tues–Sat 9am–4.30pm, Sun 9am–1pm; L3750.

On the far side of the square, enclosed in a glass box between the river and the mausoleum, the **Ara Pacis Augustae** or "Altar of Augustan Peace" is a more substantially recognizable Roman remain, built in 13 BC to celebrate Augustus's victory over Spain and Gaul and the peace it heralded. Much of this had been dug up piecemeal over the years, but the bulk of it was found during the middle half of the last century. It was no easy task to put it back together: excavation involved digging down to a depth of 10m and freezing the water table, after which many other parts had to be retrieved from museums the world over, or plaster copies made. But it's a superb example of Imperial Roman sculpture and holds on its fragmented frieze the likenesses of many familiar names, most shown in the victory procession itself, which is best preserved on the eastern side. The first part is almost completely gone, but the shape of Augustus is a little more complete, as are the figures that follow – first Tiberius, then the priests with their skull-cap headgear, then Agrippa. The women are, respectively, Augustus's wife Livia, daughter Julia, and niece Antonia, the latter caught simply and realistically turning to her husband. Around their feet run various children clutching the togas of the elders, the last of whom is said to be the young Claudius.

PIAZZA DEL POPOLO

Map 5, F5.

The other side of Piazza del Augusto Imperatore, **Via di Ripetta** was laid out by Pope Leo X to provide a straight route out of the city centre from the old river port area here. At the far end, where Via di Ripetta meets Via del Corso, the oval-shaped expanse of **Piazza del Popolo** is a dignified meeting of roads laid out in 1538 by Pope Paul III (Alessandro Farnese) to make an impressive entrance to the city; it owes its present symmetry to Valadier, who added the central fountain in 1814. The monumental **Porta del Popolo** went up in 1655, the work of Bernini, whose patron Alexander VII's Chigi family symbol – the heap of hills surmounted by a star – can clearly be seen above the main gateway.

During summer, the steps around the obelisk and fountain, and the cafés on either side of the square, are popular hangouts. But the square's real attraction is the unbroken view it gives all the way back down Via del Corso, between the perfectly paired churches of **Santa Maria dei Miracoli** and **Santa Maria in Montesanto**, to the central columns of the Vittorio Emanuele Monument. If you get to choose your first view of the centre of Rome, make it this one.

SANTA MARIA DEL POPOLO

Map 5, F4. Mon–Sat 7am–noon & 4–7pm, Sun 8am–1.30pm & 4.30–7.30pm.

On the far side of the piazza, hard against the city walls, the church of **Santa Maria del Popolo** holds some of the best Renaissance art of any Roman church. The church was originally erected here in 1099 over the burial place of Nero, in order to sanctify what was believed to be an evil place, but took its present form in the fifteenth century. Inside there are frescoes by Pinturicchio in the first chapel of the south aisle, including a lovely *Adoration of Christ*, full of tiny details receding into the distance. Pinturicchio also did some work in the Bramante-designed apse, which in turn boasts two fine tombs by Andrea Sansovino. The

Chigi chapel, the second from the entrance in the northern aisle, was designed by Raphael for Agostino Chigi in 1516 – though most of the work was actually undertaken by other artists and not finished until the seventeenth century. Michelangelo's protégé, Sebastiano del Piombo, was responsible for the altarpiece, and two of the sculptures in the corner niches, of Daniel and Habakkuk, are by Bernini. But it's two pictures by Caravaggio that attract the most attention, in the left-hand chapel of the north transept. These are typically dramatic works – one, the *Conversion of St Paul*, showing Paul and horse bathed in a beatific radiance, the other, the *Crucifixion of St Peter*, showing Peter as an aged but strong figure, dominated by the muscly figures hoisting him up. Like the same artist's paintings in the churches of San Luigi dei Francesi and Sant'Agostino (see above), both works were considered extremely risqué in their time, their heavy chiaroscuro and deliberate realism too much for the church authorities; one contemporary critic referred to the *Conversion of St Paul*, a painting dominated by the exquisitely lit horse's hindquarters, as "an accident in a blacksmith's shop".

West of Piazza Venezia

Via del Plebiscito, a dark, rather gloomy thoroughfare, forges west from Piazza Venezia. About 300m down, flanking the north side of **Piazza del Gesù**, is the dark-grey decaying bulk of the **Palazzo Altieri**, a monster of a project in its time that – a contemporary Pasquinade (see below) quipped – looked set to consume Rome by its very size. The Altieri pope, Clement X, had the palace built around the house of an old woman who refused to make way for it: the two spyhole windows that were left can still be seen above the ground-floor windows, three windows to the right of the main entrance.

THE GESÙ

Map 3, I6. Daily 6am–12.30pm & 4–7.15pm.

Lording it over the piazza proper (said, incidentally, to be the windiest in Rome), is the church of **Gesù**, a symbol of the Counter-Reformation and the Jesuit order. High and wide, with a single-aisled nave and short transepts edging out under a huge dome, it was ideal for the large and fervent congregations the Jesuits wanted to draw; indeed it has served as the model for Jesuit churches everywhere. The facade is by Giacomo della Porta, the interior the work of Vignola. Today it's still a well-patronized church, notable for its size (the glitzy tomb of the order's founder, St Ignatius, is topped by a huge globe of lapis lazuli – the largest piece in existence) and the staggering richness of its interior, especially the paintings of Baciccia in the dome and the ceiling's ingenious trompe l'oeil, which oozes out of its frame in a tangle of writhing bodies, flowing drapery and stucco angels stuck like limpets.

LARGO DI TORRE ARGENTINA

Map 3, G6.

Corso Vittorio Emanuele continues west from the Gesù, opening out eventually onto **Largo di Torre Argentina**, a good-sized square frantic with traffic circling around the ruins of four (Republican-era) temples and the channel of an ancient public lavatory, now home to a thriving colony of cats. This is not generally open to the public, but there's not a lot to see here – it's more a place to wait for a bus than to deliberately linger. On the far side of the square, the **Teatro Argentina** was in 1816 the venue for the first performance of Rossini's *Barber of Seville*, not a success at all on the night: Rossini was apparently booed into taking refuge in Bernasconi's pastry shop which used to be next door. Built in 1731, it is today one of the city's most important theatres, and has a small museum that can be visited by appointment. It is also thought, incidentally, that it was built over the spot where Caesar was assassinated.

SANT'ANDREA DELLA VALLE

Map 3, F6. Mon–Sat 7.30am–noon & 4.30–7.30pm, Sun 7.30am–12.45pm & 4.30–7.45pm.

From Largo Argentina you can either push on down Corso Vittorio Emanuele or cut left towards the Tiber and right at Piazza Cairoli into the network of streets that centres on Campo de' Fiori. Taking the Corso route, you pass the church of **Sant'Andrea della Valle**, which has the distinction of sporting the city's second-tallest dome (after St Peter's), built by Carlo Maderno. Inside, it's one of the most Baroque of Rome's churches, a high, barnlike building, in which most of your attention is drawn not only to the dome, decorated with frescoes of the Glory of Paradise by Giovanni Lanfranco, but also to a marvellous set of frescoes in the apse by his contemporary Domenichino, illustrating the life of St Andrew, and centring on the monumental scene of his crucifixion on the characteristic transverse cross. In a side chapel on the right, you may, if you've been in Rome a while, recognize some good-looking copies of not only Michelangelo's Pietà (the original is in St Peter's), but also of his figures of Leah and Rachel, from the same artist's tomb of his patron, Julius II, in the church of San Pietro in Vincoli (see p.99).

MUSEO BARRACCO

Map 3, E6. Piazza dei Baullari 1. Tues–Sat 9am–7pm, Sun 9am–1pm; L10,000.

A little further along, on the left, is the so-called Piccola Farnesina palace, built by Antonio Sangallo the Younger. The palace itself actually never had anything to do with the Farnese family, and took the name 'little Farnese" because of the lilies on the outside of the building, which were confused with the Farnese heraldic lilies. It now holds the **Museo Barracco**, a small but fine-quality collection of ancient sculpture that was donated to the city at the turn of the century by one Baron Barracco.

The first floor contains ancient Egyptian and Hellenistic pieces, including two sphinxes from the reigns of Hapsupset and Rameses II, an austere head of an Egyptian priest and a bust of a young Rameses II and statues and reliefs of the God Bes from various eras. On the second floor are ceramics and statuary from the Greek classical period – essentially the fourth and fifth centuries BC – a small but very high-quality collection. There is a lovely, almost complete figurine of Hercules; a larger figure of an athlete copied from an original by Policlitus; a highly realistic bitch washing herself from the fourth century BC; and a complete and very beautiful votive relief dedicated to Apollo. There are also, in a small room at the front of the building, later Roman pieces, most notably a small figure of Neptune from the first century BC and an odd, almost Giacometti-like column-sculpture of a very graphically drawn hermaphrodite. Look also at the charming two busts of young Roman boys opposite, which date from the first century AD,

MUSEO DI ROMA

Map 3, E5. Closed for restoration.

Across the street from the Museo Barracco, the eighteenth-century Palazzo Braschi is the home of the **Museo di Roma**, which hosts occasional exhibitions relating to the history of the city from the Middle Ages to the present day. The permanent collection – long under restoration, though due to reopen in 2000 – contains paintings showing the city during different eras, frescoes from demolished palaces, and the open railway carriage that the nineteenth-century Pope Pius IX used for journeys out of the city.

PALAZZO DELLA CANCELLERIA

Map 3 E6.

On the opposite side of the Corso is the grand **Palazzo della Cancelleria**, the seat of the papal government that once ran the city; Bramante is thought to have had a hand in its design, and it is certainly a gorgeous and well-proportioned edifice, which exudes a cool poise quite at odds with the rather grimy nature of its surroundings. You can't get in to see the interior, but you can stroll into the marvellously proportioned, multi-tiered courtyard which is treat enough in itself, although the adjacent church of **San Lorenzo in Damaso** also forms part of the complex and is open regular church hours.

PIAZZA PASQUINO AND AROUND

Map 3, E5.

Immediately behind the Palazzo Braschi, just south of Piazza Navona, the small space of **Piazza Pasquino** isn't quite what you'd expect from the scene of centuries of satire, but the battered torso of Pasquino itself, anonymous poker of fun at the rich and famous during the Middle Ages, still stands in the corner. It's most famous among a number of so-called "talking statues" in Rome, upon which anonymous comments on the affairs of the day would be attached – comments that had a serious as well as a humorous intent. Pasquino gave us our word "pasquinade", but nowadays the graffitied comments and photocopied poems that occasionally grace the statue are usually somewhat lacking in wit.

Via del Governo Vecchio leads west from here into one of Rome's liveliest quarters, the narrow streets noisy at night, and holding some of the city's most vigorous restaurants and bars.

CHIESA NUOVA

Map 3, C5.

Just off Via del Governo Vecchio the **Chiesa Nuova** is another highly ornate Baroque church – which is strange, because its founder, St Philip Neri, didn't want it decorated at all. Neri was an ascetic man, who tended the poor and sick in the streets around here for most of his life, and commissioned this church, on the site on an earlier structure – Santa Maria in Valicella – which had been donated to him and his followers by Gregory XIII, in 1577. Neri died in 1595, after a relatively normal day of saintly tasks – his last words were "Last of all, we must die." He was canonized in 1622, and this large church, as well as being his last resting-place (he lies in the chapel to the left of the apse), is his principal memorial. Inside, its principal features include three paintings by Rubens hung at the high altar, centring on the *Virgin with Angels*, and, perhaps more obviously, Pietro da Cortona's ceiling paintings, showing the *Ascension of the Virgin* in the apse, and, above the nave, the construction of the church and Neri's famous "vision of fire", which he experienced in 1544.

Behind the church, the delightful small square of **Piazza del Orologio** is so-called because of the quaint clocktower that is its main feature. The clock is part of the **Oratorio dei Filipini**, designed by Carlo Borromini, which backs onto the Chiesa Nuova and is part of the same complex: Neri's followers attended musical gatherings here as part of their worship, gifting the language forever the musical term "oratorio". Just off the square, there's a scatter of antique and bric-a-brac shops, that signal that you're just around the corner from Rome's antiques ghetto, Via dei Coronari (see p.31).

SAN GIOVANNI DEI FIORENTINI

Map 3, A4.

Borromini is buried across the way, in the church of **San Giovanni dei Fiorentini**, set on its own small square, Piazza d'Oro. Its eighteenth-century facade is as monumental as any of Rome's churches, but inside is a relatively plain affair, built originally by Sansovino on the orders of the Medici pope, Leo X, who wanted to see an expression of Florentine pride on his doorstep. The church was finished, in the early 1600s, by Carlo Maderno, who added the dome, beneath which Raggi's flamboyant seventeenth-century altarpiece depicts the Baptism of Christ. Look out also for the naive statue of a young John the Baptist, above the doorway to the sacristy, next to which there's a bust of another Florentine pope, Clement XII, carved by Bernini. It's worth knowing, too, that San Giovanni extends a special welcome to pets, and you'll often see churchgoers wandering with cat baskets and the like.

CAMPO DE' FIORI AND AROUND

Map 3, E7.

At the southern end of Piazza della Cancelleria, in front of the palace, is one of several entrances to **Piazza Campo**

de' Fiori, in many ways Rome's most appealing square. Home to a lively **fruit and vegetable market** (Mon–Sat 8am–1pm), it's flanked by restaurants and cafés, busy pretty much all day. No one really knows how the square came by its name, which means "field of flowers", but one theory holds that it was derived from the Roman Campus Martius, which used to cover most of this part of town; another claims it is after Flora, the mistress of Pompey, whose theatre used to stand on what is now the northeast corner of the square – a huge complex by all accounts, which stretched right over to Largo Argentina. You can still see the foundations in the basement of the *Da Pancrazio* restaurant, on the tiny Piazza del Biscione, and the semicircular Via di Grotta Pinta retains the rounded shape of the theatre. Later, Campo dei Fiori was an important point on papal processions between the Vatican and the major basilicas of Rome (notably San Giovanni in Laterano) and a site of public executions. The most notorious killing here is commemorated by the statue of **Giordano Bruno** in the middle of the square. Bruno was a late-sixteenth-century freethinker who followed the teachings of Copernicus and was denounced to the Inquisition; his trial lasted for years under a succession of different popes, and finally, when he refused to renounce his philosophical beliefs, he was burned at the stake.

PIAZZA FARNESE

Map 3, D7.

Just south of Campo dei Fiori, **Piazza Farnese** is a quite different square, with great fountains spurting out of lilies – the Farnese emblem – into marble tubs brought from the Baths of Caracalla, and the sober bulk of the **Palazzo Farnese** itself, begun in 1514 by Antonio di Sangallo the Younger and finished off after the architect's death by Michelangelo, who added the top tier of windows and cornice. The building now houses the French Embassy and is closed to the public, which is a pity, since it holds what has been called the greatest of all Baroque ceiling paintings, Annibale Carracci's *Loves of the Gods*, finished in 1603. However, newly restored, even from the outside it's a tremendously elegant and powerful building; indeed, of all the fabulous locations that Rome's embassies enjoy, this has got to be the best.

GALLERIA SPADA

Map 3, E7. Piazza Capo di Ferro 3. Tues–Sat 9am–7pm, Sun 9am–1pm; L10,000.

Make do instead with the Palazzo Spada, back towards Via Arenula, and the **Galleria Spada** inside (walk right through the courtyard to the back of the building) – although its four rooms, decorated in the manner of a Roman noble family, aren't spectacularly interesting unless you're a connoisseur of seventeenth- and eighteenth-century Italian painting. Best are two portraits of the cardinal Bernadino Spada by Reni and Guercino, alongside works by the odd Italian-influenced Dutch artist (Van Scorel, Honthorst), and, among bits and pieces of Roman statuary, a seated philosopher. The building itself is better: its facade is frilled with stucco adornments, and, left off the small courtyard, there's a crafty trompe l'oeil by Borromini – a tunnel whose actual length is multiplied about four times through the architect's tricks with perspective – though to see this you have to wait for one of the guided tours (held every hour, on the half-hour).

VIA GIULIA

Map 3, D8–A4.

Behind the Farnese and Spada palaces, **Via Giulia**, which runs parallel to the Tiber, was built by Julius II to connect

Ponte Sisto with the Vatican. The street was conceived as the centre of papal Rome, and Julius commissioned Bramante to line it with imposing palaces. Bramante didn't get very far with the plan, as Julius was soon succeeded by Leo X, but the street became a popular residence for wealthier Roman families, and is still packed full with stylish palazzi and antique shops and as such makes for a nice wander, with features like the playful **Fontana del Mascherone** to tickle your interest along the way. Just beyond the fountain, behind the high wall of the Palazzo Farnese, the **arch** across the street is the remnant of a Renaissance plan to connect the Farnese palace with the Villa Farnesina across the river, while further along still, the **Palazzo Falconieri**, recognizable by the quizzical falcons crowning each end of the building, now the home of the Hungarian Academy, was largely the work of Borromini, who enlarged it in 1646–49.

The Jewish Ghetto and around

By way of contrast, cross over to the far side of Via Arenula and you're in what was once the city's **Jewish Ghetto**, a crumbling area of narrow, switchback streets and alleys, easy to lose your way in, and with a lingering sense of age. There was a Jewish population in Rome as far back as the second century BC, and with the accruing of Middle Eastern colonies, their numbers eventually swelled to around 40,000. Revolts in the colonies led to a small tax on Jews and a special census, but they were never an especially persecuted group, and were only effectively ghettoized here in the mid-sixteenth century when Pope Paul IV issued a series of punitive laws that forced them into what was then one of Rome's most squalid districts: a wall was built around the area and all Jews, in a chilling omen of things to come, were made to wear yellow caps and shawls when they left the district. Later, after Unification, the ghetto was opened up, and although the Nazi occupation brought the inevitable deportations, the majority of Rome's Jewish population survived, and currently numbers 16,000 (around half Italy's total). This is nowadays, however, spread all over the city, and a couple of kosher restaurants, butchers and the like are pretty much all that remains to mark this out from any other quarter of the city.

THE SYNAGOGUE

Map 3, H9. Mon–Thurs 9am–4pm, Fri 9am–2pm, Sun 9am–noon; closed Sat & Jewish holidays; L10,000.

The Ghetto's principal (Jewish) sight is the huge **Synagogue** by the river, built in 1904 and very much dominating all around with its bulk – not to mention the carabinieri who stand guard 24 hours a day outside, ever since a PLO attack on the building in 1982 killed a two-year-old girl and injured many others. The only way to see the building is on one of the short guided tours it runs regularly in English, afterwards taking in the small two-room museum. The interior of the building is impressive, rising to a high, rainbow-hued dome, and the tours are excellent, giving good background on the building and Rome's Jewish community in general.

VIA PORTICO D'OTTAVIA AND AROUND

Map 3, H8.

The main artery of the Jewish area is **Via Portico d'Ottavia**, which leads down to the **Portico d'Ottavia**, a not terribly well-preserved second-century BC gate, rebuilt by Augustus and dedicated to his sister in 23 BC, that was the entranceway to the adjacent **Teatro di Marcello**. This has served many purposes over the years: begun by Julius Caesar, finished by Augustus, it was pillaged in the fourth century and not properly restored until the Middle Ages, after which it became a formidable fortified palace for a succession of different rulers, including the Orsini family. The theatre has been recently restored and provides a grand backdrop for classical concerts in the summer.

Retracing your steps slightly, off Piazza delle Cinque Scuole, a gloomy arch leads past one side of the **Palazzo Cenci**, which huddles into the dark streets here, a reminder of the untimely death of one Beatrice Cenci, who was executed, with her stepmother, on the Ponte Sant'Angelo in 1599 for the murder of her incestuous father – a story immortalized in verse by Shelley and in paint by an unknown artist whose portrait of the unfortunate Beatrice still hangs in the Palazzo Barberini. On a more lighthearted note, crossing to the other side of Via del Portico d'Ottavia, follow your nose to **Piazza Mattei**, whose **Fontana delle Tartarughe**, or "turtle fountain", is a delightful late-sixteenth-century creation, perhaps restored by Bernini.

SANTA MARIA IN CAMPITELLI

Map 3, I8.

Via dei Funari leads east out of the square towards Piazza Campitelli, where **Santa Maria in Campitelli** is a heavy, ornate church built by Carlo Reinaldi in 1667 to house an ancient image of the Virgin that had been deemed to have miraculous powers following respite from a plague. Everything in the church focuses on this small framed image, encased as it is in an incredibly ornate golden altar

Aldo Moro

Just around the corner from the turtle fountain, a little way up Via Caetani on the right (map 3, H7), is a memorial to the former Italian prime minister **Aldo Moro**, whose dead body was left in the boot of a car here on the morning of 9 May, 1978, 54 days after his kidnap by an Italian terrorist group. It was a carefully chosen spot, not only for the impudence it showed on the part of the terrorists, in that it was right in the centre of Rome, but also for its position midway between the headquarters of the Communist and Christian Democrat parties.

A plaque (and sometimes a wreath) marks the spot, and tells part of the story of how Moro, a reform-minded Christian Democrat, was the first right-wing politician to attempt to build an alliance with the then popular Italian Communists. Whether it was really left-wing terrorists who kidnapped him, or whether it was darker, right-wing forces allied to the establishment, or perhaps a combination of the two, there's no doubt that Moro's attempt to alleviate the Right's postwar monopoly of power found very little favour with others in power at the time – though that didn't make his death any less of a shock. Given the "mani puliti" years that have followed, and the minuscule change and the political cynicism that has resurfaced in the 1990s, it's a tragedy which must still carry a lot of resonance for Romans. The prime minister who took over after Moro's death was after all none other than the recently tried (and acquitted) elder statesman of Italian politics, Giulio Andreotti.

piece which fills the entire space between the clustered columns of the transept. There's not much else to see in the church, although the paintings, including a dramatic *Virgin with Saints* by Luca Giordano, in the second chapel on the right, represent the Baroque at its most rampant.

PIAZZA BOCCA DELLA VERITÀ

Map 7, G4.

Piazza Campitelli opens out onto the broad main drag of Via di Teatro di Marcello, which leads down to **Piazza Bocca della Verità**, past two of the city's better-preserved Roman temples – the **Temple of Portunus** and the **Temple of Hercules Victor**, the latter long known as the temple of Vesta because, like all vestal temples, it is circular. Both date from the end of the second century BC, and although you can't get inside, they're actually fine examples of republican-era places of worship; and the Temple of Hercules Victor is, for what it's worth, the oldest surviving marble structure in Rome.

More interesting is the church of **Santa Maria in Cosmedin** on the far side of the square (daily 9am–noon & 3–5pm), a typically Roman medieval basilica with a huge marble altar and a colourful and ingenious Cosmati-work floor – one of the city's finest. Outside in the portico, and giving the square its name, is the **Bocca della Verità** (Mouth of Truth), an ancient Roman drain cover in the shape of an enormous face that in medieval times would apparently swallow the hand of anyone who hadn't told the truth. It was particularly popular with husbands anxious to test the faithfulness of their wives; now it is one of the city's biggest tour-bus attractions.

On the northern side, the square peters out peacefully at the stolid **Arch of Janus**, perhaps Rome's most weathered triumphal arch, beyond which the campanile of the church of **San Giorgio in Velabro** (daily 10am–12.30pm & 4–6.30pm) is a stunted echo of that of Santa Maria across the way. Inside, recently opened after a major restoration, this is one of the city's barest and most beautiful ancient basilicas, only the late-twelfth-century fresco in the apse, the work of Pietro Cavallini, lightening the melancholy mood. Cavallini's fresco shows Christ and His mother, and various saints, including St George on the left, to whom the church is dedicated – and whose cranial bones lie in the reliquary under the high altar canopy, placed here in 749 AD, shortly after the original basilica was built.

A few steps away from here, a little way down Via San Teodoro on the right, the round church of **San Teodoro** is only open sporadically, and in any case on the inside its ancient feel has been somewhat smoothed over by the paint and plaster of later years. St Theodore was martyred on this spot in the fourth century AD, and the church dates originally from the sixth century. If you can get in, you'll be lucky enough to see the apse mosaics, which are contemporary with the original church, showing Christ with saints, including a bearded Theodore, next to St Peter on the right.

ISOLA TIBERINA

Map 3 H9.

Back by the river, you can see the remains of **Ponte Rotto** (Broken Bridge), all that remains of the first stone bridge to span the river. Built between 179 and 142 BC, it collapsed at the end of the sixteenth century. Further down is **Ponte Fabricio**, which crosses to **Isola Tiberina**. Built in 62 BC, it's the only classical bridge to remain intact without help from the restorers (the Ponte Cestio, on the other side of the island, was partially rebuilt in the last century). As for the island, it's a calm respite from the city centre proper, its originally tenth-century church of **San Bartolomeo** worth a peep on the way across the river to Trastevere, especially if you're into modern sculpture – Padre Martini, a well-known local sculptor, used to live on the island, and the church holds some wonderful examples of his elegant, semi-abstract religious pieces.

East of Via del Corso

The triangular area on the **eastern side of Via del Corso**, bound by Piazza del Popolo, the Corso, the edge of the Villa Borghese and Piazza di Spagna, is travellers' Rome, historically the artistic quarter of the city, for which eighteenth- and nineteenth-century Grand Tourists would make in search of the colourful, exotic city. Keats and Giorgio de Chirico are just two of those who used to live on Piazza di Spagna; Goethe had lodgings along Via del Corso; and institutions like *Caffè Greco* and *Babington's Tea Rooms* were the meeting-places of a local artistic and expat community for close on a couple of centuries. Today these institutions have given ground to more latter-day traps for the tourist dollar: American Express and McDonald's have settled into the area, while Via Condotti and around is these days strictly international designer territory, with some of Rome's fanciest stores; the local residents are more likely to be investment bankers than artists or poets. But the air of a Rome being discovered, even colonized, by foreigners persists, even if most of them hanging out on the Spanish Steps are mostly flying-visit InterRailers.

VIA DEL BABUINO AND AROUND

Map 5, G6.

Leading south from Piazza del Popolo, **Via del Babuino** and the narrow **Via Margutta,** where Fellini once lived, set the tone for the area, which in the 1960s was the core of a thriving art community and home to the city's best galleries and a fair number of its artists, until high rents forced out all but the most successful. Now the neighbourhood supports a prosperous trade in antiques and designer fashions. On the right, a little way down Via del Babuino, the church of **All Saints** is the official English church of Rome, its solid steeple and brick construction, erected in the late-nineteenth century, serving as a further reminder of the English connections in this part of town. It's often shut, but if you do manage to get inside you'll be rewarded with an apse mosaic by the pre-Raphaelite artist Edward Burne-Jones and tiles to a design by William Morris – truly a stronghold of English artists and craftspeople.

PIAZZA DI SPAGNA

Map 5, G6.

At the southern end of Via del Babuino is **Piazza di Spagna**, a long thin straggle of a square almost entirely enclosed by buildings and centring on the distinctive boat-shaped **Barcaccia** fountain, the last work of Bernini's father. It apparently remembers the great flood of Christmas Day 1598, when a barge from the Tiber was washed up on the slopes of Pincio Hill close by. At the southern end of the square, a **column** commemorates Pius IX's official announcement, in 1854, of the dogma of the Immaculate Conception.

Hackles were raised when **McDonald's** unveiled plans to open a branch of the world's most ubiquitous fast-food chain on the square in the early 1980s, and their presence here is proof that the American multinational won what turned out to be quite a battle. But it's to the city's credit that this is one of the most discreet examples you'll encounter, tucked into one end of the piazza, with thematically appropriate interior décor. Not surprisingly, you can now find branches of McDonald's all over the city – and most of them look much the same as they do anywhere.

KEATS-SHELLEY MEMORIAL HOUSE

Map 5, H7. Piazza di Spagna 26. Mon–Fri 9am–1pm & 3–6pm, Sat 11am–6pm; L5000.

Facing directly onto the square, opposite the fountain, is the house where the poet John Keats died in 1821. It now serves as the **Keats–Shelley Memorial House**, an archive of English-language literary and historical works and a museum of manuscripts and literary mementos relating to the Keats circle of the early nineteenth century – namely Keats himself, Shelley and Mary Shelley, and Byron (who at one time lived across the square). Among many bits of manuscript, letters and the like, there's a silver scallop shell reliquary containing locks of Milton's and Elizabeth Barrett Browning's hair, while Keats's death mask, stored in the room where he died, captures a resigned grimace. Keats didn't really enjoy his time in Rome, referring to it as his "posthumous life": he was tormented by his love for Fanny Browne, and he spent months in pain before he finally died, confined to the rooming house with his artist friend Joseph Severn, to whom he remarked that he could already feel "the flowers growing over him".

THE SPANISH STEPS

Map 5, H7.

As for the **Spanish Steps**, which sweep down in a cascade of balustrades and balconies beside the house, the only thing that is Spanish about them is the fact that they lead down to the Spanish Embassy, which also gave the piazza its name. In the last century they were the hangout of young hopefuls waiting to be chosen as artists' models; nowadays the scene is not much changed, as the venue for international posing and fast pick-ups late into the summer nights. At the top, adding to the international flavour of the square is the **Trinità dei Monti**, a largely sixteenth-century church designed by Carlo Maderno and paid for by the French king. Its rose-coloured Baroque façade overlooks the rest of Rome from its hilltop site, and it's worth clambering up just for the views. But while here you may as well pop your head around the door for a couple of faded works by Daniele da Volterra, notably a soft flowing fresco of *The Assumption* in the third chapel on the right, which includes a portrait of his teacher Michelangelo, and a poorly lit *Deposition* across the nave. Poussin considered the latter, which was probably painted from a series of cartoons by Michelangelo, as the world's third greatest painting (Raphael's *Transfiguration* was, he thought, the best).

PIAZZA BARBERINI

Map 5, J8.

From the church you can either continue left along past the Villa Medici, now housing the French Academy, to the Pincio terrace and the gardens of the Villa Borghese (see p.116), or head south down Via Sistina to **Piazza Barberini**, a busy traffic junction at the top end of the busy shopping street of Via del Tritone – named after Bernini's **Fontana del Tritone**, which gushes a high jet of water in the centre of the square. The recently restored fountain lends a unity to the square in more ways than one: traditionally, this was the Barberini quarter of the city, a family who were the greatest patrons of Gian Lorenzo

Bernini, and the sculptor's works in their honour are thick on the ground around here. He finished the Tritone fountain in 1644, going on shortly after to design the **Fontana delle Api** ("Fountain of the Bees") at the bottom end of Via Veneto. Unlike the Tritone fountain you could walk right past this, a smaller, quirkier work, its broad scallop shell studded with the bees that were the symbol of the Barberinis.

SANTA MARIA DELLA CONCEZIONE

Map 5, J7.

A little way up Via Veneto, the Capuchin church of **Santa Maria della Concezione** was another sponsored creation of the Barberini, though it's not a particularly significant building in itself, only numbering Guido Reni's androgynous *St Michael Trampling on the Devil* among its treasures. The devil in the picture is said to be a portrait of Innocent X, whom the artist despised and who was apparently a sworn enemy of the Barberini family. But the **Capuchin cemetery** (Mon–Wed & Fri–Sun 9am–noon & 3–6pm; compulsory "donation"), on the right of the church, is one of the more macabre and bizarre sights of Rome. Here, the bones of 4000 monks are set into the walls of a series of chapels, a monument to "Our Sister of Bodily Death", in the words of St Francis, that was erected in 1793. The bones appear in abstract or Christian patterns or as fully clothed skeletons, their faces peering out of their cowls in various twisted expressions of agony – somewhere between the chilling and the ludicrous.

VIA VENETO

Map 5 J6–J7.

Via Veneto, which bends north from Piazza Barberini up

to the southern edge of the Borghese gardens, is a cool, materialistic antidote to the murky atmosphere of the Capuchin grotto. The pricey bars and restaurants lining the street were once the haunt of Rome's Beautiful People, made famous by Fellini's *La Dolce Vita*, but they left a long time ago, and Via Veneto isn't really especially different to any other busy street in central Rome – a pretty tree-lined road, but with a fair share of high-class tack trying to cash in on departed glory.

GALLERIA DI ARTE ANTICA

Map 5, J8. Via Barberini 18. April–Oct Tues–Fri 9am–9pm, Sat 9am–noon, Sun 9am–8pm; Nov–March Tues–Fri 9am–5pm, Sat & Sun 9am–1pm; L12,000.

On the other side of Piazza Barberini, the **Palazzo Barberini** is home to the **Galleria di Arte Antica**, consisting of a rich patchwork of mainly Italian art from the early Renaissance to late Baroque period in the palace's converted rooms, and now hopefully completely open again now after a massive restoration. At time of writing the restoration was still in progress, and it's hard to say precisely where things will be by the time you read this. But broadly the collection proceeds chronologically across three floors of the building, starting with the first floor and ending on the third.

It's an impressive collection, and highlights include works by Titian, El Greco and Caravaggio. But perhaps the most impressive feature of the gallery is the building itself, worked on at different times by the most favoured architects of the day – Bernini, Borromini, Maderno – and the epitome of Baroque grandeur. The first floor *salone*, certainly, is guaranteed to impress, its ceiling frescoed by Pietro da Cortona in one of the best examples of exuberant Baroque trompe l'oeil work there is, a manic rendering of *The*

Triumph of Divine Providence that almost crawls down the walls to meet you.

Across the hall from the *salone*, the first floor displays early Renaissance works, notably Fra' Filippo Lippi's warmly maternal *Madonna and Child*, painted in 1437 and introducing background details, notably architecture, into Italian religious painting for the first time. Next to it is a richly coloured and beautifully composed *Annunciation* by the same artist. A further room hosts Raphael's beguiling *Fornarina*, a painting of the daughter of a Travesteran baker thought to have been Raphael's mistress (Raphael's name appears clearly on the woman's bracelet), although some experts claim the painting to be the work of a pupil. Look out also for Bronzino's portrait of Stefano Colonna, several works by Sodoma, including a dark *Mystical Marriage of St Catherine*, and an anguished *St Jerome* by Tintoretto – full of interesting detail, and clever use of light and shade.

Among the upstairs works, there is a famous painting of *Beatrice Cenci* (see p.52), fomerly attributed to Guide Reni, which moved Shelley to write a play about her tragedy, and a portrait of *Henry VIII* by Hans Holbein which feels almost as well known – probably because the painter produced so many of the monarch. Painted on the day of his marriage to his fourth wife, Anne of Cleves, he's depicted as a rather irritable but beautifully dressed middle-aged man – a stark contrast to the rather ascetic figure of *Erasmus of Rotterdam* by Quentin Matsys, which hangs next to it.

SAN CARLO ALLE QUATTRO FONTANE

Map 4, B7. Mon–Fri 9am–12.30pm & 4–6pm, Sat 9am–12.30pm.
Continue on up Via delle Quattro Fontane and you're at a seventeenth-century landmark, the church of **San Carlo alle Quattro Fontane**. This was Borromini's first real design commission, and in it he displays all the ingenuity he

Via Rasella

More or less opposite Palazzo Barberini, **Via Rasella** was the scene of an ambush of a Nazi military patrol in 1944 that led to one of the worst Italian wartime atrocities – the reprisal massacre of 35 innocent Romans at the Ardeatine Caves outside the city walls. A memorial now stands on the sight of the executions, and the event is commemorated every March 24. Oddly enough, Mussolini had a flat on Via Rasella in which he would entertain his mistresses.

later became known for, cramming the church elegantly into a tiny and awkwardly shaped site that apparently covers roughly the same surface area as one of the main columns inside St Peter's. Tucked in beside the church, the newly restored cloister is also squeezed into a tight but elegant oblong, topped with charming balustrade.

Outside the church are the four **fountains** that give the street and church their name, each cut into a niche in a corner of the crossroads that marks this, the highest point on the Quirinal Hill.

SANT 'ANDREA AND THE QUIRINALE PALACE

Map 3, N3–M4

There's another piece of design ingenuity a few steps south of here, on Via del Quirinale, which is flanked on the left by public gardens and the domed church of **Sant 'Andrea** (daily except Tues 8am–noon & 4–7pm), a flamboyant building that Bernini planned as a kind of flat oval shape to fit into its wide but shallow site.

Opposite is the featureless wall of the **Palazzo del Quirinale** (open the 2nd & 4th Sun morning each month 8am–1pm; L10,000), a sixteenth-century structure that was the official summer residence of the popes until Unification, when it became the royal palace. It's now the home of Italy's president, but you can appreciate its exceptional siting from the **Piazza del Quirinale** at the far end on the right, from which views stretch right across the centre of Rome. The main feature of the piazza is the huge statue of the **Dioscuri**, or Castor and Pollux – massive five-metre-high Roman copies of classical Greek statues, showing the two godlike twins, the sons of Jupiter, who according to legend won victory for the Romans in an important battle (see also p.76). The statues originally stood at the entrance of the Baths of Constantine, the ruins of which stood nearby, and were brought here by Pope Sixtus V in the early sixteenth century to embellish the square – part of the pope's attempts to dignify and beautify the city with many large, vista-laden squares and long straight avenues. Nowadays it forms an odd concoction with the obelisk, which tops the arrangement, originally from the Mausoleum of Augustus, and the vast shallow bowl in front, which was apparently once resident at the Roman forum – all in all a classic example of how Renaissance Rome and later periods made the most out of the classical debris that littered the city.

FONTANA DI TREVI

Map 3, K3.

Via della Dataria winds down from Piazza del Quirinale into the tight web of narrow, apparently aimless streets below, bringing you shortly to one of Rome's more surprising sights, easy to stumble upon by accident – the **Fontana di Trevi**, a huge, very Baroque gush of water over statues and rocks built onto the backside of a Renaissance palace; it's fed by the same source that surfaces at the Barcaccia fountain in Piazza di Spagna. There was a Trevi fountain, designed by Alberti, around the corner in Via dei Crociferi, a smaller, more modest affair by all accounts, but Urban VIII decided to upgrade it in line with his other grandiose schemes of the time and employed Bernini, among others, to design an alternative. Work didn't begin, however, until 1732, when Niccolò Salvi won a competition held by Clement XII to design the fountain, and even then it took thirty years to finish the project. Salvi died in the process, his lungs shot by the time spent in the dank waterworks of the fountain.

The Trevi fountain is now, of course, the place you come to chuck in a coin if you want to guarantee your return to Rome, though you might remember Anita Ekberg throwing herself into it in *La Dolce Vita* (there are police here to discourage you from doing the same thing). Newly restored, it's one of the city's most vigorous outdoor spots to hang out. Opposite, the grubby little church of **Santi Vincenzo ed Anastasio** is the parish church of the Quirinal Palace, and, bizarrely, holds in marble urns the hearts and viscera of the 22 popes who used the palace as a papal residence.

GALLERIA COLONNA

Map 3, L5. Via della Pilotta 17. Jan–July & Sept–Dec Sat 9am–1pm; L10,000.

A short stroll south from the Fontana di Trevi brings you to the **Galleria Colonna**, part of the Palazzo Colonna complex and, although outranked by many of the other Roman palatial collections, worth forty minutes or so if you happen by when it's open, if only for the chandelier-decked Great Hall where most of the paintings are displayed. Best on the whole is the gallery's collection of landscapes by Dughet (Poussin's brother-in-law), but other works that stand out are Carracci's early – and unusually spontaneous – *Bean Eater* (though this attribution has since been questioned), a *Narcissus* by Tintoretto and a *Portrait of a Venetian Gentleman* caught in supremely confident pose by Veronese.

The Forums and the Palatine

From Piazza Venezia **Via dei Fori Imperiali** cuts south through the heart of Rome's ancient sites, a soulless boulevard imposed on the area by Mussolini in 1932. Before then this was a warren of medieval streets that wound around the ruins of the ancient city centre, but as with the Via della Conciliazione up to St Peter's (see p.159) the Duce preferred to build something to his own glory rather than preserve that of another era. There has been a long-standing plan to make the entire ancient part of the city into a huge archeological park which would stretch right down to the catacombs on the Via Appia Antica. However, although excavations have been undertaken in recent years, they are continuing slowly, It's a dilemma for the city-planners: Via dei Fori Imperiali is a major traffic artery, a function which must be preserved; one way around this is to dig a tunnel under the road – an expensive option but an option that is apparently being considered. For the moment, if you want tranquil sightseeing, you'll have to settle for coming on Sunday, when a long stretch from Piazza Venezia to Via Appia Antica is closed to traffic and pedestrians take to the streets to stroll past the ruins of the ancient city.

THE IMPERIAL FORUMS

Map 3, L7.

The original Roman Forum, the Palatine Hill beyond, and of course the Colosseum, are the principal things to see here, all off to the right of the main road. In addition to these, though, scattered along on either side of Via dei Fori Imperiali, are various other remains, the **Imperial Forums**, built after the Forum proper had become too small to accommodate the needs of the ever-expanding city. Julius Caesar began the expansion in around 50 BC, building a new Senate building, and, beyond it to the northeast, a series of basilicas and temples – work that was continued after his assassination by his nephew and successor Augustus, and later by the Flavian emperors – Vespasian, Nerva and finally Trajan. In the mid-1990s, excavations were begun along the south side of the Viale dei Fori Imperiali, and further archeological work has since been conducted on the north side.

The Forum of Trajan

One of the major victims of Mussolini's redesign was the **Forum of Trajan** on the north side of the road, a complex of basilicas, monuments, apartments and shops that was in its day the most sumptuous of the imperial forums, built at what was probably the very pinnacle of Roman power and prestige, after Trajan returned from conquering Dacia (modern Romania) in 112 AD. It's currently fairly unrecognizable, the main section no more than a sunken area of scattered columns to the left of the road, fronting the semicircle of **Markets of Trajan** (summer Tues–Sat 9am–6pm,

Sun 9am–1.30pm; winter Tues–Sat 9am–4pm, Sun 9am–1.30pm; L7000), a tiered ancient Roman shopping centre that's also accessible from Via IV Novembre, and is now home to the so-called Museo degli Fori Imperiali, exhibiting fragments of the decorative marbles that once adorned this market as well as the Forum of Augustus. Down below the markets, the Basilica Ulpia was a central part of the Forum of Trajan, an immense structure, now mostly hidden below ground level. It had five aisles and a huge apse at either end, and measured 176 metres long by 59 metres wide; the central nave is discernible from the large paved area in the centre, and the column stumps give an idea of its former dimensions.

At the head of the basilica, the enormous **Column of Trajan** was erected to celebrate the emperor's victories in Dacia, and is covered top to bottom with reliefs commemorating the highlights of the campaign. The carving on the base shows the trophies brought back and there's an inscription saying that the column was dedicated by the Senate and People of Rome in 113 AD in honour of Trajan.

Behind the Forum of Trajan, the **Torre delle Milizie** is fondly imagined to be the tower from which Nero watched Rome burning, although it's actually a twelfth-century fortification left over from days when Rome was divided into warring factions within the city walls. The top was destroyed by a blast of lightning in the fifteenth century.

The Forum of Augustus

Back on Via dei Fori Imperiali, to the left, across the field of ruins, the round brick facade you can see now houses the Knights of Malta but was once part of the **Forum of Augustus**. Just beyond, the monumental staircase and platform was Augustus's Temple of Mars the Avenger, put up by Augustus in memory of his uncle and adoptive father after the last of the assassins of Julius Caesar had been killed. The temple is backed by a large wall in grey stone that was erected to prevent fire from spreading into the forums from the densely inhabited adjacent neighbourhood of Subura.

THE ROMAN FORUM

Map 3, L8. Summer Tues–Sat 9am–6pm, Sun 9am–1pm; winter Tues–Sat 9am–3pm, Sun 9am–1pm; free.

Cross the road from here and you're outside the very partially excavated remains of the **Forum of Nerva** – just a few piles of broken columns really – and the entrance to the main part of the **Roman Forum** and the **Palatine Hill** beyond.

The Forum is very near the top of most visitors' things to see in Rome. However, for many it's also one of the city's most disappointing sights, and you need an imagination and some small grasp of history to really appreciate the place at all. Certainly it holds some of the most ruined Roman ruins you'll see: the area was abandoned (and looted) for so long that very little is anything like intact. But these five or so acres were once the heart of the Mediterranean world, and are a very real and potent testament to a power that held a large chunk of the earth in its thrall for close on five centuries and whose influence reverberates right up to the present day – in language, in architecture, in political terms and systems, even in the romance that the last couple of hundred years have lent to its ruins.

Even in ancient times Rome was a very large city, stretching out as far as the Aurelian Wall in many places in a sprawl of apartment blocks or *insulae*. But the Forum was its centre, home to its political and religious institutions, its shops and market stalls, and a meeting-place for all and sundry – which it remained until the Imperial era, when Rome's increased importance as a world power led to the extensions nearby.

The Forum never really recovered from this: neglect set in, a fire in the third century AD destroyed many of the buildings, and although the damage was repaired, Rome was by this time in a general state of decay, the coming of Christianity only serving to accelerate the process, particularly with regard to its pagan temples and institutions. After the later downfall of the city to various barbarian invaders, the area was left in ruin, its relics quarried for the construction in other parts of Rome during medieval and Renaissance times and the odd church or tower being constructed *in situ* out of the more viable piles. Excavation of the site didn't start until the beginning of the nineteenth century, since when it has continued pretty much without stopping: you'll notice a fair part of the site, especially up on the Palatine, closed off for further digs.

The Via Sacra

Once inside, take some time to get orientated. Sit down on the three long steps that flank the other side of the **Via**

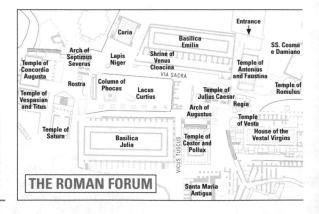

THE ROMAN FORUM

Sacra, which runs directly through the core of the Forum, from below the Capitoline Hill in the west to the far eastern extent of the site and the Arch of Titus (where there's a handy exit for the Colosseum). It was the best-known street of ancient Rome, along which victorious emperors and generals would ride in procession to give thanks at the Capitoline's Temple of Jupiter. It's possible, however, that this wasn't the original Via Sacra at all, and in fact was renamed in the 1550s, when the Holy Roman Emperor, Charles V, visited Pope Paul III and the only triumphal arch they could find to march under was the Arch of Septimus Serverus, a couple hundred yards to your left.

The Regia and around

The steps you're sitting on are part of the **Regia**, or house of the kings, an extremely ancient – and ruined – group of foundations that date probably from the reign of the second King of Rome, Numa, who ruled from 715 to 673 BC.

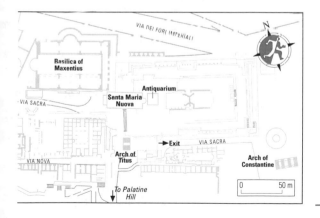

There was a shrine of Mars here, housing the shields and spears of Mars, which generals embarking on a war rattled before setting off. If the shields and spears rattled of their own accord it was a bad omen, requiring purification and repentance rites. The Regia later became the residence of Julius Caesar, who moved in here in 45 BC – an imperious act which at least in part led to his downfall.

On the other side of the road from the Regia, the Temple of Antoninus and Faustina is the best-preserved temple in the forum, mainly because of its preservation since the seventh century as the church of **San Lorenzo in Miranda**. The six huge Corinthian columns across its front are still connected by an inscribed lintel, dedicating the temple to the god Antonino and the goddess Faustina by order of the Senate – the parents of Marcus Aurelius. Above the inscription was the roof architrave, along the sides of which can be seen the original frieze of griffins, candelabra and acanthus scrolls. Otherwise, the brick stairs leading up to the floor of the temple are a modern reconstruction, while the facade of the church dates from 1602.

Next to the Regia, the pile of rubble immersed in cement with the little green roof is all that remains of the grandeur and magnificence that comprised the **temple to Julius Caesar** – the round brick stump under the roof marks the spot where Caesar was cremated, and around which the temple was built. You may hear tour guides declaiming Mark Antony's "Friends, Romans and Countrymen speech from here; if you do, bear in mind that not only was the speech made up by Shakespeare, but also that apparently Mark Antony only read Caesar's will.

The football pitch of broken columns to the right of the Via Sacra marks the site of the **Basilica Emilia**, built in the second century BC to house law courts, and, in the little booths and boutiques flanking it on the Via Sacra side, money-changers. Close by, a little marble plaque dedicated to **Venus Cloacina** marks the site of a small shrine dedicated to Venus where the Cloaca Maxima canal drained the Forum, which was originally marshland. The Cloaca Maxima reaches all the way to the Tiber from here, and still keeps the area drained.

The Curia and around

A little way beyond, the large cube-shaped building is the **Curia**, built on the orders of Julius Caesar as part of his programme for expanding the Forum – it connects up with the Forum of Caesar outside – although what you see now is a Diocletian reconstruction. The Senate met here during the Republican period, and augurs would come to announce the wishes of the gods. For centuries the Curia served as a church, only reverting to its original form earlier this century, when it was restored, and its bronze doors – which had been removed in the seventeenth century to San Giovanni in Laterno, where they remain – were replaced with reproductions.

Inside, three wide stairs rise left and right, on which about 300 senators could be accommodated with their folding chairs. In the centre is the speaker's platform, with a porphyry statue of a togaed figure. Otherwise, apart from the floor, elegantly patterned in red, yellow, green and white marble, there's not much left of its ancient decor, only the grey and white marble facing each side of the speaker's platform, which would once have covered the entire hall. The ceiling is a modern replacement, and in Roman times would have been gilded. The large marble reliefs here, the so called Plutei of Trajan – found in the Forum proper and brought here for safekeeping – show Trajan in the midst of public-spirited acts, forgiving the public debt owed by citizens to the state (porters carry large register books and place them

THE CURIA AND AROUND

before the seated emperor, where they will be burnt) and, on the right giving a woman a sack of money, a representation of Trajan's welfare plan for widows and orphans. Look closely at the reliefs and you can see how parts of the Forum would have looked at the time: in one, a fig tree, the columns and arches of the Basilica Julia, the facade of the Temple of Saturn, a triumphal arch and the Temple of Vespasian and Titus; in the other, the columns and eaves of the Temple of Castor and Pollux, and the Arch of Augustus.

....

In 667 AD, Costans II, ruler of the Eastern empire, paid a state visit to Rome. He came to the Forum, and, seeing all the temples and basilicas held together with bronze and iron cramps, decided that the metal would serve better in his war against encroaching Islam, and ordered all the metal to be transported back home and forged into spearpoints, arrowheads and armour for his forces. It took just twelve days to dismantle the metal props, and, although everything was captured en route to Constantinople by Saracen raiders, the columns and arches supporting all the buildings in the Forum fell with the next earth tremor. By the early ninth century hardly anything remained standing – ripe for the looters of later years, and one reason why so little is left today.

....

Nearby, the black, fenced-off paving of the **Lapis Niger** marks the traditional site of the tomb of Romulus, the steps beneath (usually closed) leading down to a monument that was considered sacred ground during classical times. Across the travertine pavement from the Curia, the **Column of Phocas** is one of a few commemorative columns here that retains its dedicatory inscription. To the right, the **Arch of Septimius Severus** was constructed in the early third century AD by his sons Caracalla and Galba to mark their father's victories in what is now Iran. The friezes on it recall Severus and his son, Caracalla, who ruled Rome with a reign of undisciplined terror for seven years. There's a space where Galba was commemorated – Caracalla had him executed in 213AD, and his name expediently removed from the arch altogether.

The Rostra and around

To the left of the arch, the low brown wall is the **Rostra**, facing the wide-open scatter of paving, dumped stones and beached columns that makes up the central portion of the Forum, the place where most of the life of the city was carried on, and which, in ancient times, was usually crowded with politicians, tribunes and traders. Left of the Rostra, are the long stairs of the **Basilica Julia**, built by Julius Caesar in the 50s BC after he returned from the Gallic wars. All that remains are a few column bases and one nearly complete column, and you can't mount the stairs – although you can still see the gameboards scratched in the marble of the stairs where idlers in the Forum played their pebble toss games.

A bit further along, on the right, the guard rails lead into a kind of alcove in the pavement, which marks the site of the **Lacus Curtius** – the spot where, according to legend, a chasm opened during the earliest days and the soothsayers determined that it would only be closed once Rome had sacrificed its most valuable possession into it. Marcus Curtius, a Roman soldier who declared that Rome's most valuable possession was a loyal citizen, hurled himself and his horse into the void and it duly closed. Further on, you reach the foundations of the **Temple of Saturn** – all that remains of a restoration done around 380 AD. The temple was also the Roman treasury and mint. To the right of the temple, three columns still stand from the **Temple of Vespasian and Titus** of the 80s AD. Still further to the right, behind the Arch of Septimus Severus, the large pile of brick and cement rubble is all that remains of the **Temple of Concordia Augusta**, dedicated by Tiberius in 10 AD.

The Temple of Castor and Pollux

Retracing your steps back past the Forum proper takes you to **Vicus Tuscus**, "Etruscan Street", at the end of which are public toilets and a water fountain, and the church of **Santa Maria Antiqua**, which formed the vestibule to the emperor Domitian's palace on the Palatine Hill, and was the first ancient building to be converted for Christian worship – recently open again after many years. Back around the corner to the right, the enormous pile of rubble topped by three graceful Corinthian columns is the **Temple of Castor and Pollux**, the Forum's oldest temple, dedicated in 484 BC to the divine twins or Dioscuri, the offspring of Jupiter by Leda, who appeared miraculously to ensure victory for the Romans in a key battle. The story goes that a group of Roman citizens were gathered around a water fountain on this spot fretting about the war, when Castor and Pollux appeared and reassured them that the battle was won – hence the temple, and their adoption as the special protectors of Rome.

House of the Vestal Virgins

Beyond here, the **House of the Vestal Virgins** is a second-century AD reconstruction of a building originally built by Nero. Vesta was the Roman goddess of the hearth and home, and her cult was an important one in ancient Rome. Her temple was in the charge of the so-called vestal virgins, who had the responsibility of keeping the sacred flame of Vesta alight, and were obliged to remain chaste for the thirty years that they served (they usually started at around age ten). If the flame should go out, the woman responsible was scourged; if she should lose her chastity, she was buried alive (her male partner-in-crime was flogged to death in front of the Curia). Because of the importance of their office, they were accorded special privileges; a choice section in the Colosseum was reserved for them; only they and the empress could ride in a wheeled vehicle within the confines of the city; and they had the right to pardon any criminal who managed to get close enough to one of them to beseech their mercy. A vestal virgin could resign her post if she wished, and she had the benefit of residing in a very comfortable palace: four floors of rooms around a central courtyard, with the round **Temple of Vesta** at the near end. The rooms are mainly ruins now, though they're fairly recognizable on the Palatine side, and you can get a good sense of the shape of the place from the remains of the courtyard, still with its pool in the centre and fringed by the statues or inscribed pedestals of the women themselves.

The Basilica of Maxentius

Opposite the vestals' house, the curved facade of the **Temple of Romulus** (the son of the emperor Maxentius), dating from 309 AD, has been sanctified and serves as vestibule for the church of **Santi Cosma e Damiano** behind, which sports a wide and majestic sixth-century apse mosaic showing Christ and the Apostles (entrance on Via dei Fori Imperiali). Just past the temple, a shady walkway to the left leads up to the **Basilica of Maxentius**, sometimes called the Basilica of Constantine, which rises up towards the main road – in terms of size and ingenuity probably the Forum's most impressive remains. By the early fourth century, when this structure was built, Roman architects and engineers were expert at building with poured cement. Begun by Maxentius, it was continued by his co-emperor and rival, Constantine, after he had defeated him at the Battle of the Milvian Bridge in 312 AD. It's said that Michelangelo studied the hexagonal coffered arches here when grappling with the dome of St Peter's, and apparently Renaissance architects frequently used its apse and arches as a model. It was here that the famously fragmented colossal statue of Constantine was found, before it was moved to the courtyard of Palazzo dei Conservatori, on the Capitoline Hill (see Chapter 2).

The Antiquarium and Arch of Titus

Back on the Via Sacra, past the church of Santa Maria Nova, the **Antiquarium of the Forum** (daily except Mon 9am–5pm; free) houses a collection of statue fragments, capitals, tiles, mosaics and other bits and pieces found around the Forum – none of it very interesting, apart from a number of skeletons and wooden coffins exhumed from an Iron Age necropolis found to the right of the Temple of Antoninus and Faustina.

From the basilica the Via Sacra climbs more steeply, past a grassy series of ruins that no one has been able to positively identify, to the **Arch of Titus**, which stands commandingly on a low arm of the Palatine Hill, looking one way down the remainder of the Via Sacra to the Colosseum, and back over the Forum proper. The arch was built by Titus's brother, Domitian, after the emperor's death in 81 AD, to commemorate his victories in Judea in 70 AD, and his triumphal return from that campaign. It's a much restored structure, and you can see, in reliefs on the inside, scenes of Titus riding in a chariot with Nike, goddess of Victory, being escorted by representatives of the Senate and Plebs, and, on the opposite side, spoils being removed from the

Temple in Jerusalem. It's a long-standing tradition that Jews don't pass under this arch.

THE PALATINE HILL

Map 7, I3–I4. Summer Tues–Sat 9am–6pm, Sun 9am–1pm; winter Tues–Sat 9am–3pm, Sun 9am–1pm; L12,000, last tickets 1hr before closing; L20,000 for a ticket that includes the Colosseum, Palazzo Altemps and Palazzo Massimo. Entrance either from the Roman Forum, or from Via San Gregorio .

Turning right at the Arch of Titus takes you up to the ticket booth and entrance to the **Palatine Hill**, supposedly where the city of Rome was founded and holding some of its most ancient remnants. In a way it's a more pleasant site to tour than the Forum, larger, greener and more of a park – a good place to have a picnic and relax after the rigours of the ruins below. In the days of the Republic, the Palatine was the most desirable address in Rome (from it is derived our word "palace"), and the big names continued to colonize it during the Imperial era, trying to outdo each other with ever larger and more magnificent dwellings.

Following the main path up from the Forum, the **Domus Flavia** was one of the most splendid residences, and, although it's now almost completely ruined, the peristyle is easy enough to identify, with its fountain and hexagonal brick arrangement in the centre. To the left, the top level of the gargantuan **Domus Augustana** spreads to the far brink of the hill – not the home of Augustus as its name suggests, but the private house of any emperor (or "Augustus"). You can look down from here on its vast central courtyard with maze-like fountain and wander to the brink of the deep trench of the **Stadium**. On the far side of the stadium, the ruins of the **Baths of Septimius Severus** cling to the side of the hill, the terrace giving good views over the Colosseum and the churches of the Celian Hill opposite.

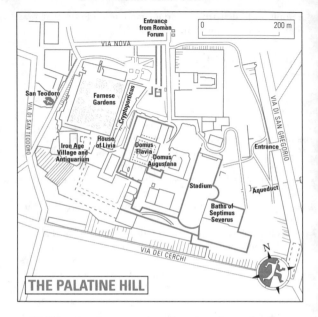

THE PALATINE HILL

Walking in the opposite direction from the Domus Flavia, steps lead down to the **Cryptoporticus** (closed for restoration), a long passage built by Nero to link the vestibule of his Domus Aurea with the Domus Augustana and other Palatine palaces, and decorated along part of its length with well-preserved Roman stucco-work. You can go either way along the passage: a left turn leads to the **House of Livia**, originally believed to have been the residence of Livia, the wife of Augustus, though now identified as simply part of Augustus's house (the set of ruins beyond). Its courtyard and some of the inner rooms are decorated with scanty frescoes.

Turn right down the passage and up some steps on the left and you're in the **Farnese Gardens**, among the first botanical gardens in Europe, laid out by Cardinal Alessandro Farnese in the mid-sixteenth century and now a tidily planted, shady retreat from the exposed heat of the ruins. The terrace here looks back over the Forum, while the terrace at the opposite end looks down on the church of San Teodoro, across to St Peter's, and down on the new excavations immediately below – the traces of an **Iron Age village** that perhaps marks the real centre of Rome's ancient beginnings. The large grey building here houses the Palatine **Antiquarium**, which contains a vast assortment of statuary, pottery, terracotta antefixes and architectural fragments that have been excavated on the Palatine during the last 150 years. Much like the Forum Antiquarium, its most interesting exhibits are the very oldest, including models of how the Palatine looked in the Iron Age.

The Colosseum, Celian Hill and beyond

On the far side of the Forum, **heading south**, are some of Rome's most ancient sights, remnants of the time when this area was mostly green, bucolic countryside. A lake lay where the Colosseum stands now, drained by a small stream that wove between the Palatine and Celian hills, curving to empty into the Tiber close by the Circo Massimo. The slopes of the Palatine and Celian hills were inhabited by people living in shanties and huts, until the great fire of 64 AD, when Nero incorporated the area into his grand design for the city, building a gigantic Nymphaeum to support his planned gardens on the Celian Hill, part of his Domus Aurea (see below), and cleaning up the slopes of the two hills. Eventually a temple to the deified Claudius was built on the Celian Hill, and the Palatine became the residence of the emperors, fed by water brought by the arched span of the Aqua Claudia.

Nowadays, this part of Rome has some of the city's most atmospheric and compelling Christan and ancient sights, in the **Colosseum**, and, beyond, the churches of **San Clemente** and **San Giovanni in Laterano**, among others. It also has some of its most pleasant corners, in particular up on the still green and peaceful **Celian Hill**.

THE ARCH OF CONSTANTINE

Map 4, B12.

Leaving the Forum by way of the Via Sacra, under the Arch of Titus (see p.78), you see the huge **Arch of Constantine** to your right, placed here in the early decades of the fourth century AD after Constantine had consolidated his power as sole emperor. The arch demonstrates the deterioration of the arts during the late stages of the Roman Empire, in that there were hardly any sculptors around who could produce original work and most of the sculptural decoration here had to be removed from other monuments. The builders were probably quite ignorant of the significance of the pieces they borrowed: the round medallions are taken from a temple dedicated to the emperor Hadrian's lover, Antinous, and show Antinous and Hadrian engaged in the hunt. The other pieces, removed from the Forum of Trajan, show Dacian prisoners captured in Trajan's war there. The large inscription in the centre was made for the arch, and dedicates the arch to Constantine for his wisdom – presumably in making Christianity the official religion of the Empire, although no one really knows what this refers to.

Between the Arch of Constantine and the Colosseum, at a pivotal point in the Via Sacra, stood a monumental fountain or **Meta Sudans**, the outline of which can still be seen today in the form of a series of recently excavated low brick walls. A "Meta" was the marker in the centre of a racecourse, and was usually an obelisk or some other large, easily visible object. In this case it was a conical fountain that was probably dedicated to Apollo, and produced a slow supply of water that resembled sweat – hence its name the "Sweating Meta".

THE COLOSSEUM

Map 4, C12. Summer Tues–Sat 9am–6pm, Sun 9am–1pm; winter Tues–Sat 9am–3pm, Sun 9am–1pm; L10,000; L20,000 for a ticket that includes the Palatine, Palazzo Altemps and Palazzo Massimo.

Across the way from here, the **Colosseum** is perhaps Rome's most awe-inspiring ancient monument, and one which – unlike the Forum – needs little historical knowledge or imagination to deduce its function. This enormous structure was so solidly built that the depredations of nearly 2000 years of earthquakes, fires, riots, wars, and, not least, being plundered for its seemingly inexhaustible supply of ready-cut travertine blocks (the Barberini and Cancelleria palaces, even St Peter's, all used stone from here), still stands between the Roman Forum and the hills immediately south and east. It's not much more than a shell now, eaten away by pollution and cracked by the vibrations of cars and metro; around the outside, the arches would originally have held statues, and there are gaping holes where metal brackets linked the great blocks together. The basic structure of the place is easy to see, however, and has served as a model for stadiums around the world ever since. You'll not be alone in appreciating it, and during summer the combination of people and scaffolding can make a visit more like touring a contemporary building-site than an ancient monument. But visit late in the evening or early morning before the tour buses have arrived, go up a level to get a real sense of the size of the building, and the arena can seem more like the marvel it really is.

Seeing the Colosseum

Originally known as the Flavian Amphitheatre (the name Colosseum is a much later invention), it was begun around 72 AD by the emperor Vespasian, who was anxious to extinguish the memory of Nero, and so chose the site of Nero's outrageous Domus Aurea (see p.97) for the stadium; the Colosseum is sited on a lake that lay in front of the vestibule of the palace, where Nero had erected a statue of himself as sun god. The lake was drained, and the Colosseum was – incredibly, given the size of the project – inaugurated by Vespasian's son Titus about eight years later, an event celebrated by 100 days of continuous games; it was finally completed by Domitian, Titus's brother, the third of the Flavian emperors.

Up until this time gladiatorial and other bloody games had been conducted in a makeshift stadium in the Roman Forum, near the Curia. The stands were temporary and constructed of wood, and had to be erected and taken down every time there were games. It is said that seventy thousand Hebrew slaves did the heavy work at the Colosseum. Fifty thousand cartloads of pre-cut travertine stone was hauled from the quarries at Tivoli, a distance of seventeen miles. In the depths of what must have been the muddy bottom of the lake, a labyrinth was laid out, walling in passages for the contestants and creating areas for assembling and storing sets, scenery and other requirements for gladiatorial contests.

The overall structure was tastefully designed, with close attention paid to decoration. On the outside, the arena's three arcades rose in strict classical fashion – with Ionic, topped by Doric, topped by Corinthian, columns – to a flat surface at the top punctuated only by windows, where there was a series of supports for masts that protruded at the upper limit. These masts, 240 in total, were used to array a

Beastly happenings
at the Colosseum

The Romans flocked to the Colosseum for many things, but **gladiatorial contests** were the big attraction. Gladiatorial combat as a Roman tradition was a direct import from the Etruscans, who thought it seemly to sacrifice a few prisoners of war or slaves at the funeral games of an important person. By the second century BC gladiatorial games had become so institutionalized in Rome that a gladiatorial school, or Ludus, was installed in the city – a rather grim affair, consisting of a residential barracks for gladiators and a ring in which they could practise with blunt weapons under supervision.

Gladiatorial combat was probably the greatest and cruellest of all bloodsports. At the start of the games the gladiators would enter through the monumental door at the eastern end of the arena. They would make a procession around the ring and halt in front of the emperor's box, where they would make their famous greeting "Hail Caesar, we who are about to die salute you." Gladiators were divided into several classes, to perform different types of combat. There was the heavily armed "Samnite", named after the types of arms that the Romans had captured on the defeat of that tribe in 310 BC, equipped with heavy armour, an oblong bronze shield, a visored helmet with crest and plumes, and a sword (gladius). Usually a Samnite would be pitted against a combatant without armour, who was equipped only with a cast net and a trident, whose main protection was that he was unencumbered and thereby could be fleet of foot. He had, however, only one cast of his net in which to entangle the Samnite and kill him with his trident. He was not allowed to flee from the arena, and, once captured, the roaring mob would be asked whether he should be killed or be allowed to live. If the opponent had put up a good fight he would usually be spared; if he had not fought as valiantly as he should, however, he would be slaughtered on the spot. The advent of Christianity brought a gradual end to the gladiatorial games, and in 404 AD the emperor Honorius abolished them altogether.

The other activities conducted in the Colosseum involved **animals**. In the hundred-day games that inaugurated the Colosseum, something like 9000 beasts were massacred – roughly twelve killings a minute – and during the 450 years of activity here several breeds of African elephant and lion were rendered extinct. There were also gladiatorial games which involved "hunting" wild animals, and sometimes animals would be pitted against each other – bears would be tied to bulls and have to fight to the finish, lions would take on tigers, dogs would be set against wolves, and so on. The last games involving animals were conducted in the year 523 AD, after which the Colosseum gradually fell into disuse and disrepair.

canvas awning over the spectators inside the arena. Inside, beyond the corridors that led up to the seats, lavishly decorated with painted stuccoes, there was room for a total of around 60,000 people seated and 10,000 or so standing; and the design is such that all 70,000 could enter and be seated in a matter of minutes – surely a lesson for designers of modern stadiums.

The seating was allocated on a strict basis, with the emperor and his attendants naturally occupying the best seats in the house, and the social class of the spectators diminishing as you got nearer the top. There were no ticket sales as we conceive of them; rather, tickets were distributed through – and according to the social status of – Roman heads of households. These "tickets" were in fact wooden tags, with the entrance, row, aisle and seat number carved on them.

BEASTLY HAPPENINGS AT THE COLOSSEUM

Inside the amphitheatre, the labyrinth below was covered over with a wooden floor, punctuated at various places for trap doors which could be opened as required and lifts to raise and lower the animals that were to take part in the games. The floor was covered with canvas to make it waterproof and the canvas was covered with several centimetres of sand to absorb blood; in fact, our word "arena" is derived from the Latin word for sand.

THE CELIAN HILL

Map 4, C13.

Some of the animals that were to die in the Colosseum were kept in a zoo up on the **Celian Hill**, just behind the arena, the furthest south of Rome's seven hills and probably its most peaceful, still clothed almost entirely in woodland and with the gorgeous park of **Villa Celimontana** at its heart. You can get in here by way of the entrance on **Piazza della Navicella**, a little way down Via Claudia, and you could do worse than take a stroll through, before moving on to a couple of worthwhile churches.

SANTI GIOVANNI E PAOLO

Map 4, C13. Daily 8.30am–noon & 3.30–6.30pm.

Continuing up to the summit of the hill, you'll come to the church of **Santi Giovanni e Paolo**, marked by its colourful campanile and set in a once-peaceful square that's been invaded by adolescent autograph hunters since Silvio Berlusconi's TV studios moved in opposite. Originally founded by a Roman senator called Pammachius, the church is in a way a memorial to conscientious objection, dedicated to two dignitaries in the court of Constantine who were beheaded here in 361 AD after refusing military service. The relics of their house are downstairs, although this is currently closed for restoration – around twenty rooms in all, frescoed with pagan and Christian subjects. Inside the church, the railed-off square in mid-nave marks the shrine where the saints were martyred and buried.

SAN GREGORIO MAGNO

Map 4, B14. Daily 9am–noon & 3–6.30pm.

From the church the road descends under a succession of brick arches to the church of **San Gregorio Magno** on the left, in a commanding position above the traffic drone of the road below, and looking over to the lollipop pines of the Palatine Hill opposite. Again, it's the story behind the church that's most interesting. It was from here that St Gregory dispatched St Augustine in the early seventh century to convert England to Christianity, and although the rather ordinary Baroque interior shows little evidence of it, the chapel of the saint does have a beautifully carved altar showing scenes from his life, and there's a room containing his marble throne.

More impressive is the structure to the left of the church, made up of three chapels and surrounded by cypress trees. **Santa Silvia** and **Sant'Andrea** contain **frescoes** by Guido Reni, Domenichino and Pomarancio, while **Santa Barbara** treasures the table at which St Gregory fed twelve paupers daily with his own hands for years.

SAN CLEMENTE

Map 4, D12. Mon–Sat 9am–12.30pm & 3–6pm, Sun opens 10am.

From the Colosseum, it's a short walk east down Via San Giovanni in Laterano to the church of **San Clemente** a cream-coloured twelfth-century basilica that perhaps encapsulates better than any other the continuity of history in the city – being in fact a conglomeration of three places of worship. Pope St Clement I, to whom the church is dedicated, was the third pope after St Peter (and in fact is said to have been ordained by him), and he reigned from 90 AD until 99 AD, when he was exiled and martyred in the Crimea. His relics are kept in this church, and have been venerated here from the very earliest times.

The basilica

The **ground-floor church** is a superb example of a medieval basilica: its facade and courtyard face east in the archaic fashion, and there are some fine, warm mosaics in the apse and a chapel with frescoes by Masolino. The choir is partitioned off with beautiful white marble slabs bearing the earliest papal insignia in the city, the monogram of Pope John II, who reigned from 533 to 535. The gilded ceiling bears the arms of Pope Clement XI, from the early years of the eighteenth century, during whose papacy the church was remodelled.

The early church and Mithraic temple

Downstairs (same hours; L4000) there's the nave of an **earlier church**, dated back to 392 AD, with a frescoed narthex depicting, among other things, the *Miracle of San Clemente*. And at the eastern end of this church, steps lead down to a third level, the remains of a Roman house – a labyrinthine set of rooms including a dank **Mithraic temple** of the late second century, set among several rooms of a Roman house built after the fire of 64 AD. In the temple is preserved a statue of Mithras slaying the bull and the seats upon which the worshippers sat during their ceremonies. The underground river that formerly fed the lake in front of the Domus Aurea can be heard rushing to its destination in the Tiber, behind the Circo Massimo, a reminder that Rome is built on very shaky foundations indeed.

Next door to the Roman house, across a narrow alley-way, are the ground-floor **rooms** of a first-century imperial building, all of which can be explored by the spooky light of fluorescent tubes set in the ceiling and along the mossy brick walls.

SANTI QUATTRO CORONATI

Map 4, D13.

An alternative route from the Colosseum to San Giovanni in Laterano takes you past the church of **Santi Quattro Coronati**, dedicated to four soldier martyrs who died because they refused to worship a statue of Aesculapius during the persecutions of Diocletian. Originally built in 1110 by Pope Paschal II, the church is a prime example of a medieval Christian building, though with an extra-wide apse and a sanctuary that contains a *matroneum* or woman's gallery – something rarely seen nowadays. A cloistered convent of Augustinian nuns lives here now, and it's they you have to ask for the key to get into the chapel of St Sylvester, which contains the oldest extant frescoes in Rome – painted in 1248 and relating the story of how the fourth century pope cured the emperor Constantine of leprosy and then baptized him.

SAN STEFANO ROTONDO

Map 4, D14.

Close by Quattro Coronati, the round church of **San Stefano Rotondo** is another truly ancient structure, built in the 460s AD and consecrated by Pope Simplicius to commemorate Christianity's first martyr. Recently open again after a lengthy restoration, its four chapels form the shape of a cross in a circle, moodily lit by the 22 windows of the clerestory. The interior has a labyrinthine feel, but the feature that will really stick in your mind is the series of stomach-turning frescoes on the walls of the outer ring: various saints being martyred in different ways: impalings, pinchings, drawings and quarterings, disembowelments, boilings in oil, hangings, beheadings – you name it.

SAN GIOVANNI IN LATERANO

Map 4, F14. Daily: summer 7am–7pm; winter 7am–6pm,

Continuing down the same street brings you out eventually at the basilica of **San Giovanni in Laterano**. Officially Rome's cathedral and the seat of the pope as bishop of Rome, this was for centuries the main papal residence. However, when the papacy returned from Avignon at the end of the fourteenth century, the Lateran palaces were in ruin and uninhabitable, and the pope moved across town to the Vatican, where he has remained ever since. The Lateran Treaty of 1929 accorded this and the other patriarchal basilicas extraterritorial status.

There has been a church on this site since the fourth century, the first established by Constantine, and the present building, reworked by Borromini in the mid-seventeenth century, evokes – like San Clemente or San Stefano – Rome's staggering wealth of history, with a host of features from different periods. The doors to the church, oddly enough, were taken from the Curia or Senate House of the Roman Forum.

The interior of the church

The **interior** has been extensively reworked over the centuries. Much of what you see today dates from 1600, when the Aldobrandini pope, Clement VIII, had the church remodelled for that Holy Year. The gilded ceiling of the nave has as its centrepiece the papal arms of Pope Pius VI, from the late 1700s; the ceiling in the crossing bears, on the left, the Aldobrandini insignia, and on the right the remembrances of Pope Innocent III, who died in 1216 and was buried here in the late 1800s at the behest of Pope Leo XIII, when he had this wing of the crossing remodelled. Leo XIII himself, who died in 1903, is buried opposite. The first pillar on the left of the right-hand aisle shows a fragment of Giotto's fresco of Boniface VIII, proclaiming the first Holy Year in 1300. Further on, a more recent monument commemorates Sylvester I – "the magician pope", Bishop of Rome during much of Constantine's reign (see above) – and incorporates part of his original tomb, said to sweat and rattle its bones when a pope is about to die. Kept secure behind the papal altar are the heads of St Peter and St Paul, the church's prize relics.

The cloisters

Outside, the **cloisters** (daily 9am–5pm; L4000) are one of the most pleasing parts of the complex, decorated with early thirteenth-century Cosmati work and with fragments of the original basilica arranged around in no particular order, including a remarkable papal throne assembly and various papal artefacts (not least the vestments of Boniface VIII) in a room off to the side.

The Lateran Palace and Baptistry

Adjoining the basilica is the **Lateran Palace**, home of the popes in the Middle Ages and also formally part of Vatican territory. Next door, the **Baptistry** (daily: summer 9am–1pm & 5–7pm; winter 9am–1pm & 4–6pm; free) has been carefully restored, along with the side of the church itself, after a car bombing in 1993. It is the oldest surviving baptistry in the Christian world, a mosaic-lined, octagonal structure built during the fifth century that has been the model for many such buildings since.

The Scala Santa and chapel of San Lorenzo

There are more ancient remains on the other side of the church, on Piazza di Porta San Giovanni, foremost of which is the **Scala Santa** (daily 6.15am–12.15pm & 3.30–6.30pm), claimed to be the staircase from Pontius Pilate's house down which Christ walked after his trial. The 28 steps are protected by boards, and the only way you're allowed to climb them is on your knees, which pilgrims do regularly – although there is also a staircase to the side for the less penitent. At the top, the chapel of **San Lorenzo** holds an ancient (sixth- or seventh-century) painting of Christ said to be the work of an angel, hence its name – *acheiropoeton*, or "not done by human hands".

SANTA CROCE IN GERUSALEMME

Map 4, I13. Daily 6am–noon & 3.30–7pm.

Across the far side of the square, the **Porta Asinaria**, one of the city's grander gateways, marks the Aurelian Wall. If you're here in the morning, you could visit the new and second-hand **clothing market** on Via Sannio (Mon–Sat until about 1.30pm). Otherwise follow the wall on the city side by way of Viale Carlo Felice to another key Roman church, **Santa Croce in Gerusalemme**, one of the seven pilgrimage churches of Rome. Built on the site of the palace of Constantine's mother St Helena, it houses the relics of the true cross she had brought back from Jerusalem. The building is mainly Baroque in style follow-ing an eighteenth-century renovation, but the relics of the cross are stored in a surreal Mussolini-era chapel at the end of the left aisle, and the Renaissance apse frescoes, recording the discovery of the fragments, are very fine indeed.

PORTA MAGGIORE

Map 4, I11.

North of here towards the rail tracks, the **Porta Maggiore** is probably the most impressive of all the city gates, built in the first century AD to carry water into Rome from the aqueducts outside, and incorporated into the Aurelian walls. The **aqueducts** that converge here are the **Aqua Claudia**, which dates from 45 AD, and the **Aqua Marcia** from 200 BC. The Roman engineers built them one on top of the other at this point to channel the water of the Aqua Claudia into the city in a manner not to interfere with the pre-existing Aqua Marcia – a feat recounted in the monumental tablet over the central arches.

The famous **Tomb of the Baker**, in white travertine, just outside the gate, is a monument from about 30 AD. The baker in question was a public contractor who made a fortune selling bread to the imperial government. The round holes in the tomb represent the openings of the baker's ovens – a style that strangely enough was picked up in the Mussolini era and can be seen time and again in Fascist architecture.

The Esquiline Hill, Termini and beyond

On the far side of the main road, Via Labacana, from the Colosseum, the **Esquiline Hill** is the highest and largest of the city's seven hills. Formerly a sparsely populated area, with vineyards, orchards and olive groves stretching out to the Aurelian wall, it was one of the most fashionable residential quarters of ancient Rome. In fact it consists of four separate summits; the *Oppian* (the part nearest the Colosseum, now a small park); the *Subura*, which was ancient Rome's most notorious inner-city suburb; the *Fagutalis*: and – the highest (65m) and largest – the *Cispius*, which is the site of the basilica of Santa Maria Maggiore. Because of these four hills, this area of the city is called "Monti". Nowadays it's a mixed area, but one which almost every traveller to Rome encounters at some point – not just because of key sights like Nero's **Domus Aurea** and the basilica of **Santa Maria Maggiore**, and the grand developments of post-Unification Rome around **Via Nazionale** and **Via XX Settembre**, but also because of **Stazione Termini**, whose tawdry environs are home to the lion's share of Rome's budget hotels.

THE DOMUS AUREA

Map 4, C11. Via Labicana 136. Daily 9am–8pm, guided tours obligatory; L10,000, plus L6000 for the obligatory tour, plus L2000 reservation fee – L18,000 in total. Booking is strongly recommended, ©06 3974 9907. The entrance is off Via Labacana, in the Parco Oppio, almost opposite the Colosseum. (Do not continue up the path into main part of the park.)

One of the Esquiline Hill's most intriguing sights is without doubt Nero's **Domus Aurea** or "Golden House", built on the summit of the Oppian and into its sides after a fire of 64 AD devastated this part of Rome. This "house" was a vast undertaking, but it was not intended to be a residence at all; rather it was a series of banqueting rooms, nymphaeums, small baths, terraces and gardens, facing what at the time was a small lake fed by the underground springs and streams that drained from the surrounding hills. Rome was used to Nero's excesses, but it had never seen anything like the Golden House before. The facade was supposed to have been coated in solid gold, there was hot and cold running water in the baths, one of the dining rooms was rigged up to shower flowers and natural scent on guests, and the grounds – which covered a full square mile – held vineyards and game. Nero didn't get to enjoy his palace for long – he died a couple of years after it was finished, and Vespasian tore a lot of the exposed facade down in disgust, draining its lake and building the Colosseum on top. Later Trajan built his baths on top of the rest of the complex, and it was pretty much forgotten until its wall paintings were discovered by Renaissance artists, including Raphael. When these artists first visited these rooms, they had to descend down ladders into what they believed at first was some kind of mystical cave, or grotto – giving us the word *grotesque*, which they used to describe their attempts to imitate this style of painting in their own work.

THE DOMUS AUREA |

Today it is possible to visit parts of the Golden House, which have recently been opened under the Trajan's baths. Tours start by taking you down a long corridor into the excavated rooms of the palace. The temperature always hovers at around 10°C and this, and the almost 100 percent humidity, makes it necessary to wear a sweater or jacket even in the dead of the Roman summer.

Inside the Domus Aurea

Tours can at first be confusing, as you become aware of just how much Trajan set out to obliterate the palace with his baths complex – the baths' foundations merge into parts of the palace, and vice versa – but a free plan, not to mention the guide, helps you sort it out. There are various covered fountains, service corridors, terraces and, most spectacularly, the Octagonal Room, domed, with a hole in the middle, which is supposed to have rotated as the day progressed to emulate the passage of the sun. Most of the rooms are decorated in the so-called Third Pompeiian style, with fanciful depictions of people looking out windows at you, garlands of flowers, fruit, vines and foliage, interspersed with mythical animals. Perhaps the best preserved frescoes are in the room of Achilles at Skyros, and illustrate Homer's story of Achilles being sent to the island of Skyros disguised as a woman to prevent him being drawn into the Trojan wars. In one fresco, Achilles is in drag at the Skyros court; another shows him putting his female clothes aside and picking up a shield, brought to him by Ulysses (in the crested helmet) to catch him out and betray his disguise.

Parco di Colle Oppio

Outside the entrance to the Golden House, the **Parco di Colle Oppio** is dotted with remnants of the various

Roman structures that once stood here: various piles of rubble, the remains of Trajan's baths, and a number of round brick stumps – well heads that led down into the Golden House. These apart, the park is a pretty unsavoury place, a gathering place for street people and fascist youths, and as such not particularly safe after dark.

SAN PIETRO IN VINCOLI

Map 4, C10. Daily 8am–12.30pm & 3.30–6pm; offering required.

Steps lead up from Colosseum metro station to Via Terme di Tito and left into Via Eudossia, which leads past Rome university's faculty of engineering to the tranquil piazza in front of the recently restored church of **San Pietro in Vincoli** – one of Rome's most delightfully plain churches, built to house an important relic, the chains that held St Peter when he was in Jerusalem and those that held him in Rome, which miraculously joined together. During the papacy of Sixtus IV, it was the cardinal seat of the pope's nephew, Giuliano della Rovere, who became Pope Julius II, of Sistine Chapel ceiling fame.

The chains of St Peter can still be seen in the confessio beneath the high altar, in a beautiful gold and rock crystal reliquary, but most people come for the tomb of Pope Julius II at the far end of the southern aisle, which occupied Michelangelo on and off for much of his career and was the cause of many a dispute with Julius and his successors. Michelangelo reluctantly gave it up to paint the Sistine Chapel, and never again found the time to return to it for very long, being always at the beck and call of successive popes – who understandably had little interest in promoting the glory of one of their predecessors.

No one knows how the tomb would have looked had it been finished – it's generally assumed that Moses would have been on one end and the risen Christ on the other, with a statue of Julius himself surmounting the whole thing – and the only statues that Michelangelo completed are the Moses, Leah and Rachel, which remain here in the church, and two Slaves which are now in the Louvre. The figure of Moses, however, pictured as descended from Sinai to find the Israelites worshipping the golden calf, and flanked by the gentle figures of Leah and Rachel, is one of the artist's most captivating works, the rest of the composition – completed by later artists – seeming dull and static by comparison. Because of a medieval mistranslation of scripture, Moses is depicted with satyr's horns instead of the "radiance of the Lord" that Exodus tells us shone around his head. Nonetheless this powerful statue is so lifelike that Michelangelo is alleged to have struck its knee with his hammer and shouted "Speak, damn you!". The rest of the group was finished by Michelangelo's pupils, while the statue of Julius II at the top, by Maso del Bosco, modelled on an Etruscan coffin lid, sadly fails in evoking the character of this apparently active, courageous and violent man.

SAN MARTINO AI MONTI

Map 4, D10.

Turn right outside the church and follow Via delle Sette Sale – named after the seven water cisterns of the nearby Baths of Trajan – to the church of **San Martino ai Monti**, another place of worship that dates back to the earliest days of Christianity. It was dedicated to the saints Sylvester and Martin in the sixth century, and incorporates an ancient Roman structure, but it was almost entirely rebuilt in the 1650s, and sports a ceiling from that time that is strangely modern in appearance, reminiscent of 1920s brushed stainless steel. The ceiling also shows the arms of the Medicis, specifically the family's last pope, Leo XI, who ruled briefly in 1605, and has a series of frescoes depicting scenes of the

Roman Campagna and the interiors of the old Roman basilicas of St Peter and St John before they were gussied up in their present Baroque splendour.

MUSEO NAZIONALE DI ARTE ORIENTALE

Map 4, E10. Via Merulana 248. Tues–Sun 9am–8pm; L12,000

It's a short walk from San Martino to the busy Largo Brancaccio, and the nineteenth-century thoroughfare of Via Merulana, where the imposing Palazzo Brancaccio houses the **Museo Nazionale di Arte Orientale**– a first-rate collection of oriental art (Italy's best) that has recently been restored. Beginning with Marco Polo in the thirteenth century, the Italians have always had connections with the Far East, and the quality of this collection of Islamic, Chinese, Indian and Southeast Asian art reflects this fact – not to mention making a refreshing break from the multiple ages of Western artistic endeavour you are exposed to in Rome. There are finds dating to 1500–500 BC from a necropolis in Pakistan; architectural fragments in painted wood, and art works and jewellery, from Tibet, Nepal and Pakistan; and a solid collection from China, with predictable Buddhas and vases, but also curiosities like imperial warming plates. Take a look, too, at the Luristan bronzes from eighth-century BC Iran, and marvel at the similarities between these and some of the Etruscan bronzes of the same age you may well have seen elsewhere in the city.

PIAZZA VITTORIO EMANUELE II

Map 4, F10.

Cross Largo Leopardi outside the museum, and walk a few yards up Via Leopardi to **Piazza Vittorio Emanuele II**, the centre of a district which became known as the "quartiere piemontese" when the government located many of its major ministries here after Unification. The arcades of the square, certainly, recall central Turin, as do the solid palatial buildings that surround it. It's more recently become the immigrant quarter of Rome, with a heavy concentration of African, Asian and Middle Eastern shops and restaurants. You'll easily hear a dozen different languages spoken as you pass through the open-air food **market** (Mon–Sat 8am–1pm) – Rome's cheapest – that surrounds the piazza.

Close to the northern end of the piazza, behind the market stalls, an eighteen-metre-high pile of Roman bricks is what is left of a monumental public fountain known as the **Nymphaeum of Alexander Severus** (emperor 222–235 AD) – a distribution point for water arriving in the city by a branch of the Acqua Claudia aqueduct.

SANTA MARIA MAGGIORE

Map 4, E9. Summer daily 7am–7pm; winter daily 7am–6pm.

Steps lead down from San Pietro in Vincoli to **Via Cavour**, a busy central thoroughfare which carves a route between the Colosseum and Termini station. After about half a kilometre the street widens to reveal the basilica of **Santa Maria Maggiore**. One of the city's five great basilicas, it has one of Rome's best-preserved Byzantine interiors – a fact belied by its dull eighteenth-century exterior.

Unlike the other great places of pilgrimage in Rome, Santa Maria Maggiore was not built on any special Constantinian site, but instead went up during the fifth century after the Council of Ephesus recognized the cult of the Virgin and churches venerating Our Lady began to spring up all over the Christian world. According to legend, the Virgin Mary appeared to Pope Liberius in a dream on the night of August 4, 352 AD, telling him to build a church on the Esquiline hill, on a spot where he would find a patch of newly fallen snow the next morning. The snow would outline exactly the plan of the church that should be built there in her honour – which of course is exactly what happened, and the first church here was called Santa Maria della Neve ("of the snow"). The present structure dates from about 420 AD, and was completed under the reign of St Sixtus III, who reigned between 432 AD and 440AD.

....

Santa Maria Maggorie is noted for two special ceremonies. One, on August 5, celebrates the miraculous snowfall: at midday mass white rose petals are showered on the congregation from the ceiling, and at night the fire department operates an artificial snow machine in the piazza in front and showers the area in snow that, naturally, melts immediately. The other takes place on Christmas morning, when the reliquary containing the crib is processed around the church and then displayed on the high altar.

....

Inside the basilica

The basilica was encased in its eighteenth-century shell during the papacy of Benedict XIV, although the campanile, the highest in Rome, is older than this – built in 1377 under Pope Gregory XI. Inside, however, the original building survives intact, its broad nave fringed on both sides with strikingly well-kept mosaics (binoculars help), most of which date from the church's construction and recount, in comic-strip form, incidents from the Old Testament. The ceiling, which shows the arms of the Spanish Borgia popes, Calixtus III and Alexander VI, was gilded in 1493 with gold sent by Queen Isabella as part payment of a loan from Innocent VIII to finance the voyage of Columbus to the New World.

The chapel in the right transept holds the elaborate tomb of Sixtus V – another, less famous, **Sistine Chapel**, decorated with marble taken from the Roman Septizodium (see box), and with frescoes and stucco reliefs portraying events from his reign. The chapel also contains the tomb of another zealous and reforming pope, St Pius V, whose statue faces that of Sixtus; Pius V is probably best known as the pope who excommunicated Queen Elizabeth I of England, in 1570.

Outside the Sistine Chapel is the tomb slab of the Bernini family, including Gian Lorenzo himself, while opposite, the **Pauline Chapel** is even more sumptuous than the Sistine Chapel, home to the tombs of the Borghese pope, Paul V, and his immediate predecessor

Sixtus V

Although he reigned only five years, **Sixtus V**'s papacy was one of Rome's most memorable. He laid out several new streets – the long straight thoroughfare that runs from the top of Trinità dei Monti to Santa Maria Maggiore (at various points Via Sistina, Via delle Quattro Fontane and Via De Pretis) is one example; he erected many of the present obelisks that dot the city, notably those in Piazza San Pietro and Piazza San Giovanni; and he launched an attack on bandits in the surrounding countryside and criminal gangs in the city. He was, like Julius II, a man of action and a Franciscan friar, and he was perhaps most famously responsible for the execution of Beatrice Cenci (see p.52). His reign was also notorious for his stripping the Roman Forum of its marbles and the Colosseum of its stone for St Peter's. He also demolished the so-called *Septizodium,* at the southeast end of the Palatine, marble from which decorated his tomb.

Clement VIII. The floor, in *opus sectile*, contains the Borghese arms, an eagle and dragon, and the magnificently gilded ceiling shows glimpses of heaven. The altar, of lapis lazuli and agate, contains a Madonna and Child dating from the twelfth or thirteenth century.

Between the two chapels, the **confessio** contains a kneeling statue of Pope Pius IX, and, beneath it, a reliquary that is said to contain fragments of the crib of Christ, in rock crystal and silver. The high altar, above it, contains the relics of St Matthew, among other Christian martyrs, and the mosaics in the apse were commissioned by the late-thirteenth-century pope, Nicolas IV, and show the Coronation of the Virgin, with angels, saints and the pope himself. Finally, the thirteenth-century mosaics of *Christ Pantocrator and the Legend of the Snow,* in the **loggia** above the main entrance, are definitely worth a look (daily 9.30am–6pm; L5000), but for L5000 extra, they're hardly a bargain.

SANTA PRASSEDE

Map 4, E9.

Behind Santa Maria Maggiore, off Via Merulana, the ninth-century church of **Santa Prassede** occupies an ancient site, where it's claimed St Prassede harboured Christians on the run from the Roman persecutions. She apparently collected the blood and remains of the martyrs and placed them in a well where she herself was later buried; a red marble disc in the floor of the nave marks the spot. In the southern aisle, the Chapel of Saint Zeno was built by Pope Paschal I as a mausoleum for his mother, Theodora, and is decorated with marvellous ninth-century mosaics that make it glitter like a jewel-encrusted bowl. The chapel also contains a fragment of a column supposed to be the one to which Christ was tied when he was scourged. In the apse are more ninth-century mosaics,

SANTA PRASSEDE

showing Christ between, on the right, saints Peter, Pudenziana and Zeno and on the left saints Paul, Praxedes and Paschal. Note that Paschal's halo is in a rectangular form, indicating that he was alive when the mosaics were placed here.

SANTA PUDENZIANA

Map 4, D8.
On the other side of Via Cavour, the church of **Santa Pudenziana** on Via Urbana has equally ancient origins, dedicated to St Prassede's supposed sister and for many years believed to have been built on the site where St Peter lived and worshipped – though this has since been entirely discredited. There were for years two relics in the church, the chair that St Peter used as his throne and the table at which he said Mass, though both have long gone – to the Vatican and the Lateran, respectively. But the church still has one feature of ancient origin, the superb fifth-century apse mosaics – some of the oldest Christian figurative mosaics in Rome, though they've been tampered with and restored over the years.

VIA NAZIONALE

Map 4, A9–D6.
A couple of minutes' walk from Santa Maria Maggiore, **Via Nazionale** connects Piazza Venezia and the centre of town with the area around Termini and the eastern districts beyond. A focus for much development after Unification, its heavy, overbearing buildings were constructed to give Rome some semblance of modern sophistication when it became capital of the new country, but most are now occupied by hotels and bland shops and boutiques.

At the corner of Via Nazionale and Via Napoli is the American Episcopal church of **St Paul's-within-the-Walls** (daily 9am–1pm & 4–7pm), the first Protestant church to be built within the walls of the city after the Unification of Italy in 1870. Dating from 1879, it was built in a neo-Gothic style by the British architect, G.E. Street, and is worth a quick peek inside for its apse mosaics by Burne-Jones, which depict one of the church's founders, the financier J.P. Morgan, as St Paul, alongside his family, Garibaldi, General Ulysces Grant, and Abraham Lincoln.

PIAZZA DELLA REPUBBLICA

Map 4, D6.

At the top of Via Nazionale, **Piazza della Repubblica** (formerly Piazza Esedra) is typical of Rome's nineteenth-century regeneration, a stern, once dignified but now rather shabby semicircle of buildings given over to cheap hotels, street vendors, travel agents and fast-food joints, and centring on a fountain surrounded by languishing nymphs and sea monsters.

SANTA MARIA DEGLI ANGELI

Map 4, D6.

The piazza actually follows the outlines of the exedra of the Baths of Diocletian, the remains of which lie across the piazza and are partially contained in the church of **Santa Maria degli Angeli** – not Rome's most welcoming church but giving the best impression of the size and grandeur of Diocletian's bath complex. It's a huge, open building, with an interior standardized by Vanvitelli into a rich eighteenth-century confection after a couple of centuries of piecemeal adaptation (started by an aged Michelangelo). The pink granite pillars, at nine feet in diameter the largest in Rome, are original, and the main transept formed the main hall of the baths; only the crescent shape of the facade remains from the original caldarium (it had previously been hidden by a newer facing), the vestibule (the tepidarium) and main transept. The meridian that strikes diagonally across the floor here was, until 1846, the regulator of time for Romans (now a cannon shot fired daily at noon from the Janiculum Hill).

AROUND PIAZZA DELLA REPUBBLICA

Map 4, D6.

The buildings that surround Santa Maria degli Angeli are also recycled parts of Diocletian's baths, including the round church of **St Bernardo**, off via XX Settembre, and the round building (now an *albergo diurnale*) at the corner of via Viminale and via di Terme di Diocleziano. Immediately to the left of the church, another caldarium was formerly used as a planetarium and is now the **Aula Ottagona** (Octagonal Hall), part of the Museo Nazionale Romano (same ticket) – a large domed room which contains marble statues taken from the baths of Caracalla and Diocletian, and two remarkable statues of a boxer and athlete from the Quirinal Hill. Excavations underground – accessible by stairs – show the furnaces for heating water for the baths and the foundations of another building from the time of Diocletian.

The rest of the Baths of Diocletian – the huge halls and courtyards on the side towards Termini – formerly housed the Museo Nazionale Romano but this has since been relocated in Palazzo Massimo and Palazzo Altemps and is now closed to the public while it is renovated as new exhibition and convention space.

PALAZZO MASSIMO

Map 4, D7. Largo di Villa Perretti 1. Tues–Sat 9am–7pm, Sun 9am–2pm; L12,000; L20,000 for Palazzo Altemps, Colosseum and Palatine.

Across from Santa Maria degli Angeli, through a seedy little park, the snazzily restored Palazzo Massimo is home to part of the **Museo Nazionale Romano** (the rest is in the Palazzo Altemps; see p.32) – a superb collection of Greek and Roman antiquities, second only to the Vatican's, which has been entirely reorganized and features many pieces that have remained undisplayed for decades.

The ground floor

The ground floor of the museum is devoted to statuary of the early Empire, including an unparalleled selection of busts of the emperors and their families. In the first long hall, look out for the so-called Statue of the Tivoli General, the face of an old man mounted on the body of a youthful athlete – sometimes believed to be a portrait of L. Munatius Plancus, the military officer who named Octavian "Augustus" (literally "Reverend") and so officially started the cult of the emperor. There are silver and gold coins from the seventh century BC to the first century AD, arranged in chronological order (though the huge money museum in the basement, detailed below, is better), and, further on, a painted frieze from the first century BC showing scenes from the Trojan War and the legend of the founding of Rome. Of some superb examples of Roman copies of Greek statuary, an altar found on Via Nomentana stands out, decorated with figures relating to the cult of Bacchus.

The first floor

A series of busts, mosaics and fresco fragments, coins and statuary lead up to the top floor gallery, where the first room is devoted to the Flavian emperors – look out for the bust of Vespasian. Beyond, there's more statuary from the

Imperial era, a room of bronze fittings from ships found at Lake Nemi, south of Rome, and some stunning frescoes from the country villa, north of Rome, of the emperor Augustus's wife Livia, depicting an orchard dense with fruit and flowers and patrolled by partridges, doves and other feathered friends. On the same floor, there are also some of the best mosaics ever found in Roman villas around the world. Room IX contains floors excavated from the Villa di Baccano on Via Cassia, a sumptuous mansion probably owned by the imperial Severi family; the right wall holds four mosaic panels taken from a bedroom, featuring four chariot drivers and their horses, so finely crafted that from a distance they look as if they've been painted. In the adjoining room is a very rare example of *opus sectile*, a mosaic technique imported from the Eastern provinces in the first century AD. Inlaid pieces of marble, mother-of-pearl, glass and hard stone are used instead of tesserae, the parts cut so as to enhance detail and give perspective depth.

....

Make sure you also catch the money collection in the basement, which you might want to do while waiting for a guide who speaks your language. Items on display include Italy's first money – in fact iron and bronze ingots – ancient Roman, Greek, Etruscan and other currencies, all displayed in glass cases equipped with magnifying glasses on runners, controlled by the buttons mounted on the front of each case.

....

STAZIONE TERMINI

Map 4, E7.

Across the street is the low white facade of **Stazione Termini** (so named for its proximity to the Baths of Diocletian, nothing to do with being the termini of

Rome's rail lines) and the vast, bus-crammed hubbub that is Piazza dei Cinquecento in front. The station is great, an ambitious piece of modern architectural design that was completed in 1950 and still entirely dominates the streets around with its low-slung, self-consciously futuristic lines. It has just received a huge and sleek renovation that has converted part of its cavernous ticket hall to retail and restaurant space and upgraded the building in general – making it a nice spot for a browse and a wander, and a marvellous place to catch a train. As for **Piazza dei Cinquecento**, it's a good place to find buses and taxis, but otherwise it and the areas around are pretty much low-life territory, and although not especially dangerous, not particularly a place to hang around for long either.

VIA XX SETTEMBRE

Map B7–E3.

Just to the north of Termini, **Via XX Settembre** spears out towards the Aurelian Wall from Via del Quirinale – not Rome's most appealing thoroughfare by any means, flanked by the deliberately faceless bureaucracies of the national government, erected after Unification in anticipation of Rome's ascension as a new world capital. It was, however, the route by which Garibaldi's troops entered the city on September 20, 1870, and the place where they breached the wall is marked with a column.

Halfway down Via XX Settembre, just north of Piazza della Repubblica, the church of **Santa Susanna** is one of an elegant cluster of facades, although behind its well-proportioned Carlo Maderno frontage it isn't an especially auspicious building, except for some bright and soothing frescoes. The headquarters of American Catholics in Rome, it looks across the busy junction to the **Fontana dell' Acqua Felice**, playfully fronted by four basking lions, and focusing on a massive, bearded figure of Moses, in the central one of three arches. Marking the end of the Acqua Felice aqueduct, the fountain forms part of Pope Sixtus V's late-sixteenth-century attempts to spruce up the city centre with large-scale public works (see p.104).

SANTA MARIA DELLA VITTORIA

Map 4, C5. Jan–July & Sept–Dec daily 6.30am–noon & 4.30–7.00pm.

Immediately opposite the fountain, the church of **Santa Maria della Vittoria** was also built by Carlo Maderno and it has an interior that is one of the most elaborate examples of Baroque decoration in Rome: almost shockingly excessive to modern eyes, its ceiling and walls are pitted with carving, and statues are crammed into remote corners as in an overstuffed attic. The church's best-known feature, Bernini's carving of the *Ecstasy of St Theresa*, the centrepiece of the sepulchral chapel of Cardinal Cornaro, continues the histrionics – a deliberately melodramatic work featuring a theatrically posed St Theresa against a backdrop of theatre-boxes on each side of the chapel, from which the Cornaro cardinals murmur and nudge each other as they watch the spectacle.

VIA NOMENTANA

Map 4, F3.

At the north end of Via XX Settembre, the **Porta Pia** was one of the last works of Michelangelo, erected under Pope Pius IV in 1561. To the left of the gate is the busy Corso d'Italia (in effect forming part of the central ring road that girdles the city centre), while straight on is the wide boulevard of **Via Nomentana**, lined with luxury villas that have long been home to some of the city's more illustrious names.

A kilometre down Via Nomentana on the right is the

nineteenth-century **Villa Torlonia**, which the banker Prince Giovanni Torlonia turned over to Mussolini to use as long as he needed it. You can't visit the house – which has seen better days – but the grounds are open to the public (daily 7am–1hr before sunset). If you do venture out this way, stop by at the **Casina delle Civette**, Via Nomentana 70 (Tues–Sun: summer 9am–7pm; winter 9am–5pm; L5000) – the "small house of the owls" – a lovely building designed by Valadier at the beginning of the eighteenth-century. It was carefully restored and opened to the public in 1997 and houses an unusual museum of notable stained-glass windows.

SANT'AGNESE FUORI LE MURA

Map 4, H1. Mon 9am–noon, Tues–Sat 9am–noon & 4–6pm, Sun 4–6pm.

Further up Via Nomentana is the church of **Sant'Agnese fuori le Mura** dedicated to the same saint who was martyred in Domitian's Stadium in 303 AD (see p.30). To get into the church, walk down the hill and through the courtyard to the narthex of the building, which apart from some very out-of-place later fixtures is much as it was built by Honorius I in the seventh century, when he reworked Constantine's original structure. The apse mosaic is Byzantine in style and contemporary with Honorius's building, showing Agnes next to the pope, who holds a model of his church.

Out of the narthex the custodian will lead you down into the **catacombs** (same hours as church; L8000) that sprawl below the church, which are among the best preserved and most crowd-free of all the city's catacombs. Indeed, if you only have time for one set of catacombs during your stay in Rome (and they really are all very much alike), these are among the best. The custodian also sells little terracotta lamps in the shape of fish, or conventional Roman-style lamps with the "Chi-Rho" sign on – probably the most ancient symbol of Christianity. They are very reasonably priced and make a nice souvenir of the place.

SANTA COSTANZA

Map 4, H1. Usually open the same hours as Sant'Agnese, or ask custodian for entrance; free.

After the catacombs the guide will show you a further part of what is really a small complex of early Christian structures, the church of **Santa Constanza**, which more than any other building in Rome, perhaps, illustrates the transition from the pagan to Christian city in its decorative and architectural features. Built in 350 AD as a mausoleum for Constantia and Helena, the daughters of the emperor Constantine, it's a round structure which follows the traditional shape of the great pagan tombs (consider those of Hadrian and Augustus elsewhere in the city), and the mosaics on the vaulting of its circular ambulatory – fourth-century depictions of vines, leaves and birds – would have been as at home on the floor of a Roman *domus* as they were in a Christian church. Unfortunately, the porphyry sarcophagus of Santa Constanza herself has been moved to the Vatican, and what you see in the church is a plaster copy.

SAN LORENZO

Map 4, H8–I8.

South and east of Via Nomentana, a short walk from Termini, the neighbourhood of **SAN LORENZO** spreads from the main campus of Rome's university, on the far side of Via Tiburtina, to the railway tracks – a solidly working-class district that retains something of its local air and is home to some good and often inexpensive local restaurants. It's also the location of the enormous **Campo Verano** cemetery – since 1830 the main Catholic burial-place in Rome, and in itself worth a visit for the grandiose tombs in which many have been laid to rest.

SAN LORENZO FUORI LE MURA

Map 4, I7. Daily: summer 7am–noon & 4–7.30pm; winter closes 5.30pm.

The area takes its name from the church of **San Lorenzo fuori le Mura** on Via Tiburtina right by the cemetery – one of the seven great pilgrimage churches of Rome, and a typical Roman basilica, fronted by a columned portico and with a lovely twelfth-century cloister to its side. The original church here was built over the site of St Lawrence's martyrdom by Constantine – the saint was reputedly burned to death on a gridiron, halfway through his ordeal apparently uttering the immortal words, "Turn me, I am done on this side." Where the church of San Lorenzo differs is that it is actually a combination of three churches built at different periods – one a sixth-century reconstruction of Constantine's church by Pelagius II, which now forms the chancel, another a fifth-century church from the time of Sixtus III, both joined by a basilica from the thirteenth century by Honorius II.

Because of its proximity to Rome's railyards, the church was bombed heavily during World War 2, but it has been rebuilt with sensitivity, and remains much as it was originally. Inside there are features from all periods: a Cosmati floor, thirteenth-century pulpits and a Paschal candlestick. The mosaic on the inside of the triumphal arch is a sixth-century depiction of Pelagius offering his church to Christ; while below stairs, catacombs (presently closed for restoration) – where St Lawrence was apparently buried – lead a dank path from the pillars of Constantine's original structure. There's also a Romanesque cloister with well-tended garden that you can get into through the sacristy.

The Villa Borghese and north

Outside the Aurelian walls, to the north and northeast of the city, was once an area of market gardens, olive groves and patrician villas abutting the Via Salaria and Via Nomentana before trailing off into open country. During the Renaissance, these vast tracts of land were appropriated as summer estates for the city's wealthy, particularly those affiliated in some way to the papal court. One of the most notable of these estates, the **Villa Borghese**, was the summer playground of the Borghese family and is now a public park, and home to the city's most significant concentration of museums. Foremost among these are the **Galleria Borghese**, housing the resplendent art collection of the aristocratic family – a Roman must-see in anyone's book – and the **Villa Giulia**, built by Pope Julius III for his summer repose and now the National Etruscan Museum. North of Villa Borghese stretch Rome's post-Unification residential districts – not of much interest in themselves, except perhaps for **Foro Italico**, which is worth visiting either to see Roma or Lazio play at its Olympic Stadium, or simply to admire Mussolini's stylish, of-its-time sports complex.

VILLA BORGHESE

Map 5.

Immediately above Piazza del Popolo, the hill known as the Pincio marks the edge of the city's core and the beginning of a collection of parks and gardens that forms Rome's largest central open space – the **Villa Borghese**, made up of the grounds of the seventeenth-century pleasure palace of Scipione Borghese, which were bought by the city at the turn of the century. It's a huge area, and its woods, lake and grass criss-crossed by roads are about as near as you can get to peace in the city centre without making too much effort. There are any number of attractions for those who want to do more than just stroll or sunbathe: a tiny boating lake, a zoo – a cruel affair well worth avoiding – and some of the city's finest museums.

The **Pincio** isn't formally part of the Villa Borghese, but its terrace and gardens, laid out by Valadier in the early nineteenth century and fringed with dilapidated busts of classical and Italian heroes, give fine views over the roofs, domes and TV antennae of central Rome, right across to St Peter's and the Janiculum Hill. Walking south from here, there are more gardens in the grounds of the **Villa Medici**, though as the villa is home to the French Academy these days, they can usually only be visited on selected days, when they host concerts and art shows. Occasionally, they throw open their doors to the curious public; check the newspapers or usual listings sources to find out when.

THE GALLERIA BORGHESE

Map 5, K3. Piazza le Scipione Borghese 5. Tues–Sat 9am–7pm, Sun 9am–5pm; pre-booked visits every 2hr; to book call ©06.32.810 – lines are open Mon–Fri 9am–7pm, Sat 9am–1pm; L12,000.

The best place to make for first, if you want some focus to your wanderings, is the Casino Borghese itself, on the far eastern side, which was built in the early seventeenth century and turned over to the state when the gardens became city property in 1902 as the **Galleria Borghese**. Recently reopened after a lengthy restoration, the Borghese has taken its place as one of Rome's great treasure houses and should not be missed.

When Camillo Borghese was elected pope and took the papal name Paul V in 1605, he elevated his favourite nephew, Scipione Caffarelli Borghese, to the cardinalate and put him in charge of diplomatic, ceremonial and cultural matters at the papal court. Scipione possessed an infallible instinct for recognizing artistic quality, and, driven by ruthless passion, he used fair means or foul to acquire the most prized works of art. He was also shrewd enough to patronize outstanding talents like Gian Lorenzo Bernini, Caravaggio, Domenichino, Guido Reni and Peter Paul Rubens. To house the works of these artists, as well as his collection of antique sculpture and other works, he built the Casino, or summer house, and predictably he spared no expense. The palace, which was built in the early 1600s, is a celebration of the ancient splendour of the Roman Empire: over the years its art collection has been added to, and its rooms redecorated – most notably during the last quarter of the eighteenth century, when the ceilings were re-done to match thematically the art works of each room. The recent restoration of the sumptuous interior seemed to go on forever, but it was finished a couple of years ago, and now the gallery's Roman-era mosaics, rich stucco decorations and trompe l'oeil ceilings provide the perfect surroundings in which to enjoy the art works which Cardinal Scipione Borghese collected so voraciously.

THE GALLERIA BORGHESE

The porch and entrance hall

Entrance is through a **porch**, which displays classical sculpture, notably several large statues of Dacian prisoners from
the time of the emperor Trajan. Inside, the **entrance hall**
has a splendid ceiling by Marino Rossi, painted in 1775–78,
depicting the foundations and early history of Rome –
Jupiter in the centre surrounded by various moral and spiritual attributes, and historical and mythological characters
like Romulus, Remus and the she-wolf. On the floor, a
series of Roman mosaics from about 320 AD depict gladiators fighting and killing various animals and each other – a
circle with a line drawn through it next to the name indi-
cates the deceased, and blood gushes gruesomely from the
pierced throats and hearts of the animals. Among a number
of notable statues, there's a Bacchus from the second century AD, a Fighting Satyr, and, on the wall facing the
entrance door, a melodramatic piece in marble of Marcus
Curtius flinging himself into the chasm (see p.75) – his
horse is a Roman sculpture and the figure is by Bernini's
father. Bernini himself also makes an appearance with a late,
in fact unfinished work, *Truth Revealed in Time*, done late in
his career when he had been accused of faulty architectural
work in part of St Peter's. Truth, with a sappy look on her
face, clutches the sun, representing time, to her breast.
There are also colossal heads of the emperors Hadrian and
Antoninus Pius, and a female head of the Antonine period,
with a lotus flower on her head to represent Isis.

The ground floor

The **ground floor** beyond the entrance hall contains
sculpture, a mixture of ancient Roman items and seventeenth-century works, roughly linked together with late-
eighteenth-century ceiling paintings showing scenes from

the Trojan War. The first room off the entrance hall, whose paintings depict the Judgement of Paris, has as its centre-piece Canova's famous statue of *Pauline Borghese* posed as Venus, with flimsy drapery that leaves little to the imagination. Pauline Borghese, the sister of Napoleon and married (reluctantly) to the reigning Prince Borghese, was a shocking woman in her day, with grand habits. There are tales of her jewels and clothes, of the Negro who used to carry her from her bath, of the servants she used as footstools, and, of course, her long line of lovers. The statue was considered outrageous by everyone but herself: when asked how she could have posed almost naked, she simply replied, "Oh, there was a stove in the studio." Interestingly, the couch on which she reposes originally had a kind of clockwork mechanism inside, which allowed the statue to rotate while the viewer remained stationary.

Next door, the so-called the Room of the Sun has a marvellous statue of David by Bernini, finished in 1624, when the sculptor was just 25. The face is a self-portrait of the sculptor, said to have been carved with the help of a mirror held for him by Scipione Borghese himself. There's more work by Bernini in the next room, where his statue of Apollo and Daphne is a dramatic, poised work that captures the split second when Daphne is transformed into a laurel tree, with her fingers becoming leaves and her legs tree trunks. Briefly, Apollo had made fun of Cupid, who had taken revenge by firing a golden arrow which infused immediate and desperate love into the breast of Apollo, and shooting Daphne with a leaden one designed to hasten the rejection of amorous advances. Daphne, the daughter of a river god, called on her father to help her avoid being trapped by Apollo, who was in hot pursuit; her father changed her into a laurel tree just as Apollo took her into his arms – a desperately sad piece of drama to which Bernini's statue does full justice. This statue also caused a great scandal when it was unveiled. The poet and playwright, Maffeo Barberini, who later became Pope Urban VIII, wrote a couplet in Latin, which is inscribed on the base, claiming that all who pursue fleshly lusts are doomed to end up holding only ashes and dust.

Next door, the walls of the Room of the Emperors are walls flanked by seventeenth- and eighteenth-century busts of Roman emperors, facing another Bernini sculpture, *The Rape of Perseopine* dating from 1622, a coolly virtuosic work that shows in melodramatic form the story of the carrying off to the underworld of the beautiful nymph Perseopine, daughter of Gaia, goddess of the earth. The brutal Pluto grasps the girl in his arms, his fingers digging into the flesh of her thigh as she fights off his advances, while the three-headed form of Cerberus snaps at their feet.

In the small room next door there's a marvellous statue of a hermaphrodite sleeping, from the first century AD, and a large porphyry Roman bathtub whose feline feet are almost modern in style. But it's back to the Berninis in the following room, where a larger-than-life statue of Aeneas, carrying his father, Anchises, out of the burning city of Troy, was sculpted by both father and his then fifteen-year-old son in 1613. The statue portrays a crucial event in Roman history, when after the defeat of the Trojans Aeneas escaped with his family and went on a long voyage that ended up on the shores of what became Latium, his descendants eventually founding the city of Rome. The old man carries the statues representing their family household gods; the small boy carrying a flaming pot with what became the Vestal Fire is Aeneas's son Ascanius.

The so-called Egyptian Room, beyond, contains artefacts, paintings and mosaics with an Egyptian theme and a statue of a satyr on a dolphin dating from the first century AD, while further on, the Room of Silenus contains a variety of paintings by Cardinal Scipione's faithful servant

Caravaggio – notably the *Madonna of the Grooms* from 1605, a painting that at the time was considered to have depicted Christ far too realistically to hang in a central Rome church, so Cardinal Scipione happily bought it for his collection. Look also at *St Jerome*, captured writing at a table lit only by a source of light that streams in from the upper left of the picture, and his *David holding the Head of Goliath*, sent by Caravaggio to Cardinal Scipione from exile in Malta, where he had fled to escape capital punishment for various crimes, in the hope of winning a reprieve. The cardinal did manage to get the artist off, but Caravaggio died of malaria after landing in Italy at Porto Ercole, north of Rome, in 1610. Goliath is apparently a self-portrait.

The first floor

Upstairs houses the Galeria Borghese's **Pinacoteca**, literally one of the richest collections of paintings in the world, although unfortunately you're only allowed half an hour up here before having to leave. Given this, you'd do well to make a second trip if possible.

First off are several important paintings by Raphael, his teacher Perugino and other masters of the Umbrian school from the late fifteenth and early sixteenth centuries, not least Raphael's *Deposition*, done in 1507 for a noble of Perugia in memory of her son, and pillaged from Perugia cathedral by associates of Cardinal Scipione. Look also for the *Lady With a Unicorn*, and *Portrait of a Man*, both also by Raphael but misattributed earlier this century, and, over the door, a copy of the artist's portrait of a tired-out Julius II, painted in the last year of the pope's life, 1513.

The next room contains more early-sixteenth-century paintings, prominent among which is Cranach's *Venus and Cupid with a Honeycomb*, of 1531, and Brescianino's

Venus and Two Cupids, from about 1520 – both remarkable at the time for their departure from classical models for their subjects. The Cranach Venus, dressed in a diaphanous robe, shows Cupid carrying a honeycomb, demonstrating the dangers of carnal love. Further into the gallery, look out for two early-sixteenth-century copies of Leonardo's *Leda and the Swan* (the original has been lost), Lorenzo Lotto's touching *Portrait of a Man*, a soulful study that hints at grief over a wife lost in childbirth symbolized by the tiny skull and rose petals under his right hand, and, in the Gallery of Lanfranco, at the back of the building, a series of self-portraits done by Bernini at various stages of his long life. Next to these are a lifelike bust of Cardinal Scipione executed by Bernini in 1632, portraying him as the worldly connoisseur of fine art and fine living that he was, and a smaller bust of Pope Paul V, also by Bernini.

Beyond here, there is a painting of *Diana* by Domechino showing the goddess and her attendants celebrating and doing a bit of target practice – one of them has just shot a pheasant through the head and everybody else is jumping with enthusiasm. In the foreground a young nymph, lasciviously bathing, looks out with a lustful expression. From here, if you can get to the Room of Psyche before the guards start herding you out, you will be able to see, along with works by Bellini and the other Venetians of the early 1500s, Titian's *Sacred and Profane Love*, painted in 1514 when he was about 25 years old, to celebrate the marriage of the Venetian noble Nicolo Aurelio (whose coat of arms is on the sarcophagus). It shows his bride, Laura Bagarotto, dressed in white representing Sacred Love, and Venus, representing Profane Love, carrying a lamp symbolizing the eternal Love of God. The bride cradles a bowl of jewels that refer to the fleeting happiness of life on earth.

THE GALLERIA NAZIONALE D'ARTE MODERNA

Map 5, H2. Via delle Belle Arti 131. Tues–Sat 9am–10pm, Sun 9am–8pm; shorter hours in winter; L8000

The Villa Borghese's two other major museums are situated on the other side of the park, along the Viale delle Belle Arti, in the so-called "Academy Ghetto" – the Romanian, British, Dutch, Danish, Egyptian and other cultural academies are all situated here. Of these, the **Galleria Nazionale d'Arte Moderna** is probably the least compulsory, a huge, lumbering, Neoclassical building housing a collection that isn't really as grand as you might expect, made up of a wide selection of nineteenth- and twentieth-century Italian (and a few foreign) names. However, it can make a refreshing change after several days of having the senses bombarded with Etruscan, Roman and Renaissance art. The nineteenth-century collection, on the upper floor, contains a lot of marginal Italian masters (as well as a Van Gogh) but really isn't that compelling unless this is one of your areas of interest. The twentieth-century collection is more appealing, and includes work by Modigliani, De Chirico, Giacomo Balla, Boccione and other Futurists, along with the odd Cézanne, Mondrian and Klimt, and some post-war canvases by the likes of Mark Rothko and Jackson Pollock.

MUSEO NAZIONALE DI VILLA GIULIA

Map 5, F2. Piazzale Villa Giulia 9. Tues–Sat 9am–7pm, Sun 9am–1.30pm; L8000

The **Villa Giulia**, five minutes' walk in the direction of Via Flaminia, a harmonious collection of courtyards, loggias, gardens and temples put together in a playful Mannerist style for Pope Julius III in the mid-sixteenth century, is perhaps more of an essential stop than the

The Etruscans

The **Etruscans** lived in central Italy from around 900 BC until their incorporation into the Roman world in 88 BC. The Romans borrowed heavily from their civilization, and thus in many ways the influence of the Etruscans is still felt today: our alphabet, for example, is based on the Etruscan system; and bishops' crooks and the "fasces" symbol, of a bundle of rods with an axe – found, among other places, behind the speaker's rostrum in the US House of Representatives – are just two other Etruscan symbols that endure. The Etruscans were masters of working in terracotta, gold and bronze, and accomplished carvers in stone, and it is these skills that make a visit to the Villa Giulia so beguiling.

Modern Art Museum. It's home to the **Museo Nazionale di Villa Giulia**, the world's primary collection of Etruscan treasures (along with the Etruscan collection in the Vatican), and a good introduction – or conclusion – to the Etruscan sites in Lazio, which between them contributed most of the artefacts on display here. It's not an especially large collection, but it's worth taking the trouble to see the whole. At the time of writing, it was split between the east and west wings and the atrium. However, since then it has been completely renovated; much of what we describe below is on show but in a different order – and to better effect.

The east wing

The entrance room of the **east wing** houses two pieces of Etruscan sculpture, one showing a man astride a seahorse, a recurring theme in ancient Mediterranean art, and an oddly amateurish centaur – basically a man pasted to the hindquarters of a horse – both from Vulci and dating from the sixth century BC. The next rooms contain bronze objects dating from the seventh and sixth centuries BC – urns used to contain the ashes of cremated persons, among which a beautiful bronze example, in the shape of a finely detailed dwelling hut, stands out – and a number of terracotta votive offerings of anatomical parts of the human body, their detail alluding to the Etruscans' accomplishments in medicine. A gold dental bridge shows their skill at dentistry too.

The next room displays items found in Veio – among them Apollo and Hercules disputing over the sacred hind which Apollo had shot and Hercules claimed. Next door, the remarkable Sarcophagus of the Married Couple (dating from the sixth century, and actually containing the ashes of the deceased rather than the bodies), is from Cerveteri, and is one of the most famous pieces in the museum – a touchingly lifelike portrayal of a husband and wife lying on a couch. He has his right arm around her; she is offering him something from her right hand, probably an egg – a recurring theme in Etruscan art. Their clothes are modelled down to the finest detail, including the laces and soles of their shoes, and the pleats of the linen and lacy pillowcases. In case you're wondering, the holes in the backs of their heads, and at other spots, are ventilation holes to prevent the terracotta from exploding when the hollow piece was fired. Beyond are more finds from Cerveteri: hundreds of vases, pots, drinking vessels and other items. Most interesting is a portrait of a man, complete with cauliflower right ear, and a finely stitched cut to the right of his mouth – clearly a tough customer.

Upstairs, you'll find mostly bronzes, mirrors, candelabra, religious statues and tools. Notice, particularly, the elongated statues of priests and priestesses, some of whom hold eels in their hands engaged in some kind of rite. There is a model of a ploughman at work plodding along behind his oxen, and a statue of a handsome young Jupiter (although this dates from the first century AD and so strictly speaking is not Etruscan), the soles of his sandals built up as if from layers of leather, each layer perfectly delineated. Further on, there is a remarkably well-preserved two-wheeled funeral chariot, and finds from Pyrgi, Cerveteri's seaport, where there was a huge temple dedicated to Venus – a miscellany of terracotta heads, and, of most interest, a series of gold leaf tablets complete with dedicatory inscriptions in Punic and Etruscan.

> To see how an Etruscan tomb would have looked at the time, take a look at the reconstruction, in the right wing, from the necropolis at Cerveteri, re-created in a glassed-in chamber. The beds on which the deceased lay are distinguished by a peaked head for the woman and a rounded head for the man. In the garden there is a reconstructed Etruscan temple, complete with sarcophagi carved with mythological themes on the sides.

The west wing

The **west wing** of the museum displays artefacts found outside Etruria proper but of obvious Etruscan provenance or heavily influenced by the Etruscans, most notably the *Cistae* recovered from tombs around Praeneste – drum-like objects, engraved and adorned with figures, that were supposed to hold all the things needed for the care of the body after death. Of these, the so-called *Cista Ficaroni*, is perhaps the most impressive, made by an Etruscan craftsman named Novios Plautios for a lady named Dindia Malconia and probably a wedding present. In the same room, look too at

THE WEST WING

the marvellously intricate pieces of gold jewellery, delicately worked into tiny horses, birds, camels and other animals. There are also gold-washed silver dishes with Egyptian motifs – the Etruscans had close relations with North Africa; ostrich eggs, an Etruscan symbol of resurrection and rebirth, also imported from Africa; and mirrors, some of which have mythological events etched on their backs. The next series of galleries has items from further south, around Lake Nemi and the Alban Hills. There is an oak log that was used as a coffin for the burial of the deceased, whose bones remain inside on display, and cases of terracotta votive offerings – anatomical parts, babies in swaddling clothes, houses, a couple of temple models.

The atrium and beyond

The museum's **atrium**, two storeys high, is devoted to the Faliscians, a people from northeast Lazio, who were closely affiliated with the Etruscans. This part of the museum was reorganized in 1998 and is clearly labelled in English, with good information in each room. There are finds from Sassi Caduti and the Sanctuary of Apollo in Civita Castellana – Etruscan artistry at its best, with gaudily coloured terracotta figures that leer, run, jump and climb; a beautiful, lifelike torso of Apollo, dating from around the turn of the fourth century BC; and a bust of Juno which has the air of a dignified matron, the flower pattern on her dress still visible, as are her earrings, her necklace and her crown. Upstairs, there are more exhibits in the same, hyperrealistic vein: a drinking horn in the shape of a dog's head that is so lifelike you almost expect it to bark; a *holmos*, or small table, to which the maker attached 24 little pendants around the edge; and a bronze disc breastplate from the seventh century BC decorated with a weird, almost modern pattern of galloping creatures.

PARIOLI AND VILLA ADA

Map 2, E3–E4.

The area north of Villa Borghese is the posh **PARIOLI** district – one of Rome's wealthier neighbourhoods, though of little interest to anyone who doesn't live there. Immediately east stretches the enormous public park of the **Villa Ada**, connected with Villa Borghese by Via Salaria – the old trading route between the Romans and Sabines, so called because the main product transported along here was salt. The Villa Ada was once the estate of King Vittorio Emanuele III and is a nice enough place in which to while away an afternoon, but otherwise not really worth the special journey from the centre of town, unless you want to visit the Egyptian embassy, housed in its grounds.

THE CATACOMBE DI PRISCILLA

Map 2, I1. Feb–Dec Tues–Sun 8.30am–noon & 2.30–5pm; L0000.

The **Catacombe di Priscilla**, which you can reach from Via Salaria, are the only real thing to see in the Villa Ada – a frescoed labyrinth of tunnels that is visitable on regular (obligatory) guided tours. No one quite knows why these catacombs are here, and whether they are Christian or pagan in origin. The so-called Greek Chapel has a number of obviously Christian frescoes – Daniel in the lions' den, the resurrection of Lazarus, Noah, the sacrifice of Isaac – painted between the second and fourth centuries AD. However, other paintings, including something that is claimed as the earliest known depiction of the *Virgin and Child*, could in fact simply be a picture of a mother and child, both of whom were probably buried here.

PONTE MILVIO

Map 2, C1.

On the far side of the Parioli district the Tiber sweeps around in a wide hook-shaped bend. These northern outskirts of Rome aren't particularly enticing, though the **Ponte Milvio**, the old, originally Roman, footbridge where the emperor Constantine defeated Maxentius in 312 AD, still stands and provides wonderful views of the meandering Tiber, with the city springing up green on the hills to both sides and the river running fast and silty below. Inside a **guardhouse** on the right (northern) bank of the Tiber a marble plaque bears the arms of the Borgia family – including, in the centre, the papal badge and shield of Alexander VI, and, on the right, the Borgia bull on a crest, placed there by Cesare Borgia,, who was at the time his father the pope's secretary of state. On the northern side of the river, **Piazzale di Ponte Milvio** sports a cheap and cheerful market (Mon–Sat 8am–1.30pm) and a handful of bars and restaurants

FORO ITALICO

Map 2, A1–B1.

It's just ten minutes' walk from the Ponte Milvio – past the huge Italian Foreign Ministry building – to the **Foro Italico** sports centre, one of the few parts of Rome to survive intact pretty much the way Mussolini planned it. This is still used as a sports centre, but it's worth visiting as much for its period value as anything else. Its centrepiece is perhaps the **Ponte Duca dí Aosta**, which connects Foro Italico to the town side of the river, and is headed by a white marble obelisk capped with a gold pyramid that is engraved MUSSOLINI DUX in beautiful 1930s calligraphy. The marble finials at the side of each end of the bridge show soldiers in various heroic acts, loading machine guns and cannons, charging into the face of enemy fire, carrying the wounded and so forth, each with the face of Mussolini himself – a very eerie sight indeed.

Beyond the bridge, an avenue patched with more mosaics revering the Duce leads up to a fountain surrounded by mosaics of muscle-bound figures revelling in healthful sporting activities. Either side of the fountain are the two main stadiums: the larger of the two, the **Stadio Olimpico** on the left, was used for the Olympic Games in 1960 and is still the venue for Rome's two soccer teams on alternate Sundays. The smaller, the **Stadio dei Marmi** ("stadium of marbles"), is ringed by sixty great male statues, groins modestly hidden by fig leafs, in a variety of elegantly macho poses – a typically Fascist monument in some ways, but in the end a rather ironic choice for a notoriously homophobic government.

The South of the City

The word romance is associated with the very name of Rome itself, and one of the most romantic parts of the city is the area to **the South**, where there are plenty of reminders of the glory of ancient Rome. This area encompasses the start of the **Via Appia,** the most famous of Rome's consular roads, which struck from the southeast end of the **Circo Massimo** straight as an arrow to the port of Brindisi 365 miles south. The road was built by the censor Appio Claudio in 312 BC, and is the only Roman landmark mentioned in the Bible. Immediately beyond the Palatine Hill, the **Baths of Caracalla** is the first major sight along the route, one of the city's grandest ruins, and the venue until recently of inspirational performances of opera. Beyond, most visitors take public transport out to see the ancient **catacombs**, which line either side of the Via Appia Antica on its way through the outlying districts of the modern city. A little way west, **Via Ostiense** was another important traffic artery, linking – as it in fact still does – Rome to its port of Ostia. It's home to a more recent, nineteenth-century attraction in the

Protestant Cemetery, where the poets Keats and Shelley are buried, and the magnificent rebuilt basilica of **St Paolo-fuori-le-Mura**.

THE CIRCO MASSIMO

Map 7, H5–I5.

On its southern side, the Palatine Hill drops down to the **Circo Massimo**, a long, thin, green expanse bordered by heavily trafficked roads that was the ancient city's main venue for chariot races. At one time this arena had a capacity of up to 400,000 spectators, and if it were still intact it would no doubt match the Colosseum for grandeur. As it is, a litter of stones at the Viale Aventino end is all that remains, together with – at the southern end – a little medieval tower built by the Frangipani family, and, behind a chain-link fence traced out in marble blocks, the outline of the **Septizodium**, an imperial structure designed to show off the glories of the city and its empire to those arriving on the Via Appia. The huge obelisk that now stands in front of the Church of San Giovanni in Laterno at 385 tonnes and over 100 feet high the largest in the world – was once the central marker of the arena, and it's known that the obelisk now in Piazza del Popolo stood here too.

THE BATHS OF CARACALLA

Map 2, G13. Viale Terme di Caracalla 52. Summer Mon & Sun 9am–1pm, Tues–Sat 9am–6pm; winter Mon & Sun 9am–1pm, Tues–Sat 9am–3pm; L8000.

Across the far side of Piazza di Porta Capena, beyond the large **UN Food and Agriculture** building, the **Baths of Caracalla**, on the right on the corner of Via Antonina, are much better preserved, and they give a far better sense of the scale and monumentality of Roman architecture than most of the extant ruins in the city – so much so that Shelley was moved to write *Prometheus Unbound* here in 1819. The baths are no more than a shell now, but the walls still rise to very nearly their original height. There are many fragments of mosaics – none spectacular, but quite a few bright and well preserved – and it's easy to discern a floor plan. As for Caracalla, he was one of Rome's worst and shortest-lived rulers, and it's no wonder there's nothing else in the city built by him.

The baths have until recently been used for occasional opera performances during the summer (one of Mussolini's better ideas), but these have largely stopped due to damage to the site. Watch out for their re-emergence, though – it's a thrilling and inexpensive way to see the baths at their most atmospheric.

THE AVENTINE HILL

Map 7, G5–F6.

Cross back over Viale Aventino after seeing the baths and scale the **Aventine Hill** – the southernmost of the city's seven hills and the heart of plebeian Rome in ancient times. These days the working-class quarters of the city are further south, and the Aventine is in fact one of the city's more upscale residential areas, covered with villas and gardens and one of the few places in the city where you can escape the traffic.

A short way up Via Santa Sabina, the church of **Santa Sabina** (daily 7am–12.45pm & 3.30–6pm) is a strong contender for Rome's most beautiful basilica: high and wide, its nave and portico restored back to their fifth-century appearance in the 1930s. Look especially at the main doors, which are contemporary with the church and boast eighteen panels carved with Christian scenes, forming a complete illustrated Bible, which includes one of the oldest representations of the Crucifixion in existence. Santa Sabina is also the principal church of the Dominicans, and it's claimed that the orange trees in the garden outside which you can glimpse on your way to the restrained cloister are descendants of those planted by St Dominic himself. Whatever the truth of this, the views from the gardens are splendid – right across the Tiber to the centre of Rome and St Peter's.

There are other churches on the Aventine, a couple of them extremely ancient, but all were remodelled in the seventeenth century and aren't especially interesting as a result. In any case it's a nice place to wander. Follow the road south past the **Priorato di Malta**, one of several buildings in the city belonging to the Knights of Malta, which has a celebrated view of the dome of St Peter's through the keyhole of its main gate. The little piazza in front of the main gate has marble triumphal insignia designed and placed here by Piranesi to celebrate the knights' dramatic history.

TESTACCIO

Map 2, D13–D14.

On the far side of Via Marmorata, below, the solid working-class neighbourhood of **TESTACCIO** groups around a couple of main squares, a tight-knit community with a market and a number of bars and small trattorias that was for many years synonymous with the slaughterhouse that sprawls down to the Tiber just beyond. In recent years the area has become a trendy place to live, property prices have soared, and some uneasy contradictions have emerged, with vegetarian restaurants opening their doors in an area still known for the offal dishes served in its traditional trattorias, and gay and alternative clubs standing cheek-by-jowl with the car-repair shops gouged into Monte Testaccio.

The slaughterhouse, or **Mattatoio**, once the area's main employer, is now home to the Centro Sociale "Villaggio Globale", a space used for concerts, raves and exhibitions, along with stabling for the city's horse-and-carriage drivers, a gymnasium and a small gypsy camp. For years there has been talk of sprucing it up into a *chi-chi* affair of shops and restaurants, but so far nothing has happened, and it's likely to remain as it is for some time to come.

Opposite the slaughterhouse, **Monte Testaccio**, which gives the area its name, is a 35-metre-high mound created out of the shards of Roman amphorae that were dumped here over some 600 years. The ancients were not aware of the fact that the terracotta amphorae could be recycled, and consequently broke them up into small shards and lay them down in an orderly manner, sprinkling quicklime on them to dissolve the residual wine or oil and so creating the mountain you see today. It's an odd sight, the ceramic curls clearly visible through the tufts of grass that crown its higher reaches, the bottom layers hollowed out by the workshops of car and bike mechanics.

THE PROTESTANT CEMETERY

Map 2, E14. Tues–Sun 9am–5pm; donation expected. Metro B Piramide.

On the opposite side of Via Zabaglia, Via Caio Cestio leads up to the entrance of the **Protestant Cemetery**, one of the shrines to the English in Rome and a fitting conclusion to a visit to the Keats-Shelley Memorial House on Piazza di Spagna (see p.58), since it is here that both poets are buried, along with a handful of other well-known names. In fact, the cemetery's title is a misnomer – the cemetery is reserved for non-Roman Catholics so you'll also find famous Italian atheists, Christians of the Orthodox persuasion, and the odd Jew or Muslim, buried here.

It's a small and surprisingly tranquil enclave, crouched behind the mossy pyramidal **tomb** of one Caius Cestius, who died in 12 BC, and home to a friendly colony of well-fed cats. Part of Cestius's will decreed that all his slaves should be freed, and the white pyramid you see today was thrown up by them in only 330 days of what must have been joyful building.

Most visitors come here to see the grave of Keats, who lies next to his friend, the painter Joseph Severn, in a corner of the old part of the cemetery near the pyramid, his stone inscribed as he wished with the words "here lies one whose name was writ in water". Severn died much later than Keats but asked to be laid here nonetheless, together with his brushes and palette.

Shelley's ashes were brought here at Mary Shelley's request and interred, after much obstruction by the papal authorities, in the newer part of the cemetery, at the opposite end – the Shelleys had visited several years earlier, the poet praising it as "the most beautiful and solemn cemetery I ever beheld". It had been intended that Shelley should rest with his young son, William, who was also buried here, but his remains couldn't be found (although his small grave remains nearby). It's worth knowing that Mary Shelley was so broken-hearted by the death of both her son and husband, that it was twenty years before she could bring herself to visit this place.

Among other famous internees, Edward Trelawny lies next door, the political writer and activist, Gramsci, on the far right-hand side in the middle, to name just two – though if you're at all interested in star-spotting you should either borrow or buy the booklet from the entrance.

THE AURELIAN WALL

From the Protestant Cemetery, you could make a long detour back into the city centre following the **Aurelian**

Wall, built by the emperor Aurelian (and his successor Probus) in 275 AD to enclose Rome's seven hills, One of the best-preserved stretches runs between Porta San Paolo and Porta San Sebastiano: walk through Porta San Paolo and turn left, and follow the walls keeping them always on your left.

It is around two kilometres from Porta San Paolo to Porta San Sebastiano, where there's a **Museum of the Walls** (Tues, Thurs & Sat 9am–1.30pm; L8000), which has displays showing why and how the walls were constructed and a walkway that allows you to walk along the top of the wall for a while before having to return. The Aurelian walls surround the city with a circumference of about 17 kilometres and if you are really an enthusiast the entire distance can be walked in an eight-hour day with a pause for lunch.

From Porta San Sebastiano you are a short walk from either San Giovanni in Laterano, or the Baths of Caracalla, on the way to which, if you're in no hurry, you could stop off at the **Tomb of the Scipios**, off Via San Sebastiano (Tues, Thurs, & Sat 9am–1.30pm; L5000). The tomb was discovered in 1780 and the Etruscan-style sarcophagus found here transported to the Vatican, where it is on display (see p.166).

SAN PAOLO FUORI LE MURA

Daily 7.30am–6.30pm.

Two kilometres or so south of the Porta San Paolo, the basilica of **San Paolo fuori le Mura** is one of the five patriarchal basilicas of Rome, occupying the supposed site of St Paul's tomb, where he was laid to rest after being beheaded at Tre Fontane (see below). Of the five, this basilica has probably fared the least well over the years. It was apparently once the grandest of them all, connected to the Aurelian Wall by a mile-long colonnade made up of 800 marble columns, but a ninth-century sacking by the Saracens and a devastating fire in 1823 (a couple of cack-handed roofers spilt burning tar, almost entirely destroying the church) means that the church you see now is largely a nineteenth-century reconstruction, sited in what is these days a rather unenticing neighbourhood.

For all that, it's a very successful if somewhat clinical rehash of the former church, succeeding where St Peter's tries (but ultimately fails) by impressing with sheer size and grandeur: whether you enter by way of the cloisters or the west door, it's impossible not to be awed by the space of the building inside, its crowds of columns topped by round-arched arcading. Also, of all the basilicas of Rome, this one gives you the feel of what an ancient Roman basilica must have been like: the huge barn-like structure, its clerestory windows and roof beams supported by enormous columns, the only natural light provided by the alabaster window panes, all combine to lend a powerful and authentic sense of occasion.

Some parts of the building did survive the fire. In the south transept, the paschal candlestick is a remarkable piece of Romanesque carving, supported by half-human beasts and rising through entwined tendrils and strangely human limbs and bodies to scenes from Christ's life, the figures crowding in together as if for a photocall; it's inscribed by its makers, Nicolo di Angelo and Pietro Bassalletto. The bronze aisle doors were also rescued from the old basilica and date from 1070, as was the thirteenth-century tabernacle by Arnolfo di Cambio, under which a slab from the time of Constantine, inscribed "Paolo Apostolo Mort", is supposed to lie – although it's hard to get a look at this. The arch across the apse is original too, embellished with mosaics donated by the Byzantine queen Galla Placidia in the sixth century that show Christ giving a blessing, angels, the symbols of the Gospels, and Ss Peter and Paul. There's also the cloister, just behind here – probably Rome's finest piece of Cosmatesque work, its spiralling, mosaic-encrusted columns enclosing a peaceful rose garden. Just off here, the Relics Chapel houses a dustily kept set of semi-august relics, and the Pinacoteca shows engravings depicting San Paolo before and after the fire.

EUR

Map 2, inset. Bus #714 from Termini or Metro line B.

From San Paolo, Via Ostiense leads south to join up with Via Cristoforo Colombo which in turn runs down to **EUR** (pronounced "eh-oor") – the acronym for the district built for the "Esposizione Universale Roma". This is not so much a neighbourhood as a statement in stone: planned by Mussolini for the aborted 1942 World's Fair and not finished until well after the war, it's a cold, soulless grid of square buildings, long vistas and wide processional boulevards linked tenuously to the rest of Rome by metro but light years away from the city in feel. Come here for its numerous museums, some of which *are* worth the trip, or if you have a yen for modern city architecture and planning; otherwise, stay well clear.

Exploring EUR

The great flaw in EUR is that it's not built for people: the streets are wide thoroughfares designed for easy traffic flow and fast driving, shops and cafés are easily outnumbered by offices. Of the buildings, the postwar development of the area threw up bland office blocks for the most part, and it's the prewar Fascist-style constructions that are of most interest. The **Palazzo della Civiltà del Lavoro** in the northwest corner stands out, Mussolini-inspired architecture at its most assured – the "square Colosseum" some have called it,

EUR
—

which sums up its mixing of modern and classical styles perfectly. To the south, **Piazza Marconi** is the nominal centre of EUR, where the wide, classically inspired boulevards intersect to swerve around an obelisk in the centre.

All the museums are within easy reach of here. On the square itself, the **Museo Nazionale delle Arti e delle Tradizioni Popolari** (Mon–Sat 9am–2pm, Sun 9am–1pm; L4000) is a run-through of applied arts, costumes and religious artefacts from the Italian regions – though everything is labelled in Italian; bring a dictionary. The **Museo Nazionale Preistorico ed Etnografico Luigi Pigorini**, Viale Lincoln 1 (Tues–Sat 9am–2pm, Sun 9am–1pm; L8000), is arranged in manageable and easily comprehensible order, but its prehistoric section is mind-numbingly exhaustive; the ethnographic collection does something to relieve things however, with artefacts from South America, the Pacific and Africa. In the same building, further down the colonnade, at Viale Lincoln 3, is the **Museo dell'Alto Medioevo** (Tues–Sat 9am–2pm, Sun 9am–1pm; L4000), which concentrates on artefacts from the fifth century to the tenth century – local finds mainly, including some beautiful jewellery from the seventh century and a delicate fifth-century gold fibula found on the Palatine Hill. But of all the museums, the most interesting is the **Museo della Civiltà Romana**, Piazza Agnelli 10 (Tues–Sun 9am–7pm, Sun 9am–2pm; L5000), which has, among numerous ancient Roman finds, a large-scale model of the fourth-century city – perfect for setting the rest of the city in context.

THE ABBAZIA DELLE TRE FONTANE

The perfect antidote to EUR is just a short walk away, at the **Abbazia delle Tre Fontane**, a complex of churches founded on the spot where St Paul was martyred; it's said that when the saint was beheaded his head bounced and three springs erupted where his head touched the ground. In those days this was a malarial area, and it was all but abandoned during the Middle Ages, but in the second half of the nineteenth century Trappist monks drained the swamp and planted eucalyptus trees in the vicinity; they still distill a eucalyptus-based chest remedy here, as well as an exquisite liqueur and wonderful chocolate bars – all sold at the small shop by the entrance.

The abbey churches

As for the churches, they were rebuilt in the sixteenth century and restored by the Trappists. They're not particularly outstanding buildings, appealing more for their peaceful location, which is relatively undisturbed by visitors, than any architectural distinction.

The first church, originally built in 625 and rebuilt and finally restored by the Trappists, is the church of **Ss Vincent and Anastasio**; this has a gloomy atmosphere made gloomier by the fact that most of the windows are of a thick marble that admits little light – although the stained glass ones, dating from the Renaissance with papal heraldry from that period, are beautiful. The three fountains in the floor are supposedly the ones of the bouncing head of the saint but they have long since run dry

Further on, to the right, the church of **Santa Maria Scala Coeli** owes its name to a vision St Bernard had here: he saw the soul he was praying for ascend to heaven; the Cosmatesque altar where this is supposed to have happened is down the cramped stairs, in the crypt, where St Paul was allegedly kept prior to his beheading. Beyond, the largest of the churches, **San Paolo alle Tre Fontane** holds the pillar to which St Paul was tied and a couple of mosaic pavements from Ostia Antica. Try to be here, if you can, in the early morning or evening, when the monks come in to sing Mass in Gregorian Chant – a moving experience.

On the way out, the **gatehouse** near the chocolate and liqueur shop contains ceiling frescoes from the thirteenth century that show the possessions of the abbey at the time. They're in a pretty bad state, but the ones that remain have been restored and are still very interesting, showing as they do a kind of picture map of Italy in the thirteenth century.

VIA APPIA ANTICA: THE CATACOMBS

Bus #218 from Piazza San Giovanni in Laterano.

During classical times the **Via Appia** was the most important of all the Roman trade routes, the so-called "Queen of Roads", carrying supplies right down through Campania to the port of Brindisi. It's no longer the main route south out of the city – that's Via Appia Nuova from Porta San Giovanni – but it remains an important part of early Christian Rome, its verges lined with the underground burial cemeteries or **catacombs** of the first Christians.

Laws in ancient Rome forbade burial within the city walls – most Romans were cremated – and there are catacombs in other parts of the city. But this is by far the largest concentration, around five complexes in all, dating from the first century to the fourth century, almost entirely emptied of bodies now but still decorated with the primitive signs and frescoes that were the hallmark of the then-burgeoning Christian movement. Despite much speculation, no one really knows why the Christians decided to bury their dead in these tunnels: the rock here, tufa, is soft and easy to hollow out, but the digging involved must still have been phenomenal, and there is no real reason to suppose that the burial places had to be secret – they continued to bury their dead like this long after Christianity became the established religion. Whatever the reasons, they make intriguing viewing now. The three principal complexes are within walking distance of each other, though it's not really worth trying to see them all – the layers of shelves and drawers aren't particularly gripping after a while.

Domine Quo Vadis and San Callisto

Via Appia Antica begins at the **Porta San Sebastiano**, built in the fifth century, a little way on from which the church of **Domine Quo Vadis** signals the start of the catacomb stretch of road. Legend has this as the place where St Peter saw Christ while fleeing from certain death in Rome and asked "Where goest thou, Lord ?", to which Christ replied that he was going to be crucified once more, leading Peter to turn around and accept his fate. Continuing on for a kilometre or so you reach the catacombs of **San Callisto** (Jan–Oct & Dec Thurs–Tues 8.30am–noon & 2.30–5pm; L8000). All third-century popes (of whom San Callisto was one) are buried here in the papal crypt, and the site features some well-preserved seventh- and eighth-century frescoes.

San Domitilla

A little way west from here, the catacombs of San **Domitilla** (Feb–Dec Mon & Wed–Sun 8.30am–noon & 2.30–5pm; L8000) are quieter than those of San Callisto and adjoin the remains of a fourth-century basilica erected here to the martyrs Achilleus and Nereus. The labyrinth itself is Rome's largest, stretching for around 17km in all, and contains more frescoes and early wall etchings.

San Sebastiano

The catacombs of **San Sebastiano** (Jan–Oct & Dec
Fri–Wed 9am–noon & 2.30–5pm; L8000), 500m further on,
are probably best for a visit, situated under a much renovated
basilica that was originally built by Constantine on the spot
where the bodies of the apostles Peter and Paul are said to
have been laid for a time. Downstairs, half-hour tours wind
around dark corridors showing signs of early Christian worship – paintings of doves and fish, a contemporary carved oil
lamp and inscriptions dating the tombs themselves. The most
striking features, however, are not Christian at all, but three
pagan tombs (one painted, two stuccoed) discovered when
archeologists were burrowing beneath the floor of the basilica
upstairs. Just above here, Constantine is said to have raised his
chapel to Peter and Paul, and although St Peter was later
removed to the Vatican, and St Paul to San Paolo fuori le
Mura, the graffiti above records the fact that this was indeed,
albeit temporarily, where the two Apostles rested.

The Villa and Circus of Maxentius

After leaving the catacombs of San Sebastiano, turn to your
right and walk about 200 metres. The group of brick ruins
trailing off into the fields to the left are the remains of the
Villa and Circus of Maxentius (daily 9am–1hr before
sunset; L8000), a large complex built by the emperor in the
early fourth century AD before his defeat by Constantine.
Clambering about in the ruins, you can make out the
twelve starting gates to the circus, or racetrack, and the
enormous towers that contained the mechanism for lifting
the gates at the beginning of the races and the remains of a
basilica. Other structures surround it, including, closer to
the road, the ruins of what was once a magnificent mausoleum of an unknown person or persons.

The tomb of Cecilia Metella

Further along the Via Appia is the circular tomb of **Cecilia Metella** (summer Mon & Sun 9am–1pm, Tues–Sat 9am–6pm; winter Mon & Sun 9am–1pm, Tues–Sat 9am–4pm; free) from the Augustan period, converted into a castle in the fourteenth century. Between here and the eleventh milestone is the best-preserved section of the ancient Via Appia, littered with remains and reconstructions of Roman tombs and fragments of the original paving. This, combined with impressive countryside to either side of the narrow road, makes it worth persevering, even though there's no bus service out here and the traffic can be heavy at times.

Trastevere and the Janiculum Hill

Across the river from the centre of town, on the right bank of the Tiber, is the district of **TRASTEVERE**. A smallish district sheltered under the heights of the Janiculum Hill, it was the artisan area of the city in classical times, neatly placed for the trade that came upriver from Ostia and was unloaded nearby. Outside the city walls, Trastevere (the name means literally "across the Tiber") was for centuries heavily populated by immigrants, and this uniqueness and separation lent the neighbourhood a strong identity that lasted well into this century. Nowadays the area is a long way from the working-class quarter it used to be, and although you're still likely to hear Travestere's strong Roman dialect here, you're also likely to bump into some of its many foreign residents, lured by the charm of its narrow streets and closeted squares. However, even if the local *Festa de' Noantri* ("celebration of we others"), held every July, seems to symbolize the slow decline of local spirit rather than celebrate its existence, there is good reason to come to Trastevere. It is among the more pleasant places to stroll in Rome, particularly peaceful in the morning, and lively come the evening, as dozens of trattorias set tables out along the cobblestone streets (Trastevere has long been known for its restaurants). The neighbourhood has also become the focus of the city's alternative scene and is home to much of its most vibrant and youthful nightlife.

PORTA PORTESE

Map 7, E6.
The obvious way to approach Trastevere is to cross over from Isola Tiberina or from the pedestrian Ponte Sisto at the end of Via Giulia, both of which leave you five minutes from the heart of the neighbourhood. On a Sunday it's worth walking over the Ponte Sublicio to Porta Portese, from which the **Porta Portese** flea market stretches down Via Portuense to Trastevere train station in a congested medley of antiques, old motor spares, cheap clothing, trendy clothing and assorted junk. Haggling is the rule, and keep a good hold of your wallet or purse. Come early if you want to buy, or even move – most of the bargains have gone by 10am, by which time the crush of people can be intense.

SANTA CECILIA IN TRASTEVERE

Map 7, E4. Daily 10am–noon & 4–5.30pm.
Further north, on Via Anicia, is the church of **Santa Cecilia in Trastevere**, a cream, rather sterile church – apart from a pretty front courtyard – whose antiseptic eighteenth-century appearance belies its historical associations. A church was originally built here over the site of the second-century home of St Cecilia, whose husband Valerian was executed for refusing to worship Roman gods and who herself was subsequently persecuted for Christian beliefs. The story has it that Cecilia was locked in the caldarium of

her own baths for several days but refused to die, singing her way through the ordeal (Cecilia is patron saint of music). Her head was finally half hacked off with an axe, though it took several blows before she finally succumbed. Below the high altar, Stefano Maderno's limp, almost modern statue of the saint shows her incorruptible body as it was found when exhumed in 1599, with three deep cuts in her neck – a fragile, intensely human piece of work that has helped make Cecilia one of the most revered Roman saints.

The excavations of the baths and the caldarium, in the crypt, were at time of writing closed for restoration, but should be open by the time you read this. On Tuesday and Thursday mornings (10–11.30am; donation expected), you can still visit the singing gallery, where some delicately painted and beautifully coloured frescoes by Pietro Cavallini (c.1293) are all that remains of the decoration that once covered the entire church.

PIAZZAS SAN COSIMATO AND SANTA MARIA

Map 7, C4 & D3.

Santa Cecilia is situated in the quieter part of Trastevere, on the southern side of **Viale Trastevere**, the wide boulevard that cuts through the centre of the district. There's more life on the far side of here, centred – during the day at least – around two main squares. The first of these, **Piazza San Cosimato**, holds a medium-sized produce market (Mon–Sat 8am–1pm), while the other, **Piazza Santa Maria in Trastevere**, a short walk north, is the heart of old Trastevere, named after the church in its northwest corner.

SANTA MARIA IN TRASTEVERE

Map 7, C3. Daily 7.30am–12.40pm & 4–7pm.

The church of **Santa Maria in Trastevere** is held to be

the first Christian place of worship in Rome, built on a site where a fountain of oil is said to have sprung on the day of Christ's birth. The greater part of the structure now dates from 1140, after a rebuilding by Innocent II, a pope from Trastevere. These days people come here for two things. The church's mosaics are among the city's most impressive: those on the cornice by Cavallini were completed a century or so after the rebuilding and show the Madonna surrounded by ten female figures with lamps – once thought to represent the Wise and Foolish Virgins. Inside, there's a nineteenth-century copy of a Cosmatesque pavement of spirals and circles, and apse mosaics contemporary with the building of the church – Byzantine-inspired works depicting a solemn yet sensitive parade of saints thronged around Christ and Mary. Beneath the high altar on the right, an inscription – "FONS OLIO" – marks the spot where the oil is supposed to have sprung up, close by which there is a chapel that is crowned with the crest of the British monarchy – placed here by Henry, cardinal of York, when he and his family, the Stuarts, lived in exile in Rome.

PALAZZO CORSINI

Map 7, B1. Via della Lungara 10 Tues–Fri 9am–7pm, Sat 9am–2pm, Sun 9am–1pm; L8000.

Cutting north through the backstreets towards the Tiber, the **Galleria Nazionale di Palazzo Corsini** is an unexpected cultural attraction on this side of the river. Built originally for Cardinal Riario in the fifteenth century, the palace was totally renovated in 1732–36 by Ferdinando Fuga for the cardinal and art collector Neri Maria Corsini, who gathered most of the paintings on display. It's rather a highbrow collection, perhaps of more interest to the art historian rather than the layperson, but among its highlights are works by Rubens, Van Dyck, Guido Reni and Caravaggio.

Among a host of works from the late 1400s and early 1500s, there is a particularly gruesome *St George and the Dragon* by Francesco Raibolini and, in the next room, a *St John the Baptist* by Caravaggio and *Madonna and Child* by Gentileschi, along with a charming double portrait of Clement XII with his nephew, the gallery's founder Neri Corsini. Beyond here, look out for a depiction of the Pantheon by Charles Clérisseau, when there was a market held in the piazza outside – though it's a rather fanciful interpretation, squeezing the Pyramid of Cestius and Arch of Janus into the background. You can also visit the chambers of Queen Christina, who renounced Protestantism, and, with it, the Swedish throne in 1655, and brought her library and fortune to Rome, to the delight of the Chigi pope, Alexander VII. She died here, in the palace, in 1689, and she is one of only three women to be buried in St Peter's. Her bedroom is decorated with frescoes by an unknown artist – grotesques with scenes of the miracles of Moses as well as the Riario coats of arms.

Later rooms are chock-full of paintings from the seventeenth and eighteenth centuries, but apart from a famous portrayal of *Salome With the Head of St John the Baptist* by Guido Reni, and *Prometheus Chained* by Salvatore Rosa – the latter one of the most vivid and detailed expositions of human internal anatomy you'll see – the main thing to look for is the curious Corsini Throne, thought to be a Roman copy of an Etruscan throne of the second or first century. Carved out of marble, its back is carved with warriors in armour and helmets, below which is a boar hunt, with wild boars the size of horses pursued by hunters. The base is decorated with scenes of a sacrifice, notably the minotaur devouring a human being – only discernible by the kicking legs that protrude from the feasting beast.

THE ORTO BOTANICO

Map 7, B2. Mon–Sat: 9.30am–5.30pm; L4000.

The park of the Palazzo Corsini is now the site of the **Orto Botanico**, which, after Padua's botanical gardens, is the most important in Italy – and a good example of eighteenth-century garden design. Its highlights are a wood of century-old oaks, cedars and conifers, a grove of acclimatized palm-trees, in front of the so-called Fountain of the Tritons, a herbal garden with medicinal plants, a collection of orchids that bloom in springtime and early summer – and, a nice touch, a garden of aromatic herbs put together for the blind people; the plants can be identified by their smell or touch, and are accompanied by signs in braille. The garden also has the distinction of being home to one of the oldest plane trees in Rome, between 350 and 400 years old.

VILLA FARNESINA

Map 7, C1. Mon–Sat 9am–1pm; L6000.

Much more interesting is the **Villa Farnesina** across the road from the Palazzo Corsini, built during the early sixteenth century by Baldassare Peruzzi for the Renaissance banker Agostino Chigi and known for its Renaissance frescoes. Inside you can view the Raphael-designed painting of *Cupid and Psyche* in the now glassed-in loggia, completed in 1517 by the artist's assistants, Giulio Romano, Francesco Penni and Giovanni da Udine. Vasari claims Raphael didn't complete the work because his infatuation with his mistress – "La Fornarina", whose father's bakery was situated nearby – was making it difficult to concentrate, and says that Chigi arranged for her to live with the painter in the palace while he worked on the loggia. More likely he was simply so overloaded with commissions that he couldn't possibly finish them all. He did, however, manage to finish the *Galatea* in the room next door, which he fitted in between his Vatican commissions for Julius II; "the greatest evocation of paganism of the Renaissance", Kenneth Clark called it, although Vasari claims that Michelangelo, passing by one day while Raphael was canoodling with La Fornarina, finished the painting for him. In the same room, the lunettes feature scenes from Ovid's *Metamorphoses* by Sebastiano del Piombo, while the ceiling illustrates Chigi's horoscope constellations, frescoed by the architect of the building, Peruzzi, who also decorated the upstairs *Salone delle Prospettive*, where trompe l'oeil balconies give views onto contemporary Rome – one of the earliest examples of the technique.

THE JANICULUM HILL

Map 2, B10–B11.

From the Villa Farnesina, it's about a fifteen-minute walk up Via Garibaldi (bus #870 goes up from Piazza della Rovere) to the summit of the **Janiculum Hill** – not one of the original seven hills of Rome, but the one with the best and most accessible views of the centre. Via Garibaldi leads up past the church of **San Pietro in Montorio** (daily 7.30am–noon & 4–6pm), built on a site once – now, it's thought, wrongly – believed to have been the place of the saint's crucifixion. The compact interior is particularly intimate – it's a favourite for weddings – and features some first-rate paintings, among them Sebastiano del Piombo's graceful *Flagellation*. Don't miss Bramante's little **Tempietto** (daily 9am–noon & 4–6pm) in the courtyard on the right, one of the seminal works of the Renaissance, built on what was supposed to have been the precise spot of St Peter's martyrdom. The small circular building is like a classical temple in miniature, perfectly proportioned and neatly executed.

The Janiculum was the scene of a fierce 1849 set-to between Garibaldi's troops and the French, and the white marble **memorial** opposite the church is dedicated to all those who died in the battle. A little further up the hill, the **Acqua Paola** – constructed for Paul V with marble from the Roman Forum – gushes water at a bend in the road. At the top, the **Porta San Pancrazio** was built during the reign of Urban VIII, destroyed by the French in 1849, and rebuilt by Pope Pius IX five years later. It has recently been restored to house the new **Museum of the Roman Republic 1848–49** – yet to open at time of writing. Afterwards, take the weight off your feet at **Bar Gianicolo**, a cool hangout for Italian media stars, writers and academics from the nearby Spanish and American academies.

Just beyond here is the entrance to the grounds of the **Villa Doria Pamphili**, which stretch down the hill alongside the old Via Aurelia. This is the largest and most recent of Rome's parks, laid out in 1650 and acquired for the city in the Seventies. It's a good place for a picnic, but most people turn right along the **Passeggiata del Gianicolo** to the crest of the hill, where, on Piazzale Garibaldi, there's an equestrian monument to Garibaldi – an ostentatious work from 1895. Just below is the spot from which a cannon is fired at noon each day for Romans to check their watches. Further on, the statue of Anita Garibaldi recalls the important part she played in the 1849 battle – a fiery, melodramatic work (she cradles a baby in one arm, brandishes a pistol with the other, and is galloping full speed on a horse) which also marks her grave. Spread out before her are some of the best views over the city.

A little further on is the Renaissance **Villa Lante**, a jewel of a place that is now the home of the Finnish Academy in Rome. Descending from here towards the Vatican and Saint Peter's, follow some steps off to the right and, next to a small amphitheatre, you'll find the gnarled old oak tree where the sixteenth-century Italian poet **Tasso**, friend of Cellini and author of *Orlando Furioso*, is said to have whiled away his last days. Further down the hill, past the Jesuit children's hospital, the church of **Sant'Onofrio** (Sun 9am–1pm) sits on the road's hairpin, its L-shaped portico fronting the church where Tasso is buried. To the right of the church is one of the city's most delightful small cloisters; you can visit the poet's cell, which holds some manuscripts, his chair, his death mask and personal effects.

The Vatican

n the west bank of the Tiber, directly across from Rome's historic centre, the **VATICAN CITY** was established as an independent sovereign state in 1929, a tiny territory surrounded by high walls on its far, western side and on the near side opening its doors to the rest of the city and its pilgrims in the form of St Peter's and its colonnaded piazza.

The Latin name *Mons Vaticanus* (Vatican Hill) is a corruption of an Etruscan term, indicating a good place for observing the flights of birds and lightning on the horizon that was believed to prophesy the future. It's believed that later St Peter himself was buried in a pagan cemetery here, giving rise to the building of a basilica to venerate his name and the siting of the headquarters of the Catholic Church here. After reaching an uneasy agreement with Mussolini, the Vatican became a sovereign state in 1929, and nowadays has its own radio station, newspaper, currency and postal service, and indeed security service in the colourfully dressed Swiss Guards. However, its relationship with the Italian state is not surprisingly anything but straightforward.

You wouldn't know at any point that you had left Rome and entered the Vatican; indeed the area around the Vatican, known as the **Borgo**, is one of the most cosmopolitan districts of Rome, full of hotels and restaurants,

Vatican practicalities

The Vatican Museums and the Basilica of St Peter's are open to visitors, and it's also possible to visit the **Vatican Gardens**, though only on one guided tour a day (Mon–Tues & Thurs–Sat except religious holidays 10am; L18,000); visits last about two hours and tickets must be bought a few days ahead from the **Vatican Information Office** in Piazza San Pietro (Mon–Sat 8.30am–6pm; ©06.6988.4466). You can also, if you wish, attend a **papal audience**: these happen once a week, usually on Wednesdays at 11am in the Audiences Room, and are by no means one-to-one affairs. It's often possible to get a place on one if you apply not more than a month and not less than two days in advance, by sending a fax with your name, your home address, your Rome address, and your preferred date of audience, to the Prefettura della Casa Pontificia (©06.6988.3273, fax 06.6988.5863). Finally, if you want to send a postcard with a Vatican postmark, there are Vatican **post offices** on the north side of Piazza San Pietro and inside the Vatican Museums.

and scurrying tourists and pilgrims – as indeed it always has been since the king of Wessex founded the first hotel for pilgrims here in the eighth century. You may find yourself staying in one of many mid-range hotels located here, although unless you're a pilgrim it's a better idea to base yourself in the more atmospheric city centre and travel back and forth on the useful bus #64. However much you try, one visit is never anywhere near enough.

CASTEL SANT'ANGELO

Map 6, G4. Tues–Sat 9am–10pm, Sun 9am–8pm; L12,000.
The best route to the Vatican and St Peter's is across **Ponte**

Sant'Angelo, flanked by angels carved to designs by Bernini (his so-called "breezy maniacs"). On the far side is the great circular hulk of the **Castel Sant'Angelo**, designed and built by the Emperor Hadrian as his own mausoleum (his ashes were interred here until a twelfth-century pope appropriated the sarcophagus, which was later destroyed in a fire). It was a grand monument, faced with white marble and surrounded with statues and topped with cypresses, similar in style to Augustus's mausoleum across the river. Renamed in the sixth century, when Pope Gregory the Great witnessed a vision of St Michael here that ended a terrible plague, the mausoleum's position near the Vatican was not lost on the papal authorities, who converted the building for use as a fortress and built a passage-way to link it with the Vatican as a refuge in times of siege or invasion – a route utilized on a number of occasions, most notably when the Medici pope, Clement VII, sheltered here for several months during the Sack of Rome in 1527.

Inside, from the monumental entrance hall a spiral ramp leads up into the centre of the mausoleum itself, passing through the chamber where the emperor was entombed, over a drawbridge, one of the defensive modifications made by the Borgia pope, Alexander VI, in the late fifteenth century, to the main level at the top, where a small palace was built to house the papal residents in appropriate splendour. After the Sack of Rome, Pope Paul III had some especially fine renovations made, including the beautiful *Sala Paolina*, which features frescoes by Pierno del Vaga, among others. The gilded ceiling here displays the Farnese family arms, on the wall is a tromp-l'oeil fresco of one of the family's old retainers, whose name is unknown, coming through a door from a darkened room. You'll also notice Paul III's personal motto, *Festina Lenta* ("make haste slowly"), scattered throughout the ceilings and in various corners of all his rooms.

Elsewhere, rooms hold swords, armour, guns and the like, others are lavishly decorated with grotesques and paintings (don't miss the bathroom of Clement VII on the second floor, with its prototype hot and cold water taps and mildly erotic frescoes). Below are dungeons and storerooms (not visitable), which can be glimpsed from the spiralling ramp, testament to the castle's grisly past as the city's most notorious Renaissance prison – Benvenuto Cellini and Cesare Borgia are just two of its more famous detainees. From the quiet bar upstairs you'll also get one of the best views of Rome and excellent coffee.

PIAZZA SAN PIETRO

Map 6, D4.

Beyond here, the approach to St Peter's – **Via della Conciliazione** – is disappointing: typically, Mussolini swept away the houses of the previously narrow street and replaced them with this wide sweeping avenue, and nowadays St Peter's somehow looks too near, the vast space of Bernini's **Piazza San Pietro** not really becoming apparent until you're right on top of it.

In fact, in tune with the spirit of the Baroque, the church was supposed to be even better hidden than it is now: Bernini planned to complete the colonnade with a triumphal arch linking the two arms, so obscuring the view until you were well inside the square, but this was never carried out and the arms of the piazza remain open, symbolically welcoming the world into the lap of the Catholic Church. The obelisk in the centre was brought to Rome by Caligula in 36 AD, and it stood for many years in the centre of Nero's Circus on the Vatican Hill (to the left of the church); according to legend, it marked the site of St Peter's martyrdom. It was moved here in 1586, when Sixtus V ordered that it be erected in front of the basilica, a task that took four months and was apparently done in silence, on pain of death.

The matching fountains on either side are the work of Carlo Maderno (on the right) and Bernini (on the left). In between the obelisk and each fountain, a circular stone set into the pavement marks the focal points of an ellipse, from which the four rows of columns on the perimeter of the piazza line up perfectly, making the colonnade appear to be supported by a single line of columns.

BASILICA DI SAN PIETRO

Map 6, C4–D4. Daily: summer 7am–7pm; winter 7am–6pm.

The piazza is so grand that you can't help but feel a little let down by the **Basilica di San Pietro** (St Peter's), its facade – by no means the church's best feature – obscuring the dome that signals the building from just about everywhere else in the city. Amid a controversy similar to that surrounding the restoration of the Sistine chapel a few years ago, the facade has also recently been restored, leaving the previously sober travertine facade a decidedly yellowish grey.

Some history

Built to a plan initially conceived at the turn of the fifteenth century by Bramante and finished off, heavily modified, over a century later by Carlo Maderno, St Peter's is a strange hotchpotch of styles, bridging the gap between the Renaissance and Baroque eras with varying levels of success. It is, however, the principal shrine of the Catholic Church, built as a replacement for the rundown structure erected here by Constantine in the early fourth century on the site of St Peter's tomb. As such it can't help but impress, having been worked on by the greatest Italian architects of the sixteenth and seventeenth centuries, and occupying a site rich with historical significance. In size, certainly, Saint Peter's beats most other churches hands down. Bramante had originally conceived a Greek cross plan rising to a high central dome, but this plan was altered after his death and only revived with the (by then) very elderly Michelangelo's accession as chief architect. Michelangelo was largely responsible for the dome, but he too died shortly afterwards, in 1564, before it was completed. He was succeeded by Vignola, and the dome was completed in 1590 by Giacomo della Porta. Carlo Maderno, under orders from Pope Paul V, took over in 1605, and stretched the church into a Latin cross plan, which had the practical advantage of accommodating more people and followed more directly the plan of Constantine's original basilica. But in so doing he completely unbalanced all the previous designs, not least by obscuring the dome (which he also modified) from view in the piazza. The inside, too, is very much of the Baroque era, largely the work of Bernini, who created many of the most important fixtures. The church was finally completed and reconsecrated on 18 November, 1626, 1300 years to the day after the original basilica was first consecrated.

Inside St Peter's

You need to be properly dressed to enter St Peter's, which means no bare knees or shoulders – a rule that is very strictly enforced. Inside on the right is Michelangelo's other legacy to the church, his **Pietà**, completed at the opposite end of his career when he was just 24. Following an attack by a vandal a few years back, it sits behind glass, strangely remote from the life of the rest of the building. Looking at the piece, its fame comes as no surprise: it's a sensitive and individual work, and an adept one too, draping the limp body of a grown man across the legs of a woman with grace and ease. Though you're much too far away to read it, etched into the strap across Mary's chest are words proclaiming the work as Michelangelo's – the only piece ever signed by the sculptor and apparently done after he heard his work, which had been placed in Constantine's basilica, had been misattributed by onlookers. You can see it properly on the plaster cast of the statue in the Pinacoteca of the Vatican Museums.

As you walk down the **nave**, the size of the building becomes more apparent – and not just because of the bronze plaques set in the floor that make comparisons with the sizes of other churches. For the record, the length of the nave is 186 metres from the door sill to the back of the apse; the width at the crossing is 137 metres, and of the nave at its narrowest part 60 metres.

In the north transept is the wonderful gilded Baroque Chapel of the Blessed Sacrament, designed by Borromini with work by Pietro da Cortona, Domenichino and Bernini. This chapel is not open to the casual sightseer but it is worthy of a visit, which can be managed if you go there to pray along with the clergy, who maintain a vigil there during the time the basilica is open.

The **dome** is breathtakingly imposing, rising high above the supposed site of St Peter's tomb. With a diameter of 44 metres it is only 1.5 metres smaller than the Pantheon (the letters of the inscription inside its lower level are over six feet high); it is supported by four enormous piers, decorated with reliefs depicting the basilica's so-called "**major relics**": St Veronica's handkerchief, which was used to wipe the face of Christ, and is adorned with His miraculous image; the lance of St Longinus, which pierced Christ's side; and a piece of the True Cross, in the pier of St Helen (the head of St Andrew, which was returned to the Eastern

Church by Pope Paul VI in 1966, was also formerly kept here). On the right side of the nave, near the pier of St Longinus, the bronze statue of **St Peter** is another of the most venerated monuments in the basilica, carved in the thirteenth century by Arnolfo di Cambio and with its right foot polished smooth by the attentions of pilgrims. On holy days this statue is dressed in papal tiara and vestments.

Bronze was also the material used in Bernini's **baldacchino**, the centrepiece of the sculptor's Baroque embellishment of the interior, a massive 26m high (the height, apparently, of Palazzo Farnese), cast out of 927 tonnes of metal removed from the Pantheon roof in 1633. To modern eyes, it's an almost grotesque piece of work, with its wild spiralling columns copied from columns in the Constantine basilica. But it has the odd personal touch, not least in the female faces expressing the agony of childbirth and a beaming baby carved on the plinths – said to be done for a niece of Bernini's patron (Urban VIII), who gave birth at the same time as the sculptor was finishing the piece.*

Bernini's feverish sculpting decorates the apse too, his

---

* The baldacchino and confessio just in front are supposed to mark the exact spot of the **tomb of St Peter**, and excavations earlier this century did indeed turn up – directly beneath the baldacchino and the remains of Constantine's basilica – a row of Roman tombs with inscriptions confirming that the Vatican Hill was a well-known burial ground in classical times. Whether the tomb of St Peter was found is less clear: a shrine was discovered, badly damaged, that agrees with some historical descriptions of the saint's marker, with a space in it through which ancient pilgrims placed their heads in prayer. Close by, the bones were discovered of an elderly but physically fit man, and, although these have never been claimed as the relics of the apostle, speculation has been rife. It is possible to take an English-language tour of the Vatican necropolis; contact the Vatican Information Office (see above) for details.

cattedra enclosing the supposed (though doubtful) chair of St Peter in a curvy marble and stucco throne, surrounded by the doctors of the Church (the two with bishops' mitres are St Augustine of Hippo and St Ambrose, representing the Western Church; the two to the rear are portraits of St John Chrysosthom and St Athanasius of the Eastern Church). Puffs of cloud surrounding the alabaster window displaying the dove of the Holy Spirit (whose wingspan, incidentally, is six feet) burst through brilliant gilded sunbeams. On the right, the **tomb of Urban VIII**, also by Bernini, is less grand but more dignified. On the left, the **tomb of Paul III**, by Giacomo della Porta, was moved up and down the nave of the church before it was finally placed here as a counter to that of Urban VIII. More interesting is Bernini's **monument to Alexander VII** in the south transept, with its winged skeleton struggling underneath the heavy marble drapes, upon which the Chigi pope is kneeling in prayer. The grim reaper significantly clutches an hourglass – the Baroque at its most melodramatic, and symbolic. On the left sits Charity, on the right, Truth Revealed in Time; to the rear are Hope and Faith.

There are innumerable other tombs and works of art in the basilica, and you could spend days here if you tried to inspect each one. Further down the south transept, on the east side of the crossing is an enormous **mosaic** of Raphael's *Transfiguration*, significantly larger than the original painting – which is in the Vatican Pinacoteca (oil paintings would be ruined by the high water table under St Peter's). Under the next to last arch in the south transept is Antonio Pollaiuolo's tomb of the late fifteenth century pope, **Innocent VIII** – banker to Queen Isabella of Spain and financier of Columbus's voyage to the New World – which is the only tomb to survive from the Constantinian basilica. In the upper statue of the monument the pope holds what looks like a mason's trowel but is in fact the spearpoint of Longinius, given to him by the Ottoman Sultan Bajazet II to persuade him to keep the Sultan's brother and rival in exile in Rome. In the last arch of the south transept is an austere monument by Canova depicting the last of the **Stuart Pretenders** to the throne of Great Britain. Over the door to the lift is the monument to **Clementina Sobieska**, the wife of James III (Stuart pretender to the English throne) – one of only three women buried in St Peter's.

The Treasury

An entrance off the aisle leads to the steeply priced **Treasury** (daily: summer 9am–6pm; winter 9am–5pm; L8000). Along with more recent additions, this holds artefacts from the earlier church: a spiral column (the other survivors form part of the colonnade around the interior of the dome); a wall-mounted tabernacle by Donatello; a rich blue-and-gold dalmatic that is said once to have belonged to Charlemagne (though this has since been called into question); the vestments and tiara for the bronze statue of St Peter in the nave of the basilica; and the massive, though fairly ghastly, late-fifteenth-century bronze tomb of Sixtus IV by Pollaiuolo – said to be a very accurate portrait.

The Grottoes

Back at the central crossing, steps lead down under Bernini's statue of St Longinus to the **Grottoes** (daily: summer 8am–6pm; winter 7am–5pm), where a good number of popes are buried, though to be honest none are particularly interesting.

Ascending to the roof and dome

Far better is the **ascent to the roof and dome** (daily:

May–Sept 8am–6pm; Oct–April 8am–5pm; L8000 with lift); the entrance is in the northern courtyard between the church and the Vatican Palace, on your way out as you exit through the crypt. You'll probably need to queue and, even with the lift, it's a long climb up a narrow stairway that spirals up the dome. The views from the gallery around the interior of the dome give you a sense of the enormity of the church. From there, the roof grants views from behind the huge statues onto the piazza below, before the ascent to the lantern at the top of the dome, from which the views over the city are as glorious as you'd expect. Remember that it is over 300 fairly claustrophobic steps through the double shell of the dome to reach the lantern; indeed you should probably give it a miss if you're either in ill health or uneasy with heights or confined spaces.

THE VATICAN MUSEUMS

Map 6, C2. Viale Vaticano 13. Dec–March Mon–Sat 8.45am–12.45pm, last exit 1.45pm; rest of year Mon–Sat 8.45am–3.45pm, last exit 4.45pm; L18,000, reduced rate L12,000. Closed Sun, hols and religious holidays, except the last Sunday of each month when admission is free.

A fifteen-minute walk out of the northern side of the piazza takes you up to the only part of the Vatican Palace you can visit independently, the **VATICAN MUSEUMS** – quite simply, the largest, richest, most compelling and perhaps most exhausting museum complex in the world. If you have found any of Rome's other museums disappointing, the Vatican is probably the reason why: so much booty from the city's history has ended up here, from both classical and later times, and so many of the Renaissance's finest artists were in the employ of the pope, that not surprisingly the result is a set of museums so stuffed with antiquities as to put most other European collections to shame.

The museums' layout

The Vatican Museums are composed of four principal structures: the **Vatican Palace** itself, at the end nearest St Peters, the oldest part of the complex; the **Belvedere Palace** to the north, constructed in the late 1400s by Pope Innocent VIII, as a summer casino amidst the meadows that in those days surrounded this part of the city (and from which the modern neighbourhood, Prati, – "pastures" – gets its name); and the two long **galleries** built in the 1500s to make passage between the two palaces easier.

In the middle of all this are three **courtyards**: the **Cortile del Belvedere** at the far end, the small **Cortile della Biblioteca** in the middle, created by the construction of the Vatican Library and Braccio Nuovo, and, the northernmost of the three, the **Cortile della Pigna** – named after the huge bronze pine cone ("pigna" in Italian) mounted in the niche at the end, an ancient Roman artefact that was found close to the Pantheon. In classical times this was a fountain with water pouring out of each of its points. Also in this courtyard is a large modern bronze sculpture of a sphere within a sphere, which occasionally rotates – though to an erratic schedule. If you're on a guided tour, you'll stop here to be talked through the Sistine Chapel paintings before going in, as it's forbidden to speak inside. Even if you're not, it can be worth listening in, if there's one being given in English, but be discreet.

Until the new entrance is finished, you enter by a **main entrance** to the museums that was created by Pope Pius XI, in 1932, its huge bronze spiral staircase leading up to the ticket offices above. On it are displayed the heraldic arms of all the popes from 1447 (Nicholas II) to Pius XI's predecessor (Benedict XV). The staircase is in the form of a double helix, one half ascending, the other descending.

As its name suggests, the Vatican Palace actually holds a collection of museums on very diverse subjects – displays of classical statuary, Renaissance painting, Etruscan relics, Egyptian artefacts, not to mention the furnishings and decoration of the palace itself. There's no point in trying to see everything, at least not on one visit. Once inside, you have a choice of **routes**, but the only features you really shouldn't miss are the Raphael Stanze and the Sistine Chapel. Above all, decide how long you want to spend here, and what you want to see, before you start; you could spend anything from 45 minutes to the better part of a day here, and it's easy to collapse from museum fatigue before you've even got to your most important target of interest. Be conservative – the distances between different sections alone can be vast and very tiring.

Museo Pio-Clementino

To the left of the entrance, the small **Museo Pio-Clementino** and its octagonal courtyard is home to some of the best of the Vatican's classical statuary, including two statues that influenced Renaissance artists more than any others – the serene Apollo Belvedere, a Roman copy of a fourth-century BC original, and the first century BC Laocoon. The latter was discovered near Nero's Golden House in 1506 by a ploughman who had inadvertently dug through the roof of a buried part of Trajan's Baths. It depicts the prophetic Trojan priest being crushed with his sons by serpents sent to punish him for warning his fellow citizens of the danger of the Trojan horse. It is perhaps the most famous classical statue ever, referred to by Pliny who thought it carved from a single piece of marble, and written about by Byron – who described its contorted realism as "dignifying pain". It was restored by Michelangelo, who replaced the missing

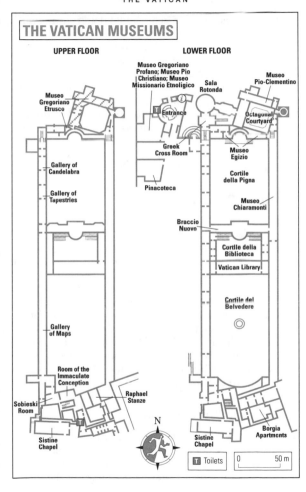

THE VATICAN MUSEUMS

UPPER FLOOR

LOWER FLOOR

Museo Gregoriano Etrusco

Gallery of Candelabra

Gallery of Tapestries

Gallery of Maps

Room of the Immaculate Conception

Raphael Stanze

Sobieski Room

Sistine Chapel

Museo Gregoriano Profano; Museo Pio Christiano; Museo Missionario Etnoligico

Sala Rotonda

Museo Pio-Clementino

Entrance

Octagonal Courtyard

Greek Cross Room

Museo Egizio

Pinacoteca

Cortile della Pigna

Museo Chiaramonti

Braccio Nuovo

Cortile della Biblioteca

Vatican Library

Cortile del Belvedere

Sistine Chapel

Borgia Apartments

N

Toilets

0   50 m

right arm – since in turn replaced by the original, which was found in the 1950s.

Also in the museum, the frescoed Hall of the Muses has as its centrepiece the so-called Belvedere Torso, which was found in the Campo de' Fiori during the reign of Julius II. It's signed by one Apollonius the son of Nestor, a Greek sculptor of the first century BC, and is generally thought to be a near-perfect example of male anatomy. Its portrayal, either of Hercules sitting on his lion skin or Ajax resting, was studied by most key Renaissance artists, including Michelangelo, who incorporated its turning pose as Christ's in the *Last Judgement* in the Sistine Chapel.

The Sala Rotonda

A brief corridor leads next to the **Sala Rotonda**, whose floor is paved with a second century AD Roman mosaic from the town of Otricoli, north of Rome, depicting battles between men and sea monsters. There is more classical statuary around the room, notably a huge gilded bronze statue of a rather dim-witted looking Hercules also from the second century AD, the only surviving gilded bronze statue on display in the Vatican Museums. Each side of the statue are busts of the emperor Hadrian and his lover, Antinous – who is also depicted in the same room as a huge statue dressed as Bacchus. There is also a beautiful white marble statue of Claudius, in the guise of Jupiter, with his oak leaf crown and an eagle.

The Greek Cross Room

Beyond here, the **Greek Cross Room** is decorated in Egyptian style, although the pharaonic statues flanking the entry door are nineteenth-century imitations. There's another Roman mosaic, showing the phases of the moon, from the second century AD, and two huge porphyry boxes – the sarcophagi of queens Helen and Constanza. On Helen's, soldiers vanquish their enemies, a reference to the fact that she was the mother of Constantine, while that of Costanza, the daughter of the emperor, shows putti carrying grapes, loaves of bread and lambs – a reference to the eucharist, as she was a devout Christian. Look behind the sarcophagus, on the left, at the lifesize statue of a striding woman – believed to be the only surviving likeness of Cleopatra.

Museo Egizio

The **Museo Egizio**, founded in the nineteenth century by Gregory XVI, isn't one of the Vatican's highlights. It has some vividly painted mummy cases (and two mummies), along with *canopi*, the alabaster vessels into which the entrails of the deceased were placed. There is also a partial reconstruction of the Temple of Serapis from Hadrian's Villa near Tivoli, along with another statue of his lover, Antinous, who drowned close to the original temple in Egypt and so inspired Hadrian to build his replica. The Egyptian-style statues in shiny black basalt next door to the mummies were also found in Tivoli, and are also Roman imitations, although Hadrian collected some original Egyptian bits and pieces too, some of which are housed in the room which curves around the niche containing the pinecone – various Egyptian deities including the laughing fat ogre, Bes. The next rooms contain Egyptian bronzes from the late pharaonic period and early days of the Roman Empire, including a group of items from the cult of Isis which became popular in Rome itself. There is also, beyond here, a series of rooms with clay tablets inscribed in cuneiform writing from Mesopotamia, and Assyrian, Sumerian and Persian bas-reliefs on stone tablets.

MUSEO EGIZIO

Museo Gregoriano Etrusco

Past the entrance to the Egyptian Museum a grand staircase, the Simonetti Stairs, leads up to the **Museo Gregoriano Etrusco**, which holds sculpture, funerary art and applied art from the sites of southern Etruria – a good complement to Rome's specialist Etruscan collection in the Villa Giulia. Especially worth seeing are the finds from the Regolini-Galassi tomb, from the seventh century BC, discovered near Cerveteri, which contained the remains of three Etruscan nobles, two men and a woman; the breastplate of the woman and her huge fibia (clasp) are of gold. Take a look at the small ducks and lions with which they are decorated, fashioned in the almost microscopic beadwork for which Etruscan goldsmiths were famous. There's also armour, a bronze bedstead, a funeral chariot and a wagon, as well as a great number of enormous storage jars, in which food, oil and wine were contained for use in the afterlife.

Beyond here are Etruscan bronzes, including weapons, candelabra, barbecue sets (skewers and braziers); beautiful women's makeup cases known as *cistae*, and, most notably, the so-called Mars of Todi, a three-quarters lifesize votive statue found in the Umbrian town of Todi. On a flap of the figure's breastplate an inscription gives the name of the donor. Further on, there is a large collection of Etruscan sarcophagi and stone statuary from Vulci, Tarquinia and Tuscania in northern Lazio. Particularly interesting here are the finely carved horses' heads from Vulci and the sarcophagus of a magistrate from Tarquinia which still bears traces of the paint its reliefs were coloured with. There are also two rooms of Etruscan jewellery, with exquisite goldsmith work, crowns of golden oak and laurel leaves, necklaces, earrings and rings set with semiprecious stones and a fibula complete with the owner's name etched on it in such small writing that a magnifying glass is provided for you to read it.

If you haven't had your fill of the Etruscans by now, go back downstairs to see another huge collection, housed in a series of large rooms on the north side of the Belvedere Palace which offer stunning views of Monte Mario, and comprising lots of vases, assorted weapons and items of everyday household use, and a magnificent terracotta statue of Adonis melodramatically lying on a lacy couch, found near the town of Tuscania in the 1950s. Finally, don't miss the Greek krater, among a lot of Greek pottery found in Etruscan tombs, which shows Menelaus and Ulysses asking the Trojans for the return of Helen. It's housed in a special display case and can be rotated by pressing the electrical switch on the bottom of the case.

The Galleries of Candelabra, Tapestries and Maps

Outside the Etruscan Museum, the large monumental staircase leads back down to the main route, taking you first through the **Gallery of Candelabra**, the niches of which are adorned with huge candelabra taken from Imperial Roman villas. This gallery is also stuffed with ancient sculpture, its most memorable piece being a copy of the famous statue of Diana of Ephesus, whose the multiple breasts are, according to the Vatican official line, in fact bees' eggs. Beyond here the **Gallery of Tapestries** has on the left Belgian tapestries to designs by the school of Raphael which show scenes from the life of Christ, and on the right tapestries made in Rome at the Barberini workshops during the 1600s, showing scenes from the life of Maffeo Barberini, who became Pope Urban VIII.

Next, the **Gallery of Maps**, which is as long (175m) as the previous two galleries put together, was decorated in the late sixteenth century at the behest of Pope Gregory XIII, the reformer of the calendar, to show all of Italy, the major islands in the Mediterranean, the papal possessions in France, as well as the siege of Malta, the battle of Lepanto and large-scale maps of the maritime republics of Venice and Genoa. This gallery is considered by many to be the most beautiful area in the entire Vatican Museums, and its ceiling frescoes, illustrating scenes that took place in the area depicted in each adjacent map, are perhaps one reason why.

After the Gallery of the Maps, there is a hall with more tapestries, and, to the left, the **Room of the Immaculate Conception**, which sports nineteenth-century frescoes of Pope Pius IX declaring the Doctrine of the Immaculate Conception of the Blessed Virgin Mary on December 8, 1854. From here all visitors are directed to a covered walkway suspended over the palace courtyard of the Belvedere which leads through to the Raphael Stanze.

The Raphael Stanze

The first of the **Raphael Stanze** that you come to, the Stanza di Constantino was not in fact done by Raphael at all, but painted in part to his designs about five years after he died, by his pupils, Giulio Romano, Francesco Penni and Raffello del Colle, between 1525 and 1531. It shows scenes from the life of the emperor Constantine, who made Christianity the official religion of the Roman Empire. The enormous painting on the wall opposite the entrance is the *Battle of the Milvian Bridge* by Giulio Romano and Francesco Penni – a depiction of a decisive battle in 312 AD between the warring co-emperors of the West, Constantine and Maxentius. With due regard to the laws of propaganda, the victorious emperor is in the centre of the painting mounted on his white horse while the vanquished Maxentius drowns in the river to the right, clinging to his black horse. The painting to your left as you enter, the

Vision of Constantine by Giulio Romano, shows Constantine telling his troops of his dream-vision of the Holy Cross inscribed with the legend "In this sign you will conquer". Opposite, the *Baptism of Constantine*, by Francesco Penni, is a flight of fancy – Constantine was baptized on his deathbed about thirty years after the battle of the Milvian Bridge. Beyond the Stanza di Constantine, the **Room of the Chiaroscuri** was originally painted by Raphael, but curiously Pope Gregory XIII had those paintings removed and the room repainted in the rather gloomy style you see today – although there is a magnificent gilded and painted ceiling which bears the arms of the Medici.

A small door from here leads into the little **Chapel of Nicholas V**, with wonderful frescoes by Beato Angelico painted between 1448 and 1450, showing scenes in the lives of Ss Stephen and Lawrence. But the real attraction is to head straight through the souvenir shop to the **Stanza di Eliodoro**, the first of the Raphael rooms proper, which in proper, in which the fresco on the right of the entrance, *The Expulsion of Heliodorus from the Temple*, tells the story of Heliodorus, the agent of the eastern king, Seleucus, who was slain by a mysterious rider on a white horse while trying to steal the treasure of Jerusalem's Temple. An exciting piece of work, painted in 1512–1514 for Pope Julius II, the figures of Heliodorus, the horseman and the flying men are adeptly done, the figures almost jumping out the painting into the room, but the group of figures on the left is more interesting – Pope Julius II, in his papal robes, Giulio Romano, the pupil of Raphael, and, to his left, Raphael himself in a rare self-portrait

On the left wall as you enter, the *Mass of Bolsena* is a bit of anti-Lutheran propaganda, and relates a miracle that occurred in the town in northern Lazio in the 1260s, when a German priest who doubted the transubstantiation of Christ found the wafer bleeding when he broke it during a service. (The napkin onto which it bled is preserved in Orvieto's cathedral.) The pope facing the priest is another portrait of Julius II. The composition is a neat affair, the colouring rich, the onlookers kneeling, turning, gasping, as the miracle is realized. On the window wall opposite is the *Deliverance of St Peter*, showing the saint being assisted in a jail-break by the Angel of the Lord – a night scene, whose clever chiaroscuro, predates Caravaggio by nearly one hundred years. It was painted by order of Pope Leo X, as an allegory of his imprisonment after a battle that took place in Ravenna a few years earlier. Finally, on the large wall opposite Heliodorus, *Leo I Repulsing Attila the Hun* is an an allegory of the difficulties that the papacy was going through in the early 1500s, and shows the chubby cardinal, Giovanni dei Medici, who succeeded Julius II as Leo X in 1513 – Leo later had Raphael's pupils paint a portrait of himself as Leo I, so, confusingly, he appears twice in this fresco, as pope and as the equally portly Medici cardinal just behind.

The next room, the **Stanza della Segnatura** or Pope's study, is probably the best known – and with good reason. Painted in the years 1508–11, when Raphael first came to Rome, the subjects were again the choice of Julius II, and, composed with careful balance and harmony, it comes close to the peak of the painter's art. The *School of Athens*, on the near wall as you come in, steals the show, a representation of the triumph of scientific truth (to pair with the *Disputation of the Sacrament* opposite, which is a reassertion of religious dogma), in which all the great minds from antiquity are represented. Plato and Aristotle discuss philosophy at the centre of the painting: Aristotle, the father of scientific method, motions downwards; Plato, pointing upward, indicating his philosophy of otherworldly spirituality, is believed to be a portrait of Leonardo da Vinci. On the far right, the crowned figure holding a globe was meant to represent the Egyptian geographer, Ptolemy; to his right is Raphael, the young man in the black beret, while in front, demonstrating a theorem to his pupils on a slate, the figure of Euclid is a portrait of Bramante. Spread across the steps is Diogenes, lazily ignorant of all that is happening around him, while to the left Raphael added a solitary, sullen portrait of Michelangelo — a homage to the artist, apparently painted after Raphael saw the first stage of the Sistine chapel almost next door. Other identifiable figures include the beautiful youth with blonde hair looking out of the painting, Francesco Maria Della Rovere, placed here by order of Julius II. Della Rovere also appears as the good-looking young man to the left of the seated dignitaries, in the painting opposite, the *Disputation on the Holy Sacrament*, an allegory of the Christian religion and the main element of the mass, the Blessed Sacrament — which stands at the centre of the painting being discussed by all manner of popes, cardinals, bishops, doctors, even the poet Dante.

The last room, the **Stanza Incendio**, was the last to be decorated, to the orders and general glorification of Pope Leo X, and in a sense it brings together three generations of work. The ceiling was painted by Perugino, Raphael's teacher, and the frescoes were completed to Raphael's designs by his pupils (notably Giulio Romano), most striking of which is the *Fire in the Borgo*, facing the main window — an oblique reference to Leo X restoring peace to Italy after Julius II's reign but in fact describing an event that took place during the reign of Leo IV, when the pope stood in the loggia of the old St Peter's and made the sign of the cross to extinguish a fire. As with so many of these paintings, the chronology is deliberately crazy: Leo IV is in fact a portrait of Leo X, while on the left, Aeneas carries his aged father Anchises out of the burning city of Troy, 2000 years earlier. This last Raphael Room is connected back to the Sobieski Room by the small **Chapel of Urban VI**, with frescoes and stuccoes by Pietro da Cortona.

THE RAPHAEL STANZE

The Borgia Apartments

Outside the Raphael Stanze, on the other side of the Sistine Chapel steps, the **Borgia Apartments** were inhabited by Julius II's hated predecessor, Alexander VI – a fact which persuaded Julius to move into the new set of rooms he called upon Raphael to decorate. Nowadays host to a large collection of modern religious art (see below), the Borgia rooms were almost exclusively decorated by Pinturicchio in the years 1492–95, on the orders of Alexander VI. The ceiling frescoes in the *Sala dei Santi* are especially worth seeing, typically rich in colour and detail and depicting the legend of Osiris and the Apis bull – a reference to the Borgia family symbol, a bull. Among other images is a scene showing St Catherine of Alexandria disputing with the emperor Maximillian, in which Pinturicchio has placed his self-portrait behind the emperor – and also, clearly visible in the background, the Arch of Constantine. The figure of St Catherine is said to be a portrait of Lucrezia Borgia, and the room was reputedly the scene of a decidedly un-papal party to celebrate the first of Lucrezia's three marriages, which ended up with men tossing sweets down the fronts of the women's dresses.

The religious collection includes a variety of works by some of the most famous names in the modern art world – liturgical vestments designed by Matisse; a fascinating *Landscape with Angels* by Salvador Dalí, donated by King Juan Carlos of Spain; one of Francis Bacon's studies of Innocent X after Valazquez (a list is available at the door) – but really isn't that interesting by comparison.

The Sistine Chapel

Steps lead up from here to the **Sistine Chapel**, a huge barn-like structure built for Pope Sixtus IV between 1473 and 1481. It serves as the pope's official private chapel and the scene of the conclaves of cardinals for the election of each new pontiff. The ceiling paintings here, and the Last Judgement on the wall behind the altar, together make up arguably the greatest masterpiece in Western art, and the largest body of painting ever planned and executed by one man – Michelangelo. They are also probably the most viewed paintings in the world: it's estimated that on an average day about 15,000 people trudge through here to take a look; and during the summer and on special occasions the number of visitors can exceed 20,000. It's useful to carry a pair of binoculars with you in order to see the paintings better, but bear in mind that it is strictly forbidden to take pictures of any kind in the chapel, including video, and it is also officially forbidden to speak – although this is something that is rampantly ignored.

The wall paintings

Upon completion of the structure, Sixtus brought in several prominent painters of the Renaissance to decorate the **walls.** The overall project was under the management of Pinturicchio and comprised a series of paintings showing (on the left as you face the altar) scenes from the life of Moses and, on the right, scenes from the life of Christ. Sixtus didn't have just anybody work on these: there are paintings by, among others, Perugino, who painted the marvellously composed cityscape of *Jesus giving St Peter the Keys to Heaven*, Botticelli – *The Trials of Moses* and *Cleansing of the Leper* – and Ghirlandaio, whose *Calling of St Peter and St Andrew* shows Christ calling the two saints to be disciples, surrounded by onlookers, against a fictitious medieval landscape of boats, birds, turrets and mountains. Some of the paintings were in fact collaborative efforts, and it's known that Ghirlandaio and Botticelli in particular contributed to each other's work. Recently restored after a thorough restoration, anywhere else they would be pored over very closely indeed. As it is, they are entirely overshadowed by Michelangelo's more famous work.

The ceiling paintings

The **ceiling** at this time was painted as a blue background with gold stars to resemble the night sky. Over the altar there were two additional paintings by Perugino and a large picture of the Virgin Mary. Pope Sixtus IV was succeeded by Innocent VIII, who was followed by Alexander VI, the Borgia pope, who was later, in 1503, after the brief reign of Pius III, succeeded by Giuliano della Rovere, who took the name Julius II. Though a Franciscan friar, he was a violent man with a short temper, and his immediate objective as pope was to try to regain the lands that had been taken away from the papacy during the reigns of Innocent VIII and Alexander VI by the French, Germans and Spanish. For this purpose he started a series of wars and secret alliances.

He was also an avid collector and patron of the arts, and he summoned to Rome the best artists and architects of the day. Among these artists was Michelangelo, who, through a series of political intrigues orchestrated by Bramante and Raphael, was assigned the task of decorating the Sistine Chapel. Work commenced in 1508. Oddly enough, Michelangelo hadn't wanted to do the work at all: he considered himself a sculptor, not a painter, and was more eager to get on with carving Julius II's tomb (now in San Pietro in Vincoli, see p.99) than the ceiling, which he regarded as a chore. Pope Julius II, however, had other plans, drawing up a design of the twelve Apostles for the vault and hiring Bramante to design a scaffold for the artist from which to work. Michelangelo was apparently an awkward, solitary character: he had barely begun painting when he rejected Bramante's scaffold as unusable, fired all his staff, and dumped the pope's scheme for the ceiling in favour of his own. But the pope was easily his match, and there are tales of the two men clashing while the work was going on – Michelangelo would lock the doors at crucial points, ignoring the pope's demands to see how it was progressing; and legend has the two men at loggerheads at the top of the scaffold one day, resulting in the pope striking the artist in frustration.

The **frescoes** depict scenes from the Old Testament, from the *Creation of Light* at the altar end to the *Drunkenness of Noah* over the door. The sides are decorated with prophets and sibyls and the ancestors of Jesus. Julius II lived only a few months after the Sistine Chapel ceiling was finished, but the fame of the work he had commissioned soon spread far and wide. Certainly, it's staggeringly impressive, all the more so for its recent restoration (financed by a Japanese TV company to the tune of $3 million in return for three years' world TV rights), which has lifted centuries of accumulated soot and candle grime off the paintings to reveal a much brighter, more vivid painting than anyone thought existed. The restorers have also been able to chart the progress of Michelangelo as he moved across the vault. Images on fresco must be completed before the plaster dries, and each day a fresh layer of plaster would have been laid, on which Michelangelo would have had around eight hours or so before having to finish for the day. Comparing the different areas of plaster, it seems the figure of Adam, in the key *Creation of Adam* scene, took just four days; God, in the same fresco, took three days. You can also see the development of Michelangelo as a painter when you look at the paintings in reverse order. The first painting, over the door, the *Drunkenness of Noah*, is done in a stiff and formal style, and is vastly different from the last painting he did, over the altar, *The Creation of Light*, which shows the artist at his best, the perfect master of the technique of fresco painting.

Entering from behind the altar, you are supposed, as you

THE CEILING PAINTINGS

look up, to imagine that you are looking into heaven through the arches of the fictive architecture that springs from the sides of the chapel, supported by little putti cary-atids and *ignudi* or nudes, bearing shields and della Rovere oakleaf garlands. Look at the pagan sibyls and biblical prophets which Michelangelo also incorporated in his scheme – some of the most dramatic figures in the entire work, and all clearly labelled by the painter, from the sensitive figure of the Delphic Sybil, to the hag-like Cumaean Sybil, whose biceps would put a Bulgarian shotputter to shame. Look out too for the figure of the prophet Jeremiah – a brooding self-portrait of an exhausted-looking Michelangelo.

We've detailed the paintings of the central panels in the chart, but, specifically, they start with a large portrait of *Jonah and the Whale*, and move on, respectively, to *God Separating Light from Darkness* – His arms bowed, beard flowing, as he pushes the two qualities apart; *God Creating the Sun, the Moon and the Planets* – in which Michelangelo has painted God twice, once with his back to us hurling the moon into existence and simultaneously displaying another moon to the audience; *God Separating Land from Water*; and, in the fourth panel, probably most famous of all these paintings, the *Creation of Adam*, in which God sparks Adam into life with the touch of his finger. God's cape billows behind him, where a number of figures stand – representatives of all the unborn generations to come after Adam. The startled young woman looking at Adam is either Eve or the Virgin Mary, here as a witness to the first events in human history.

The fifth panel from the altar shows the *Creation of Eve*, in which Adam is knocked out under the stump of a della Rovere oak tree and God summons Eve from his side as he sleeps. She comes out in a half-crouch position with her hands clasped in prayer of thanksgiving and awe. The sixth panel is the powerful *Temptation and Expulsion from the Garden of Eden*, with an evil spirit, depicted as a serpent, leaning out from the tree of knowledge and handing the fruit to Adam. On the right of this painting the angel of the Lord, in swirling red robes is brandishing his sword of original sin at the nape of Adam's neck as he tries to fend the angel off, motioning with both hands. The eighth panel continues the story, with the *Story of the Flood*, and the unrighteous bulk of mankind taking shelter under tents from the rain while Noah and his kin make off for the Ark in the distance. Panel seven shows Noah and his family making a *Sacrifice of Thanksgiving* to the Lord for their safe arrival after the flood; one of the sons of Noah kneels to blow on the fire to make it hotter, while his wife brings armloads of wood. Lastly, there's the *Drunkenness of Noah* in which Noah is shown getting drunk after harvesting the vines and exposing his genitals to his sons (it is strictly prohibited in the Hebrew canon that a father should show his organs of reproduction to his children) – although oddly enough Noah's sons are naked too.

The Last Judgement

The **Last Judgement**, on the altar wall of the chapel, was painted by Michelangelo more than twenty years later, between 1535 and 1541. Michelangelo wasn't especially keen to work on this either – he was still engaged on Julius II's tomb, under threat of legal action from the late pope's family – but Pope Paul III, a old acquaintance of the artist, was keen to complete the decoration of the chapel. Michelangelo tried to delay by making demands that were likely to cause the pope to give up entirely, insisting on the removal of two paintings by Perugino and the closing of a window that pierced the end of the chapel. Furthermore he insisted that the wall be replastered, with the top six inches out of the perpendicular to prevent the accumulation of soot and dust.

THE SISTINE CHAPEL

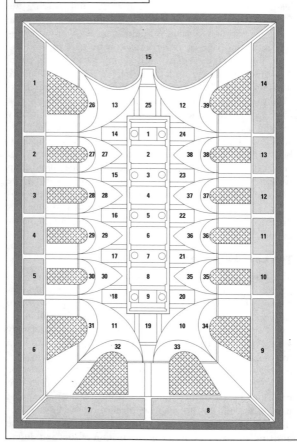

WALL PAINTINGS

1 Perugino
Moses' Journey into Egypt

2 Botticelli
The Trials of Moses

3 Rosselli
Crossing of the Red Sea

4 Rosselli
Moses and the Law

5 Botticelli
Punishment of the Rebels

6 Signorelli
Testament and Death of Moses

7 Matteo da Lecce
Fight over the Body of Moses

8 Arrigo Palludano
Resurrection of Christ

9 Rosselli
Last Supper

10 Perugino
*Jesus giving St Peter
the keys of Heaven*

11 Rosselli
Sermon on the Mount

12 Ghirlandaio
*Calling of St Peter
and St Andrew*

13 Botticelli
Cleansing of the Leper

14 Perugino
Baptism of Christ

15 Michelangelo
The Last Judgement

CEILING PAINTINGS

1 The Creation of Light
2 The Creation of the Sun and the Moon
3 The Separation of Land and Water
4 The Creation of Adam
5 The Creation of Eve
6 The Temptation and Expulsion from
 the Garden of Eden
7 The Sacrifice of Noah
8 The Story of the Flood
9 The Drunkenness of Noah

10 David and Goliath
11 Judith and Holofernes
12 The Punishment of Haman
13 The Brazen Serpent

14 The Libyan Sibyl
15 Daniel
16 The Cumaean Sibyl
17 Isaiah
18 The Delphic Sibyl
19 Zachariah

20 Joel
21 The Erythraean Sibyl
22 Ezekiel
23 The Persian Sibyl
24 Jeremiah
25 Jonah

26 Aminadab
27 Salmon, Booz, Obed
28 Roboam, Abia
29 Ozias, Joatham, Achaz
30 Zorobabel, Abiud, Elichiam
31 Achim, Eliud
32 Jacob, Joseph
33 Eleazar, Matthan
34 Azor, Sadoch
35 Josias, Jechonias, Salathiel
36 Ezekias, Manasses, Amon
37 Asa, Josophat, Joram
38 Jesse, David, Solomon
39 Naasson

THE SISTINE CHAPEL |

The painting took five years, again single-handed, but it is probably the most inspired and most homogeneous large-scale painting you're ever likely to see, the technical virtuosity of Michelangelo taking a back seat to the sheer exuberance of the work. The human body is fashioned into a finely captured set of exquisite poses: even the damned can be seen as a celebration of the human form. Perhaps unsurprisingly, the painting offended some, and even before it was complete Rome was divided as to its merits, especially regarding the etiquette of introducing such a display of nudity into the pope's private chapel. But Michelangelo's response to this was unequivocal, lampooning one of his fiercer critics, the pope's master of ceremonies at the time, Biago di Cesena, as Minos, the doorkeeper of hell, with ass's ears and an entwined serpent in the bottom right-hand corner of the picture. Later the pope's zealous successor, Pius IV, objected to the painting and would have had it removed entirely had not Michelangelo's pupil, Daniele da Volterra, appeased him by carefully – and selectively – adding coverings to some of the more obviously naked figures, earning himself forever the nickname of the "breeches-maker". During the recent work, most of the remaining breeches have been discreetly removed, restoring the painting to its former glory.

Briefly, the painting shows the last day of existence, when the bodily resurrection of the dead takes place and the human race is brought before Christ to be either sent to eternity in Paradise or condemned to suffer in Hell. The centre is occupied by Christ, turning angrily as he gestures the condemned to the underworld. St Peter, carrying his gold and silver keys, looks on in astonishment at his Lord filled with rage, while Mary averts her eyes from the scene. Below Christ a group of angels blasts their trumpets to summon the dead from their sleep. Somewhat amusingly, one angel holds a large book, the book of the damned, while another carries a much smaller one, the book of the saved. On the left, the dead awaken from their graves, tombs and sarcophagi and are levitating into the heavens or being pulled by ropes and the napes of their necks by angels who take them before Christ. At the bottom right, Charon, keeper of the underworld, swings his oar at the damned souls as they fall off the boat into the waiting gates of hell. Among other characters portrayed are many martyred saints, the apostles, Adam, and, peeking out between the legs of the saint on the left of Christ, Julius II, with a look of fear and astonishment.

The Library of Sixtus V

Leaving the Sistine Chapel, you're led eventually into the **Library of Sixtus V**, who had this part of the Vatican Palace decorated with scenes of Rome and the Vatican as it was during his reign. Over the doors of the corridor you can see the facade of St Peter's as it was in the late 1500s, before Maderno's extension of the nave. Over the next door you can see the erection of the obelisk outside in the Piazza San Pietro, showing the men, ropes, animals and a primitive derrick, with the obelisk being drawn forward on a sled. Otherwise, there are sometimes exhibits of books from the main Vatican Library here.

Braccio Nuovo and Museo Chiaramonti

The **Braccio Nuovo** and **Museo Chiaramonti** both hold classical sculpture, although be warned that they are the Vatican at its most overwhelming – close on a thousand statues crammed into two long galleries – and you need a keen eye and much perseverance to make any sense of it all. The **Braccio Nuovo** was built in the early 1800s to display classical statuary that were particularly prized, and it contains, among other things, probably the most famous extant image of Augustus, and a bizarre-looking statue depicting the Nile, whose yearly flooding was essential to the fertility of the Egyptian soil. It is this aspect of the river that is represented here: crawling over the hefty river god are sixteen babies, thought to allude to the number of cubits the river needed to rise to fertilize the land.

The 300-metre-long **Chiaramonti gallery** is especially unnerving, lined as it is with the chill marble busts of hundreds of nameless, blank-eyed ancient Romans, along with the odd deity. It pays to have a leisurely wander, for there are some real characters here: sour, thin-lipped matrons with their hair tortured into pleats, curls and spirals; kids, caught in a sulk or mid-chortle; and ancient old men with flesh sagging and wrinkling to reveal the skull beneath. Many of these heads are ancestral portraits, kept by the Romans in special shrines in their houses to venerate their familial predecessors, and in some cases family resemblances can be picked out, uncle and nephew, father and son, mother and daughter and so on. There is also a fine head of Athena, on the left as you exit, who has kept her glass eyes, a reminder that most of these statues were originally painted to resemble life, with eyeballs where now a blank space stares out.

The Pinacoteca

The **Pinacoteca** is housed in a separate building on the far side of the Vatican's main spine and ranks possibly as Rome's best picture gallery, with works from the early to High Renaissance right up to the nineteenth century.

Among early works, there are pieces by Crivelli, Lippi and the stunning Simoneschi triptych by Giotto of the *Martyrdom of SS Peter and Paul*, painted in the early 1300s for the old St Peter's, where it remained until 1506 when it was removed for the rebuilding of the new church. Beyond the rich backdrops and elegantly clad figures of the Umbrian School painters, Perugino and Pinturicchio, Raphael has a room to himself, including three very important oil paintings, and, in climate-controlled glass cases, the tapestries that were made to his designs to be hung in the Sistine Chapel during conclave. (The cartoons from which these tapestries were made are now in the Victoria and Albert Museum in London.) Of the three paintings, there is the *Transfiguration*, which he had nearly completed when he died in 1520, and which was finished by his pupils; the *Coronation of the Virgin*, done when he was only 19 years old; and, on the left, the *Madonna of Foglino*, showing Ss John the Baptist, Francis of Assisi, and Jerome – painted as an offering from the donor for his life being spared after his house was struck by a cannonball (seen flying into the house in the centre of the painting).

Leonardo's *St Jerome*, in the next room, is unfinished too, but it's a remarkable piece of work, with Jerome a rake-like ascetic torn between suffering and a good meal. Look closely at this painting and you can see that a ten-inch square, the saint's head, has been reglued to the canvas after the painting was used as upholstery for a stool in a cobbler's shop in Rome for a number of years. Caravaggio's *Descent from the Cross* in the next room but one, however, gets more attention, a warts 'n' all canvas that unusually shows the Virgin Mary as a middle-aged mother grieving over her dead son, while the men placing Christ's body on the bier are obviously models that the artist recruited from the city streets – a realism that is imitated successfully by Reni's *Crucifixion of St Peter* in the same room. Take a look also at the most gruesome painting in the collection, Poussin's *Martyrdom of St Erasmus*, which shows the saint stretched out on a table with his hands bound above his head in the process of having his small intestine wound onto a drum – basically being "drawn" prior to "quartering".

The Museos Gregoriano Profano, Pio Cristiano and Missionario Etnologico

Leaving the Pinacoteca, you're well placed for the further grouping of museums in the modern building next door. The **Museo Gregoriano Profano** holds more classical sculpture, mounted on scaffolds for all-round viewing, including mosaics of athletes from the Baths of Caracalla and Roman funerary work, notably the Haterii tomb friezes, which show backdrops of ancient Rome and realistic portrayals of contemporary life. It's thought the Haterii were a family of construction workers and that they grabbed the opportunity to advertise their services by including reliefs of the buildings they had worked on (including the Colosseum), along with a natty little crane, on the funeral monument of one of their female members.

The adjacent **Museo Pio Cristiano** has intricate early Christian sarcophagi and, most famously, an expressive third-century AD statue of the *Good Shepherd*. And the **Museo Missionario Etnologico** displays art and artefacts from all over the world, collected by Catholic missionaries, and seems to be inspired by the Vatican's desire to poke fun at non-Christian cults as well as pat itself on the back for its own evangelical successes.

Out from the City

You may find there's quite enough of interest in Rome to keep you occupied during your stay. But Rome can be a hot, oppressive city, its surfeit of churches and museums intensely wearying, and if you're around long enough you really shouldn't feel any guilt about freeing yourself from its weighty history to see something of the countryside around. Two of the main attractions visitable on a day trip are, it's true, Roman sites, but just the process of getting to them can be energizing.

Tivoli, about an hour by bus east of Rome, is a small provincial town famous for the travertine quarries nearby and its fine ancient Roman villa, complete with landscaped gardens and parks. **Ostia**, in the opposite direction from the city near the sea, and similarly easy to reach on public transport, is the city's main seaside resort (though one worth avoiding), but was also the site of the port of Rome in classical times, the ruins of which – **Ostia Antica** – are well preserved and worth seeing.

TIVOLI

Just 40km from Rome, perched high on a hill and looking back over the plain, **TIVOLI** has always been something of

Beaches

Rome's nearest **beach** is at **Lido di Ostia**, half an hour away by train, and this is where the tourist board will try to point you. However, as you'll see from the account below, it's not by any means the best place to head for. The beaches on the road **south from Ostia** toward Torvaianica and Capocotta have recently been cleaned up; to get there, take the Ostia train to the Cristoforo Colombo stop, then take bus #071 or #061. Also, if you're making a day of it, it's worth travelling south to **Anzio** or **Nettuno** – an hour away by frequent train from Termini (every hour), where you'll find clean, if fairly crowded beaches – and, in Anzio, a nice selection of seafood restaurants.

a retreat from the city. In classical days it was a retirement town for wealthy Romans; later, during Renaissance times, it again became the playground of the moneyed classes, attracting some of the city's most well-to-do families out here to build villas. Nowadays the leisured classes have mostly gone, but Tivoli does very nicely on the fruits of its still-thriving travertine business, exporting the precious stone worldwide (the quarries line the main road into town from Rome), and supports a small airy centre that preserves a number of relics from its ritzier days. To do justice to the gardens and villas – especially if Villa Adriana is on your list – you'll need time; set out *early*.

The town

Most people head first for **Villa d'Este** (summer daily 9am–1hr before sunset; winter Tues–Sun 9am–1hr before sunset; L8000), across the main square of Largo Garibaldi – the country villa of Cardinal Ippolito d'Este that was transformed from a convent by Pirro Ligorio in 1550 and is now often thronged with visitors even outside peak season. The gardens, rather than the villa itself – a parade of dim, scruffy rooms decorated with faded Mannerist murals – are what they come to see, peeling away down the hill in a succession of terraces: probably the most contrived garden in Italy, but also the most ingenious, almost completely symmetrical, its carefully tended lawns, shrubs and hedges interrupted at decent intervals by one playful fountain after another. In their day some of these were quite amazing – one played the organ, another imitated the call of birds – though nowadays the emphasis is on the quieter creations. At time of writing the fountains were undergoing a thorough cleanup, and although this was primarily for the year 2000, it's possible it will not have been completely finished by the time you read this – check before you go that they're viewable. If you do manage to see them, make sure that you don't *touch or drink* the water in the fountains – it comes directly from the operating sanitary sewers of Tivoli.

Among the fountains, the central, almost Gaudi-like Fontana del Bicchierone, by Bernini, is one of the simplest and most elegant; on the far left, the Rometta or "Little Rome" has reproductions of the city's major buildings and a boat holding an obelisk; while perhaps the best is the Fontana dell'Ovato on the opposite side of the garden, fringed with statues, behind which is a rather dank arcade, in which you can walk.

Even if Villa d'Este is still not accessible, you may find that Tivoli's other main attraction, the **Villa Gregoriana** (daily 10am–1hr before sunset; L3500), a park with waterfalls created when Pope Gregory XVI diverted the flow of the river here to ease the periodic flooding of the town in 1831, is more interesting and beautiful. Less well known and less touristed than the d'Este estate, it has none of the latter's conceits – its vegetation is lush and overgrown, descending into a gashed-out gorge over 60m deep.

There are two main waterfalls – the larger Grande Cascata on the far side, and a small Bernini-designed one at the neck of the gorge. The path winds down to the bottom of the canyon, passing ruined Roman resting pavilions and shrines to the sylvan and faunal gods. The path winds down to the bottom of the canyon and the water, and scales the drop on the other side past two grottoes, where you can get right up close to the roaring falls. The dark, torn shapes of the rock glowers overhead. It's harder work than the Villa d'Este – if you blithely saunter down to the bottom of the gorge, you'll find that it's a long way back up the other side – but it is in many ways more rewarding; the path leads up on the far side to an exit and the substantial remains of a **Temple of Vesta**, which you'll have seen clinging to the side of the hill. This is now incorporated into the gardens of a restaurant, but it's all right to walk through and take a look, and the view is probably Tivoli's best – down into the chasm and across to the high green hills that ring the town.

Villa Adriana

Once you've seen these two sights you've really seen Tivoli – the rest of the town is nice enough but there's not that much to it. But just outside town, at the bottom of the hill, fifteen minutes' walk off the main Rome road (ask the Rome–Tivoli bus to drop you or take the local CAT #4 from Largo Garibaldi), **Villa Adriana** (daily 9am–1hr before sunset; L8000) casts the invention of the Tivoli popes and cardinals very much into the shade. This was probably the largest and most sumptuous villa in the Roman Empire, the retirement home of the emperor Hadrian for a short while between 135 AD and his death three years later, and it occupies an enormous site. You need time to see it all; there's no point in doing it at a gallop and, taken with the rest of Tivoli, it makes for a long day's sightseeing.

The site is one of the most soothing spots around Rome, its stones almost the epitome of romantic, civilized ruins. The imperial palace buildings proper are in fact one of the least well preserved parts of the complex, but much else is clearly recognizable. Hadrian was a great traveller and a keen architect, and parts of the villa were inspired by buildings he had seen around the world. The massive Pecile, for instance, through which you enter, is a reproduction of a building in Athens. The Canopus, on the opposite side of the site, is a liberal copy of the sanctuary of Serapis near Alexandria, its long, elegant channel of water fringed by sporadic columns and statues leading up to a temple of Serapis at the far end.

Nearby, a museum displays the latest finds from the usually ongoing excavations, though most of the extensive original discoveries have found their way back to Rome. Walking back towards the entrance, make your way across the upper storey of the so-called Pretorio, a former warehouse, and down to the remains of two bath complexes. Beyond is a fishpond with a *cryptoporticus* (underground passageway) winding around underneath. It is great to walk through the *cryptoporticus* and look up at its ceiling, picking out the names of the seventeenth- and eighteenth-century artists (Bernini, for one) who visited here and wrote their signatures here using a smoking candle. Behind this are the relics of the emperor's imperial apartments. The Teatro Maríttimo, adjacent, with its island in the middle of a circular pond, is the place to which it's believed Hadrian would retire at siesta time to be sure of being alone.

Practicalities

Buses leave Rome for Tivoli and Villa Adriana every 20 minutes from Ponte Mammolo metro station (line B) – journey time 50 minutes. In Tivoli, the **bus station** is in

Piazza Massimo near the Villa Gregoriana, though you can get off earlier, on the main square of Largo Garibaldi, where you'll find the **tourist office** (Mon 9am–3pm, Tues–Fri 9am–6.30pm, Sat 9am–3pm; ℭ0774.334.522), which has free maps and information on **accommodation** if you're planning to stay over.

OSTIA

There are two Ostias: one an overvisited seaside resort, the so-called **Lido di Ostia**, which is well worth avoiding; the other, one of the finest ancient Roman sites – the excavations of the port of **Ostia Antica** – which are on a par with anything you'll see in Rome itself and easily merit a half-day journey out.

Lido di Ostia

The **LIDO DI OSTIA**, reachable by overground train from Magliana metro station on line B, has for many years been the number-one seaside resort for Romans. The beaches are OK, and have recently been cleaned up, but the town is on the whole a poor outpost of the city, with little, if anything, to recommend it – you're probably better off making the slightly longer journey to Anzio or Nettuno if you want to swim (see above). If you do come here, the water is most inviting along the coastal road between Ostia and Torvaianica, and there are nudist areas around the 8- or 9km marker.

Ostia Antica

The stop before Lido di Ostia on the train from Rome, the site of **OSTIA ANTICA** marked the coastline in classical times, and the town which grew up here was the port of ancient Rome, a thriving place whose commercial activities were vital to the city further upstream. The **excavations** (Tues–Sun 9am–1hr before sunset; L8000) remain relatively unvisited; indeed until the 1970s the site was only open one day a week and few people realized how well the port had been preserved by the Tiber's mud. Still relatively free of the bustle of tourists, it's an evocative site, and it's much easier to reconstruct a Roman town from this than from any amount of pottering around the Forum – or even Pompeii. It's also very spread out, so be prepared for a fair amount of walking; and carry some water, so as to avoid the not very well situated snack bar near the entrance.

From the entrance, the **Decumanus Maximus**, the main street of Ostia, leads west, past the **Baths of Neptune** on the right (where there's an interesting mosaic) to the town's commercial centre, otherwise known as the **Piazzale delle Corporazioni** for the remains of shops and trading offices that still fringe the central square. These represented commercial enterprises from all over the ancient world, and the mosaics just in front denote their trade – grain merchants, ship-fitters, ropemakers and the like.

Flanking one side of the square, the **theatre** has been much restored but is nonetheless impressive, enlarged by Septimius Severus in the second century AD to hold up to 4000 people. On the left of the square, the **House of Apulius** preserves mosaic floors and, beyond, a dark-aisled *mithraeum* with more mosaics illustrating the cult's practices. Behind here – past the substantial remains of the *horrea* or warehouses that once stood all over the city – the **Casa di Diana** is probably the best-preserved private house in Ostia, with a dark, mysterious set of rooms around a central courtyard, and again with a *mithraeum* at the back. You can climb up to its roof for a fine view of the rest of the site, afterwards crossing the road to the **Thermopolium**– an

OSTIA ANTICA

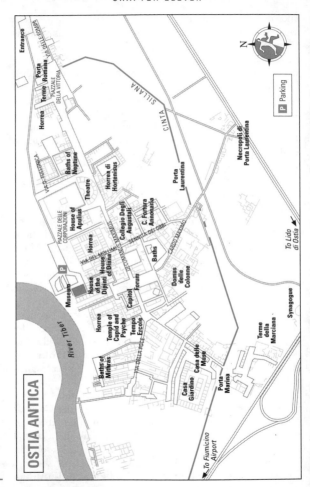

OSTIA ANTICA

River Tiber

Entrance

Porta Romana
Terme del
PIAZZALE DELLA VITTORIA

Horrea

VIA DELLA FOCE
Baths of Neptune

Theatre

Horrea di Hortensius

House of Apulius
PIAZZALE DELLE CORPORAZIONI

Horrea
VIA DEL MOLINI

House of Diana
DECUMANUS MAXIMUS
Collegio Degli Augustali

C. Fortura Annonaria

SEMITA DEI CISII

Baths

Museum
P

House of the Dipinti
Forum
Capitol

Temple of Cupid and Psyche
Tempio Ercole

Baths of Mithras
VIA DELLE FOCE

Horrea

Domus delle Colonne

CARDO MAXIMO

Casa Giardino
Casa delle Muse

Porta Marina

Terme della Marciana

Synagogue

Porta Laurentina

CINTA SILIANA

Necropoli di Porta Laurentina

To Lido di Ostia

To Fiumicino Airport

N

P Parking

ancient Roman café, complete with seats outside, a high counter, display shelves and even wall paintings of parts of the menu.

North of the Casa di Diana, the **museum** holds a variety of articles from the site, including wall paintings depicting domestic life in Ostia and some fine sarcophagi and statuary. Left from here, the **Forum** centres on the **Capitol** building, reached by a wide flight of steps, and is fringed by the remains of baths and a basilica. Continuing on down the main street, more **horrea** superbly preserved and complete with pediment and names inscribed on the marble merit a detour off to the right; although you can't enter, you can peer into the courtyard. Beyond, the **House of Cupid and Psyche** has a courtyard you can walk into, its rooms clearly discernible on one side, a colourful marbled floor on the other.

LISTINGS

Accommodation

As you might expect, there is plenty of **accommodation** in Rome, and for much of the year you can usually expect to find something, although it's always worth booking in advance, especially when the city is at its busiest – from Easter to the end of October, and over the Christmas period. During the year 2000, it's likely that things will be more difficult – the city is expecting somewhere between twenty and thirty million Catholic pilgrims, and although, in order to accommodate this influx, new hotels and hostels are popping up all over the city, you really would be mad not to book as far in advance as possible.

If for some reason you haven't booked, the **Enjoy Rome** office (see p.7) is your best bet; or try the **Free Hotel Reservation Service** (daily 7am–10pm; ©06.699.1000), where multilingual staff will check out vacancies for you. The rooms offered by touts at Termini are rarely a good deal, and can often be rather dodgy; be sure you establish the (full) price beforehand, in writing if necessary, and only use them as a last resort. It might be worth getting hold of the free booklet issued by the tourist office, which lists all hotels and campsites with their current prices.

HOTELS AND PENSIONS

Many of the city's cheaper places are located conveniently close to **Termini**, and you could do worse than hole up in one of these, so long as you can tolerate the seediness of this district. The streets both sides of the station – Via Amendola, Via Principe Amedeo, Via Marghera, Via Magenta, Via Palestro – are stacked full of bargain hotels, and some buildings have several pensions to choose from, though you should be somewhat circumspect in the streets to the southwest of the station, parts of which can be a little *too* unsavoury, especially if you're a woman travelling alone. If you want to stay somewhere more central and picturesque, there are many hotels in the **centro storico**, some of them not that expensive, but they fill quickly – best phone in advance before heading down there. For more luxury surroundings, the area **east of Via del Corso**, towards Via Veneto and around the Spanish Steps, is the city's prime hunting ground for beautiful, upscale accom-

Accommodation price codes

Prices given for **youth hostels** are per person and assume Hostelling International (HI) membership. **Hotel** accommodation is graded on a scale from ① to ⑨; all are **high-season rates** (most hotels are keeping the same rates for the full jubilee year, but always call to be sure) and indicate the cost of the **cheapest double room.** The price bands to which these codes refer are as follows:

① Up to L60,000	⑥ L200,000–250,000
② L60,000–90,000	⑦ L250,000–300,000
③ L90,000–120,000	⑧ L300,000–400,000
④ L120,000–150,000	⑨ L400,000 and above
⑤ L150,000–200,000	

modation – although there are a few affordable options close by Piazza Spagna. Consider also staying across the river in **Prati,** a pleasant neighbourhood, nicely distanced from the hubbub of the city centre proper, and handy for the Vatican and St Peter's, or in the lively streets of **Trastevere**, on the same side of the river but an easy walk into the centre of town.

CENTRO STORICO

Arenula

Map 3, G8. Via S. Maria de'Calderari 47 ©06.687.9454, fax 06.689.6188, *hotel.arenula@flashnet.it* Bus #H or #63.
Simple, clean rooms, each with their own bath, television and telephone. A great location, just a few minutes' walk from Trastevere, the Jewish Ghetto, and Campo de' Fiori. ⑥

Abruzzi

Map 3, G4. Piazza della Rotonda 69 ©06.679.2021. Bus #64 or #492.
Bang in front of the Pantheon, and as such you pay for the location. Rooms are clean but very simple, all with wash basins but none with private baths. No credit cards; to reserve a room you must send an unsigned traveller's cheque. ④

Campo de' Fiori

Map 3, E7. Via del Biscione 6 ©06.6880.6865, fax 06.687.6003. Bus #64 or #492.
A friendly place in a great location close to Campo de' Fiori. Rooms come in all shapes and colours but are all clean and pleasant. Climb the six floors of stairs and catch your breath – and some great views – on their large roof terrace. ⑤

Hotel Cesàri

Map 3, H4. Via di Pietra 89a ©06.679.2386, fax 06.679.0882 *www.venere.it/roma/cesari*. Bus #492 or #64.

In a perfect location close to the Pantheon, the *Cesàri* has been a hotel since 1787; as they will be sure to tell you, Stendhal stayed here once. Totally renovated in 1999, the rooms are quiet and comfortable, and have all the modern touches. ⑧

Della Lunetta

Map 3, F6. Piazza del Paradiso 68 ℂ06.686.1080, fax 06.689.2028. Bus #64 or #492.

An unspectacular hotel, but in a nice location close to Campo de' Fiori. Simple, smallish rooms surround a green courtyard, and if you look up you will see the dome of San Andrea della Valle looming above. No breakfast. ④

Mimosa

Map 3, H5. Via Santa Chiara 61 ℂ06.6880.1753, fax 06.683.3557. Bus #64 or #492.

Clean, if slightly scruffy rooms, most without bathrooms. In a good position, on a quiet street, close to Santa Maria sopra Minerva and the Pantheon, and popular with groups of visiting students. Rooms are charged per person, not per room. No credit cards, only lire or US dollars. ④–⑤

Navona

Map 3, F5. Via dei Sediari 8 ℂ06.686.4203, fax 06.6880.3802. Bus #64 or #492.

Completely renovated *pensione*-turned-hotel housed in a building that dates back to the first century AD, built on the ancient Roman baths of Agrippa. Very close to Piazza Navona and run by a friendly Italian-Australian couple. No credit cards; a/c available for L30,000 extra a night. ⑤

Nazionale a Montecitorio

Map 3, H3. Piazza Montecitorio 131 ℂ06.695.001, fax 06.678.6677, *www.nazionaleamontecitorio.it*. Bus #492.

Luxury hotel housed in a sixteenth-century palazzo, perfectly located between the Piazza Navona and Piazza di Spagna, in peaceful Piazza Montecitorio. Inevitably, given its position next door to the Italian parliament, it's popular with visiting politicians and dignitaries, and the rooms are accordingly luxurious, with every modern convenience. ⑨

Pantheon

Map 3, H4. Via Pastini 131 ℂ06.678.7746, fax 06.678.7755, *www.venere.it/roma/pantheon* Bus #64 or #492.

This comfortable four-star is, as you might expect from the name, a stone's throw from the Pantheon. The well-equipped rooms are quite pleasant, with beamed wooden ceilings, and often exquisite. Some rooms have two floors, with an upstairs portion given over to a skylighted sitting room. ⑨

✗Piccolo

Map 3, F7. Via dei Chiavari 32 ℂ06.6880.2560. Bus #64 or #492.

In a nice part of town, central but very quiet, quite close to Campo de' Fiori. Many rooms look down to a bakery below and enjoy the smell of fresh baked bread. Run by a sweet, efficient Italian couple, who keep their pleasant, clean rooms to a high standard. ④

✗Pomezia

Map 3, F7. Via del Chiavari 12 ℂ & fax 06.686.1371, *www.hotelpomezia@uni.net.* Bus #64 or #492.

Down the street from the *Piccolo,* and slightly more expensive, though not necessarily any better. A small bar occupies half of the reception area, and Maurizio, the owner, keeps it open all night for those who want it. ⑤

✗Primavera — BOOKED

Map 3, E6. Piazza San Pantaleo 3 ℂ & fax 06.6880.3109. Bus #64.

Worth it for the location alone, in a grand building whose

peaceful courtyard seems a world away from the noisy Piazza San Pantaleo outside. Its simple rooms overlook Corso Vittorio Emanuele, and are a couple of minutes' walk from both Piazza Navona and Campo de' Fiori. ⑤

Santa Chiara

Map G5. Via di Santa Chiara 21 ©06.687.2979, fax 06.687.3144. Bus #64 or #492.

A friendly, family-run hotel in a great location, on a quiet piazza behind the Pantheon. Nice rooms too, some of which overlook the church of Santa Maria sopra Minerva. Hard to do better for the price, which includes breakfast. ⑧

Smeraldo

Map 3, F7. Via dei Chiodaroli 11 ©06.687.5929, fax 06.6880.5495. Bus #64.

Clean and comfortable hotel with a modern interior. All rooms have been recently renovated, with shiny new baths, televisions and a/c. Some rooms have lovely views over Rome's rooftops. Breakfast is not included in the price but is available for L10,000. ⑤

Sole

Map 3, E7. Via del Biscione 76 ©06.687.9446, fax 06.689.3787. Bus #64.

Almost overlooking Piazza del Campo de' Fiori, this place enjoys one of the best locations in the centre, and has pleasant rooms with televisions and phones. The real treat here, though, is the small roof terrace with a spectacular view of the domed churches of San Andrea delle Valle and San Carlo ai Catinan. No breakfast, no credit cards. ⑥

Teatro di Pompeo

Map 3, F6. Largo del Pallaro 8 ©06.687.2812, fax 06.688.05531. Bus #64.

Built above the remains of Pompey's ancient Roman theatre, in a quiet piazza close to Campo de' Fiori, the rooms here are classy and comfortable, with high beamed wooden ceilings, marble-topped furniture and some with great views. ⑧

Zanardelli

Map 3, E3. Via G. Zanardelli 7 ℂ06.6821.1392, fax 06.6880.3802. Bus #70.

A brand new hotel run by the same family as the *Navona* – to which it is a more lavish alternative. Located just north of Piazza Navona, the building used to be a papal residence and has many original fixtures and furnishings. The rooms are elegant, with antique iron beds, silk-lined walls, and all modern amenities. ⑦

EAST OF VIA DEL CORSO

Condotti

Map 5, G6. Via Mario de'Fiori 37 ℂ06.679.4661, fax 06.679.0457. Metro A Spagna

A cosy and inviting hotel with comfortable rooms, if a bit devoid of personality – although this is somewhat compensated for by the staff, who are cheery and welcoming. ⑧

Eden

Map 5, I6. Via Ludovisi 49 ℂ06.478.121, fax 06.482.1584, Bus #63.

Just off Via Veneto, this former private residence, on a quiet tree-lined street, is one of Rome's most enchanting hotels, with a lobby decorated with understated luxury – fresh flowers, marble floors, etc. All the rooms have everything you would expect from a luxury hotel, although those on the fifth floor are a bit more special – with private balconies offering spectacular views of the city. Even if you can't get one of these, the rooftop bar or restaurant is just as good, if not as private. ⑨

Eradelli

Map 5, H7. Via due Macelli 28 ✆06.679.1265. Metro A Spagna.
A rather plain hotel with no-frills rooms, but well priced for its location just up the street from the Spanish Steps. ⑥

Excelsior

Map 5, J6. Via Veneto 125 ✆06.47.081, fax 06.482.6205. Bus #63.
This grand white palace on Via Veneto was recently renovated to its original turn-of-the-century Empire style, and it's once again the choice of royalty when they visit Rome, who favour the antiques, crystal chandeliers, and tapestries that decorate each room – along with, of course, every modern-day convenience. ⑨

Firenze

Map 5, H7. Via due Macelli 106 ✆06.797.240, fax 06.785.636. Metro A Spagna.
Just up the street from *Eradelli*, this recently renovated hotel is a bit more expensive but is worth it for its smart new rooms. ⑥

Grand Hotel Palace

Map 5, J7. Via Veneto 62 ✆06.47.493, fax 06.474.3601, Bus #63.
Built in the 1920s, this has a more sophisticated atmosphere than its grand turn-of-the-century neighbours, with large rooms furnished in an Art Deco style without a lot of clutter; most overlook the lush green courtyard, while some have views of the centre of Rome. Don't miss the murals in the bar, some of which depict Mussolini's mistress Clara Petacci. ⑨

Hassler

Map 5, H7. Trinità dei Monti 6 ✆06.69.93.40, fax 06.67.89.991, *www.hotelhasslerroma.com*. Metro A Spagna
Location, location, location. At the top of the Spanish Steps, you can't get much closer to the heart of Rome than this. A luxury hotel, with simple elegant rooms and every convenience

a guest could possibly require, but what you are paying for above all is the location and its view. ⑨

Majestic Roma

Map 5, J7. Via Veneto 50 ℂ06.421.441, fax 06.488.0984. Bus #63.

Opened in 1889, this is Via Veneto's oldest hotel, and, with its precious antiques and sumptuous furnishings, it set the standard for hotels that would follow on Rome's most fashionable street. The reception is as ostentatious as you would expect, with ceiling frescoes, silk hangings, and big, comfy couches. Each room is a bit different, but all are elegant and roomy, with huge marble baths. ⑨

Manfredi

Map 5, G6. Via Margutta 61 ℂ06.320.7676, fax 06.320.7736. Metro A Spagna.

Occupying a sixteenth-century building, this is a first-class hotel with an ideal location on Via Margutta, moments from the Spanish Steps. ⑧

Margutta

Map 5, F5. Via Laurina 34 ℂ06.322.3674, fax 06.320.0395. Metro A Spagna.

Popular hotel handily located in the Corso/Piazza del Popolo shopping area. Three rooms have tiny private balconies. Reserve well ahead. ⑤

Piazza di Spagna

Map 5, G7. Via Mario de'Fiori 61 ℂ06.679.3061, fax 06.679.0654. Metro A Spagna.

A small hotel just a few minutes' walk from the Spanish Steps – a good alternative to the sumptuous palaces that characterize this area. Rooms are comfortable, all have a/c, minibar, phone, and some have jacuzzis. Friendly staff too. ⑧

HOTELS AND PENSIONS: EAST OF VIA DEL CORSO

Scalinata di Spagna Hotel

Map 5, H7. Piazza Trinità dei Monti 17 ℭ06.679.3006, fax 06.6994.0598. Metro A Spagna.

A wonderful location, just up from the Spanish Steps, and all the amenities you would expect at this price, plus a terrace for breakfast. ⑨

TERMINI AND AROUND

Astoria Garden

Map 4, F6. Via Bachelet 8 ℭ06.446.9908, fax 06.445.3329. Metro Termini.

In a peaceful area east of Termini, a newly renovated hotel that was once the home of an Italian count. Rooms are pleasant, quiet and some have balconies that look onto the large garden below. ⑤

Britannia

Map 5, C7. Via Napoli 64 ℭ06.488.3153, fax 06.488.3243. Metro A Repubblica.

A suprisingly peaceful hotel minutes from Termini and Piazza della Repubblica. The Neoclassical interior was renovated last year, and rooms have all modern amenities, lovely furnishings, and are decorated with pictures of ancient Rome. ⑧

Casa Kolbe

Map 2, E11. Via di San Teodoro 44 ℭ06.679.4974, fax 06.699.41550. Metro B Colosseo.

In a quiet location not far from the Colosseum, this is a favourite with students and tour groups. Its rooms are simple, clean, and good value for the location. Half- and full-board possible. ④

Cervia

Map 4, F5. Via Palestro 55 ℭ06.491.057, fax 06.491.056,

hotelcervia@wnt.it. Metro B Castro Pretorio.

Pleasant rooms in a lively *pensione* in the same building as the *Restivo* and *Mari* (see below). If you don't mind lugging your bags a few more steps, ask for the discounted rooms on the third floor. ④

Hotel des Artistes

Map 4, F5. Via Villafranca 20 ⓒ06.445.4365, fax 06.446.2368, *www.hoteldesartistes.com*. Metro B Castro Pretorio.

One of the better hotels in the Termini area. Exceptionally good value, spotlessly clean, and recently redecorated. Eat breakfast or recover from a long day of sightseeing on a breezy roof terrace; there's also email and Internet services for guests' use for L10,000 per hour. Also has dorm beds for L35,000. ⑤

Elide

Map 4, C7. Via Firenze 50 ⓒ06.474.1367, fax 06.48904318. Metro A Repubblica.

A *pensione* for the last fifty years, with clean, simple rooms and a friendly staff, a few minutes' from Piazza della Repubblica. Several of the rooms are right on a busy street, though; if noise bothers you, ask for a room in the back. ③

Fawlty Towers

Map 4, F6. Via Magenta 39 ⓒ06.445.4802. Metro Termini

Playfully named accommodation, owned by the people who run *Enjoy Rome*, this place has both beds (L35,000) and clean and comfortable hotel rooms, some with private bath. There's a communal kitchen, Internet access, and a pleasant roof terrace. ④

Katty

Map 4, F5. Via Palestro 35 ⓒ06.490079, fax 06.444.1216. Metro B Castro Pretorio.

A good-value *pensione* located in one of the nicer buildings on the east side of Termini. Rooms are quite pleasant and some have shiny new bathrooms. If you want to spend a bit extra, go up a floor to *Katty 2*, where all rooms have private baths, mini-bar, TV, phone, and a/c. ③–④

Mari

Map 4, F5. Via Palestro 55 ©06.446.2137, fax 06.482.8313. Metro B Castro Pretorio.

Clean rooms in a friendly hotel across the landing from the *Restivo*, run by three women. No private bathrooms. ③

Mari II

Map 4, E5. Via Calatafimi 38 ©06.474.0371, fax 06.4470.3311. Metro Termini.

Sister hotel to the Mari, and equally clean, though poorly situated east of Termini on a nasty little alley near a porno cinema. ④

Marsala

Map 4, E6. Via Marsala 36 ©06.444.1262, fax 06.441.397. Metro Termini.

Handily situated two-star, hotel 50m east of the station. Very clean, good-value rooms, and a friendly English-speaking staff. ④

Positano

Map 4, F5. Via Palestro 49 © & fax 06.446.9101. Metro Termini.

Not glamorous, but certainly reasonably priced, with comfortable rooms two minutes' walk from Termini. Helpful management too. ②

Restivo

Map 4, F5. Via Palestro 55 ©06.446.2172. Metro B Castro Pretorio.

Spotless rooms in a small *pensione* run by a sweet old lady. She stays up until all guests are safely back home, so it's best avoided if you're planning to party into the small hours. No private bathrooms. ②–③

Raccuia

Map 4, I4. Via Treviso 37 ℭ06.4423.1406. Metro B Policlinico.
A clean and family-run *pensione*, just a short walk from the Policlinico metro stop. A particularly good deal if there are three of you – L90,000 for triples. ②

Rosetta

Map 4, B10. Via Cavour 295 ℭ & fax 06.478.23069. Metro B Colosseo.
Family-run *pensione* in a nice location very close to the Colosseum The small rooms are a bit shabby, but they're comfortable enough, and have private baths, TV, and telephone. No breakfast. ④

TRASTEVERE

Brunella

Map 2, C14. Via Pacinotti 8 ℭ06.557.7219, fax 06.557.1626. Bus #170, tram #8.
Good-value, comfortable small hotel situated at the end of Viale Trastevere, not far from the nightlife of the Testaccio area, but well connected to the historical centre by public transport. ③

Carmel

Map 7, C4. Via G. Mameli 11 ℭ06.580.9921. Bus #H or #63.
Pleasant rooms, with private bathrooms and two with their own terrace, at the southern end of Trastevere. There's also a leafy roof terrace for all guests. If you arrange it ahead of time they can provide a kosher kitchen for your own use. Don't arrive on spec as the owner closes if she's not expecting anyone. ③

Cisterna

Map 7, D4. Via della Cisterna 7/8/9 ℭ06.581.7212, fax 06.581.0091. Bus #H or #63.
Friendly hotel with a homely feel, bang in the middle of

HOTELS AND PENSIONS: TRASTEVERE

Trastevere. Twelve rooms, some with colourful tiled floors, wooden beamed ceilings, and all with private bathrooms. The peaceful terrace garden out the back is a treat when the weather is nice. ⑥

Trastevere

Map 7, D4. Via Luciano Manara 24a/25, ℗06.581.4713, fax 06.588.1016. Bus #H or #63.

The place to come if you want to be in the heart of Trastevere, this hotel was totally renovated in 1998, with all new furnishings, wood panelling, terracotta floors, and newly installed bathrooms in every room. Especially good value are their four apartments with kitchens and private entry. ④

Atlante Star

Map 6, F3. Via Vitelleschi 34 ℗06.687.3233, fax 06.687.2300. Metro A Ottaviano or bus #23.

Just steps away from the Vatican, this is a truly luxurious hotel. Rooms are decorated with rich wood panelling and antiques, and each marble bathroom has a jacuzzi so you can soak your tired feet. Perhaps the most impressive feature of this hotel is the rooftop terrace, which offers a 360-degree view of Rome; it's also the home of the very popular *Les Etoiles* restaurant (see p.255). ⑨

Alimandi

Map 6, C1. Via Tunisi 8 ℗06.3972.3948, fax 06.3972.3943. Metro A Ottaviano

Close to the Vatican, this place boasts a friendly staff, a roof-top garden, and nicely furnished, good-value doubles, all with telephone and TV. ⑥

Arcangelo

Map 6, F2. Via Boezio 15 ℗06.687.4143, fax 06.689.3050. Metro A Ottaviano

Clean, reliable hotel, with comfortable rooms in a quiet street not far from the Vatican. ⑤

Colors

Map 6, F2. Via Boezio 31 ℂ and fax 06.687.4030. Metro A Ottaviano.

Run by the friendly people from *Enjoy Rome*, this is a smaller version of their popular *Fawlty Tours*, a hostel/hotel in a quiet neighbourhood near the Vatican. Dorm beds (L35,000) and private rooms, are available. Everyone is very friendly, and there are kitchen facilities, a lounge with satellite TV, and a small terrace. ④

Davos

Map 6, F1. Via degli Scipioni 239 ℂ06.321.7012, fax 06.323.0367. Metro A Lepanto.

Simple, affordable *pensione* on a quiet street not far from the Vatican. Rooms are clean and quite basic, but all except one has a private bath. No credit cards. ④

Farnese

Map 6, H1. Via Alessandro Farnese 30 ℂ06.321.1953, fax 06.321.5129. Metro A Lepanto.

Another grand aristocratic residence that has been turned into an upscale hotel. All the rooms have recently been renovated, adding touches like soundproof windows and doors, handmade walnut furniture, and marble bathrooms. Some rooms have private balconies, and there is a roof-top terrace with a great view of the Vatican. ⑧

Gerber

Map 6, F1. Via degli Scipioni 241 ℂ06.321.6485, fax 06.322.1001. Metro A Lepanto.

A friendly staff and elegant comfortable rooms make this hotel great value for its convenient location on a quiet street not far from the Vatican. Even better, they give a 10 percent discount to *Rough Guide* readers. ⑥

Giulio Cesare

Map 6, H1. Via degli Scipioni 287 ℂ06.321.0751, fax 06.321.1736, *giulioce@uni.net.* Metro A Lepanto.

This charming hotel is no longer the *Villa Patricia,* home of an Italian countess, but you will feel like royalty once you step into the foyer, with its glistening golden ceiling. An attentive staff will lead you down mirror-lined hallways to elegantly decorated rooms with marble baths. ⑧

Isa

Map 6, H2. Via Cicerone 39 ℂ06.321.2610, fax 06.321.5882. Metro A Lepanto.

A fairly short walk from the Vatican, the grim exterior of this hotel is deceptive, hiding moderately large rooms that have been newly renovated with warm wooden panelling, brightly coloured beds and shiny marble basins. ⑧

Ottaviano

Map 6, E2. Via Ottaviano 6 ℂ06.3973.7253, *www.pensioneottaviano.com.* Metro A Ottaviano.

A simple *pensione*-cum-hostel near to the Vatican that is very popular with the backpacking crowd; book well in advance, fluent English spoken. No private bathrooms. Dorm beds L35,000; rooms ②

HOSTELS, CONVENTS, AND STUDENT ACCOMMODATION

Franciscan Sisters of Atonement

Map 2, A10. Via Monte del Gallo 105 ℂ06.630.782, fax 06.638.6149. Bus #64 to Piazza Cavour then bus #34.

Pleasant rooms, all with private bath and close to the large

Short-Term Rentals

Renting an apartment in Rome has many advantages; for families with children or small groups, it can be a cheaper option than a hotel. Short-term rentals are becoming very popular, however, so you must book well in advance. All the places listed below have helpful Web sites, with pictures of their accommodation in Rome, which ranges from small city-centre apartments to grand villas outside the city. You can also find a good array of options in the weekly magazine, *Wanted in Rome*.

Holidays in Apartments, Via Porta di Fabrica 49, Rome 00165; ℂ06.8632.9153, fax 06.8638.4905. .

Homes in Rome, Via Valadier 36 Rome 00193; ℂ06.323.0166, fax 06.322.1484.

Rome Sweet Home, Via delle Vite 32 Rome 00187; ℂ06.6992.4833, fax 06.6920.2142.

Ulysse Holidays, Via Rutilio Namaziano 50 Rome 00121; ℂ06.561.1746, fax 06.4080.0701.

peaceful garden, this place, near St Peter's, is run by American and Canadian nuns. It's popular with groups, and welcomes men and women, so it's best to book ahead; 11pm curfew; L55,000 per person, with breakfast.

Nostra Signora di Lourdes
Map 5, I5. Via Sistina 113 ℂ06.474.5324. Bus #175.
A swankily located convent – a couple of minutes' walk from the Spanish Steps – with singles and doubles for women or married couples who can put up with a 10.30pm curfew. ③

Ostello del Foro Italico
Map 2, B2. Viale delle Olimpiadi 61 ℂ06.324.2571. Metro A to

Ottaviano, then bus #32 to the hostel – ask the driver for the "*ostello*". Rome's official HI hostel, though not particularly central or easy to get to from Termini. You can call ahead to check out availability, but they won't take phone bookings. L25,000, including breakfast. You can join here if you're not a HI member already.

Sandy

Map 4, D9. Via Cavour 136 ©06.488.4585. Metro B Cavour.
Run by the same folk as the *Ottaviano*, but with dormitories only. No breakfast; L37,000.

Suore Pallotini

Map 6, D6. Viale della Mura Aurelie 7B ©06.635.697, fax 06.3936.6943. Bus #64.
Simple, clean accommodation near the Vatican, run by nuns, but open to both women and men. The first night you are there, there is a 10pm curfew, after that they give you a key. L100,000 for a double without bath, L150,000 with bath.

Suore Pie Operaie

Map 3, G6. Via di Torre Argentina 76 ©06.686.1254. Bus #64.
For women only, this place offers the cheapest beds in the city centre, although you need to book well in advance and there's a 10.30pm curfew. Closed Aug. L25,000 per person.

Villa Santa Cecilia

Map 2, E14. Via Argeleto 54–58 ©06.5237.1688, fax 06.5237.0880. Metro B Magliana, where you change for Lido and the overground train to Vitinia.
Thirty minutes by metro from Termini, a religious-run hostel/hotel (no curfew) with singles, doubles, triples and four-bedded rooms, all with private bathrooms. Singles L65,000; doubles L110,000; triples L125,000; quadruples L165,000. All include breakfast.

YWCA

Map 4, D8. Via C. Balbo 4 ℂ06.488.0460, fax 06.487.1028. Metro Termini.

Though only open to women and married couples, this is more conveniently situated than the HI hostel, just ten minutes' walk from Termini. A mixture of singles and doubles, along with three-bedded rooms. Singles L80,000 with bath, L60,000 without; doubles L120,000 with bath, L100,000 without; triples L120,000 without bath; all rooms include breakfast except Sun mornings and August. Midnight curfew.

CAMPING

All Rome's **campsites** are some way out of the city, and, although easy enough to get to, are not especially cheap. The closest site is *Camping Flaminio*, 8km north of the centre on Via Flaminia Nuova (March–Oct, L16,000 plus L13,000 per person; ℂ06.333.2604); take bus #910 to Piazza Mancini, then transfer to Bus #200 (ask the driver to drop you at the "fermata più vicina al campeggio").

Camping Tiber, on Via Tiberina at Km1400 (March–Oct, L16,500 plus 12,500 per person; ℂ06.3361.2314), is another good bet – spacious and friendly, with a bar/pizzeria, a swimming pool and really hot showers. It offers a free shuttle service (every 30min) to and from the nearby Prima Porta station, where you can catch the Roma-Nord service to Piazzale Flaminio (about 20min).

Eating: cafés and restaurants

Although Rome is undeniably a major-league cultural and historic city, it just doesn't compare to London or Paris for cutting-edge sophistication and trendiness. In many ways it's like an overgrown village. This can be bad news for nightlife, but it's great news for **food**. Romans, as a group, are still very much in touch with the land – many even have small farms of their own in the countryside nearby, or they return to their home villages regularly. So the city's denizens know a good deal about freshness and authenticity, and can be very demanding when it comes to the quality of the dishes they are served.

Consequently, eating out is a major, often hours-long, activity in Rome, and the meals you'll enjoy generally range from good to truly remarkable. You'll find that most city-centre **restaurants** offer standard Italian dishes, although a few more adventurous restaurants have been popping up of late. At the geographical centre of the country, Italy's capital city also has numerous establishments dedicated to a variety of **regional cuisines**, and a reasonable number of excellent **ethnic restaurants**, though many of these are in outlying areas. Rome is also blessed with an abundance of good, honest **pizzerias**, churning out thin, crispy-baked pizza from wood-fired ovens. House wine is usually drinkable, but rarely memorable, but there are also any number of *enoteche* – **wine bars** – who really know their business (we've listed some of the best of these in chapter 14). We've also listed a range of places serving **snacks** — though most **bars** serve *panini* and *tramezzini* — and, at the end of the chapter, the best of the city's **gelaterie** and **pasticcerie**.

Vegetarians will find plenty of options in virtually all Italian eateries. Many pastas and pizzas, of course, are made entirely without meat; lentils and other beans and pulses are a part of traditional cookery; and wonderful fresh vegetables and cheeses are always available. Even so, there are a number of restaurants that specialize in vegetarian cuisine, and some of them are among the most appealing places in Rome.

One final caveat: generally speaking it's hard to find truly bad food and rip-off prices in Rome. However, it may be wise to avoid places that are adjacent to some major monuments, such as the Pantheon, Piazza Navona, or the Vatican. The food in these places can be poor, and the prices truly outlandish, sometimes as much as three times the going rate. Near major sights, use the guide!

Opening hours have been given for all restaurants and cafés; note, however, that many places are closed during August.

LUNCH, SNACKS, SANDWICHES

Just about all **bars and cafés** in town sell snacks like *tramezzini* and pizza bianca (best eaten toasted), with fillings

Roman Food and Wine

Roman cooking is traditionally dominated by the offal-based earthy cuisine of the working classes, with a little influence from the city's centuries-old Jewish population thrown in. Although you'll find all sorts of **pasta** served in Roman restaurants, spaghetti is probably the most popular, as it stands up well to the coarse, gutsy sauces the Romans prefer: *aglio e olio* (oil and garlic), *cacio e pepe* (pecorino and ground black pepper), *alla carbonara* (with beaten eggs, cubes of pan-fried *guanciale* — cured pork jowl — or bacon, and pecorino or parmesan), and *alle vongole* (best when a little peperoncino is added to give the clams an extra kick). There's also *maccheroni alla ciociara*, with *guanciale*, slices of sausage, prosciutto and tomato; *bucatini all'Amatriciana* (thick spaghetti with tomato and *guanciale*); and *gnocchi*, usually with a meat sauce, which are traditionally eaten on Thursday.

Fish is an integral, though usually pricey, part of Roman cuisine, and is most frequently eaten in Rome as salt cod — *baccalà*; best eaten Jewish-style, deep-fried. **Offal** is also important and although it has been ousted from many of the more refined city-centre restaurants, you'll still find it on the menus of more traditional places, especially those in Testaccio. Most favoured is *pajata*, the intestines of an unweaned calf, but you'll also find *lingua* (tongue), *rognone* (kidney), *milza* (spleen — delicious as a paté on toasted bread) and *trippa* (tripe). Look out too for *coda alla vaccinara*, oxtail stewed in a rich sauce of tomato and celery; *testerelle d'abbacchio*, lamb's head baked in the oven with herbs and oil; and *coratella*, lamb's heart, liver, lungs and spleen cooked in olive oil with lots of black pepper and onions. More conventional **meat** dishes include *abbacchio*, milk-fed lamb roasted to melting tenderness with rosemary, sage and garlic; *scottadito*, grilled lamb chops **eaten** with the fingers; and *saltimbocca alla romana*, thin slices of veal cooked with a slice of prosciutto and sage on top, served plain or with a Marsala sauce. Outside Rome there's quite a bit of game served — wild boar (*cinghiale*), hare (*lepre*), pigeon (*piccione*), rabbit (*coniglio*), and pheasant (*fagiano*).

Artichokes (*carciofi*) are the quintessential Roman **vegetable**, served "alla romana" (stuffed with garlic and roman mint and stewed) and in all their unadulterated glory as *alla giudea* — flattened and deep fried in olive oil. Another not-to-be-missed side dish is batter-fried squash or courgette blossom, stuffed with mozzarella and a sliver of marinated anchovy. Roman pizza has a thin crust and is best when baked in a wood-burning oven (*cotta a legna*), but you can also find pizza by the slice (*pizza al taglio*), always sold by weight.

Wine comes mainly from the Castelli Romani (most famously Frascati) to the south, and from around Montefiascone (Est! Est! Est!) in the north. Both are basic, straightforward whites, fine for sunny lunchtimes but otherwise not all that noteworthy. However, in most places you'll find a complete selection of Italy's best and most famous wines.

like mozzarella and prosciutto, mozzarella and spinach, and *bresaola e rughetta* (cured beef and wild arugula). **Rosticcerias** have a whole range of Roman specialities, including *supplì* (deep-fried rice balls), roast chicken and potatoes, and even green vegetables, and a complete meal for two can cost as little as L12,000. Expect to pay around L4000 for a decent-sized pizza slice from one of the many **pizza al taglio** or **pizza rustica** outlets scattered throughout the city. If money is very tight you can picnic off bread, tomatoes, salad and sheep's-milk ricotta bought from street markets and bakeries. All **alimentari** will make up sandwiches for you, usually starting at about L5000; for

LUNCH, SNACKS, SANDWICHES

hot snacks, go to a **tavola calda** or **gastronomia**, but expect to pay quite a bit more.

CENTRO STORICO

Brek

Map 3, G6. Largo di Torre Argentina 1 ©06.6821.0353. Bus #64 or #492.

Daily 8am–midnight.

Brand-new semi-fast-food, but a lot more fun. Colourful cinema-theme decor and everything is actually prepared for you fresh. Good for both a snack or a full meal.

Caffé Sant'Eustachio

Map 3, G5. Piazza Sant'Eustachio 82 ©06.686.1309. Bus #63 or #492.

Tues–Sun 8.30am–1am.

Just behind the Pantheon you'll find what many feel is absolutely Rome's best coffee, usually served Neopolitan-style – that is, very, very sweet. You can ask for it without sugar, but they'll think you're weird.

Camilloni

Map 3, G5. Piazza Sant'Eustachio 54 ©06.686.4995. Bus #63 or #492.

Tues–Sun 8.30am–midnight.

The rival for Rome's best coffee, larger than the *Sant'Eustachio*, across the square, and with great cakes.

Il Delfino

Map 3, G6. Corso V. Emanuele 67 ©06.686.4053. Bus #64 or #492.

Daily 8am–9pm.

Central and very busy cafeteria right on Largo Argentina with huge choice of snacks and full meals. Good for a fast fill-up between sights.

Filetti di Baccalà

Map 3, E7. Largo dei Librari 88 ℂ06.686.4018. Bus #64 or #492.
Mon–Sat 5.30–10.30pm.

A fish-and-chip shop without the chips. Paper-covered Formica tables (outdoors in summer), cheap wine, beer and fried cod, a timeless Roman speciality. Located near Campo de' Fiori. Closed in August.

Il Forno di Campo de' Fiori

Map 3, E6. Campo de' Fiori 22 ℂ06.6880.6662. Bus #64 or #492.
Mon–Sat 7am–1.30pm & 5.30–8pm; closed Sat evening in summer, Thurs evening in winter.

The pizza bianca here (just drizzled with olive oil on top) is a Roman legend and their pizza rossa (with a smear of tomato sauce) follows close behind. Get it hot from the oven.

Roma Rosa

Map 3, I4. Via di Pietra 88 ℂ06.678.6789. Bus #63.
Daily 8am–midnight.

A new refuge, tucked just off overwhelming Via del Corso. Tea, snacks, and full lunch.

La Scaletta

Map 3, G4. Via della Maddalena 46–49 ℂ06.679.2149. Bus #63.
Tues–Sun Noon–3.30pm & 6pm–12.30am.

Very centrally placed *birreria* that's good for its great, reviving snacks, hot meals, or just a drink between sights.

La Tazza d'Oro

Map 3, H4. Via degli Orfani 84/86 ℂ06.679.2768. Bus #63 or #492.
Mon–Sat 7am–8pm.

Straight off Piazza del Pantheon, this is by common consent the home of one of Rome's best cups of coffee, plus decent iced coffee and sinfully rich *granita di caffè*, with double dollops of whipped cream.

LUNCH, SNACKS, SANDWICHES: CENTRO STORICO

Zi Fenizia

Map 3, G8. Via Santa Maria del Pianto 64–65. Bus #63 or #H.

Sun–Thurs 8am–8pm, Fri 8am–3pm.

Kosher pizza to go in the heart of the Jewish Ghetto, and also roasted chicken. The speciality of the house is pizza filled with fresh anchovies and *indivia*, a kind of salad. Also *supplì*, burgers and *shawarma*.

EAST OF VIA DEL CORSO

Antico Forno

Map 3, K3. Via delle Muratte 8 ✆06.679.2866. Bus #63 or Metro A Barberini.

Daily 7am–9pm.

The last thing you'd expect just by the Trevi Fountain: fresh pizza, a sandwich bar, fresh fruits & salads, a bakery and grocery store, all rolled into one – and open on Sundays!

Babington's Tea Rooms

Map 5, G6. Piazza di Spagna 23 ✆06.678.6027. Metro A Spagna.

Daily 9am–8.30pm.

Over one hundred years of tradition in the very heart of Rome. Light lunches, and scones and other English delicacies for tea. Rather expensive, but very handy.

Ciampini al Café du Jardin

Map 5, H6. Viale Trinità dei Monti (no street number) ✆06.678.5678. Metro A Spagna.

Thurs–Tues 8am–1am, closes earlier in early spring, closed Nov–March.

A secluded outdoor setting with a view, opposite Villa Medici, just up the Spanish Steps, a perfect place to relax if you're not too hungry. Salads, sandwiches, ice cream, and, of course, coffee, don't come cheap – resting your feet in Rome's most fashionable quarter has its price – but the location can't be beaten.

Defa
Map 5, F6. Via del Corso 51 ©06.679.3548. Metro A Flaminia.
Daily 8am–midnight.
Tavola calda with *pizza al taglio*, to eat on the premises or take away.

Caffé Greco
Map 5, G7. Via Condotti 86 ©06.678.5474. Metro A Spagna.
Mon–Sat 8am–9pm.
Founded in 1742, and patronized by, among others, Casanova, Byron, Goethe and Stendhal. Now, however, it's a rather dubious tourist joint. Curiosity value only, although the coffee granita is a hit on a hot summer day.

Herbier Natura
Map 3, I2. Via San Claudio 87 ©06.678.5847. Bus #63 or #492.
Mon–Sat 8am–8pm.
Just off Piazza San Silvestro, inside a lovely inner courtyard, this is a real oasis of calm away from the hectic and fumy traffic. Snacks or even a full lunch.

Pizza House
Map 3, J2. Via della Mercede 46 ©06.679.7584. Bus #63 or #492.
Daily 11am–11pm.
Rosticceria and *tavola calda* with seating inside. Good choices and prices, at least for this part of town.

Self-Service Luncheonette
Map 4, C6. Salita di San Nicola da Tolentino 19/21 ©06.474.0029.
Metro A Barberini or Bus #492.
Mon–Sat 8am–3pm.
Just up from Bernini's spouting Triton fountain at Piazza Barberini, this place has great food served cafeteria-style. It caters to the office workers in the area and so is delicious and cheap. It can be very crowded, so best get there early.

LUNCH, SNACKS, SANDWICHES: EAST OF VIA DEL CORSO

Caffé Fantini

Map 4, D8. Via A. Depretis 77b ℂ06.474.6866. Bus #75.
Mon–Sat 6.30am–6pm.

Cafeteria-style service, sandwiches, and a hot and cold buffet – a complete menu that's different every day. A convenient place to break after seeing Santa Maria Maggiore. Just go down the grand staircase at the back of the Basilica, cross Via Cavour and continue straight on about a block. No smoking policy during the lunch hour.

Enoteca Cavour 313

Map 4, B10. Via Cavour 313 ℂ06.678.5496. Metro B Cavour or Bus #75.
Mon–Sat 12.30–2.30 & 7.30–12.30.

At the Forum end of Via Cavour, a lovely old wine bar that makes a handy retreat after seeing the ancient sites. Lots of wines and delicious (though not cheap) snacks and salads.

Trimani

Map 4, D5. Via Cernaia 37b ℂ06.446.9630. Bus #63.
Mon–Sat noon–midnight.

Classy wine bar (Rome's biggest selection of Italian regional vintages) good for a lunchtime tipple and gastronomic indulgence. You'll spend around L30,000 to sample a range of good-quality cheeses and cured pork meat, or a soup and salad, including a glass of wine.

Akropolis

Map 7, D5. Via S. Francesco a Ripa 103 ℂ06.5833.2600. Bus #75 or #H.

Tues–Sun noon–2.30 & 7pm–midnight.

A fairly new Greek takeaway, featuring souvlaki and all the usual snacks and honeyed sweets.

Fidelio

Map 7, E3. Via degli Stefaneschi 3/7 ©None. Bus #H or #63.

Daily noon–2am.

Tucked away just behind Piazza Sonino in Trastevere, a *vineria* with lunch and dinner possibilities, too. Sandwiches go for L5000, big salads for about L8000. A nice selection of Italy's best wines. See also p.270.

Il Mondo in Tasca

Map 7, E3. Via della Lungaretta 169 ©06.588.6040. Bus #63 or #H.

Tues–Sun 11am–3pm & 6pm–midnight.

This great little place, whose name translates as "The World in Your Pocket", offers *shawarma*, felafel, hummus, curry, pizza, chili con carne, couscous, salads, tandoori, moussaka, goulash, etc. Plus you can check your email and get a tarot reading. Home-made pitta bread, too. Located just behind Piazza Sonino, down and across from *The Open Door* English bookshop.

Ombre Rosse

Map 7, C3. Piazza Sant'Egidio 12 ©06 588.4155. Bus #H or #75.

Mon–Sat 7am–2.30am, Sun 5pm–2.30am.

This has become something of a Trastevere institution, especially for a morning cappuccino, but also for interesting light meals. A great place to people watch; everybody walks by here eventually.

Panificio La Renella

Map 7, D3. Via del Moro 15 ©06.581.7265. Bus #H or #75.

Daily 8am–9pm.

Arguably the best bakery in Rome, right in the heart of Trastevere. Superb *pizza al taglio*: ask for *pizza al tonno*, *pomodoro e rughetta* (tuna fish, tomatoes and wild arugula) – they'll make it for you on the spot if there isn't any left on the counter – or wait around to taste *pizza e patate* (with potatoes and rosemary) hot from the oven. Don't go away without a loaf of *filone* bread. Take a number and be prepared to wait at certain hours on certain days.

Caffé del Seme e la Foglia

Map 2, D14. Via Galvani 18 ©06.574.3008. Bus #75.
Mon–Sat 8am–1.30am, Sun 6pm–1.30am.

Pleasantly low-key café popular with Testaccio trendies and students from the nearby music school. During the day good for sandwiches and big salad lunches – they do fairly exotic things like avocados with shrimp or crab, and curried turkey sandwiches – and in the evenings a mellow place to relax before visiting the area's more energetic offerings.

Da Venanzo

Map 7, D4. Via San Francesco a Ripa 137 ©06.589.7110. Bus #75 or #H.
Mon–Sat 11am–11pm, closed holidays.

Located just half a block from Viale Trastevere, there's no sign outside this *pizza al taglio* hole-in-the-wall, which is ironic as it may very well have the best pizza by the slice in Rome. Also roast chickens and potatoes, *supplì* and all the usual *rosticceria* fare. Try their unique chopped spicy green olive pizza.

VATICAN AND AROUND

Franchi

Map 6, F2. Via Cola di Rienzo 200 ©06.686.4576. Metro A Lepanto or Ottaviano.

Mon–Sat 8am–9pm.

One of the best delis in Rome — a triumph of cheeses, sausages and an ample choice of cold or hot food to go, including roast chicken. They'll make up customized lunches for you, and they also have the wines to go with it.

Non Solo Pizza
Map 6, E1. Via degli Scipioni 95–97 ℂ06.372.5820. Metro A Ottaviano.
Tues–Sun 8.30am–10pm.

Try a slice of pizza with sausage and broccoli or with courgette flowers. There's also the whole range of Roman fritters — *supplì, olive ascolane, fiori di zucca, crochette*, etc. — and also a complete selection of hot dishes *tavola calda* style. Starting at 7pm, they offer made-to-order round pizzas, too. No extra charge to sit, inside or out.

RESTAURANTS AND PIZZERIAS

There are lots of good places to eat in the **centro storico**, and it's still surprisingly easy to find places that are not tourist traps – prices in all but the really swanky places remain pretty uniform throughout the city. The area around **Via Cavour and Termini** is packed with cheap restaurants, although some of them are of dubious cleanliness; if you are not in a hurry, you might do better heading up to the nearby student area of **San Lorenzo**, where you can often eat far better for the same money. South of the centre, the **Testaccio** neighbourhood is also well endowed with good, inexpensive trattorias, and, across the river, **Trastevere** is Rome's traditional restaurant enclave. Even though the number of authentic "Trasté" trattorias has declined over recent years, you'll easily find good-to-great meals there, at all price levels.

Eating Italian: the essentials

Most Italians start their day in a bar, their breakfast consisting of a coffee with hot milk (a cappuccino) and a *cornetto* – a jam, custard- or chocolate-filled croissant. At other times of the day, **sandwiches** (*panini*) can be pretty substantial, and cost about L3000–5000; bars also offer *tramezzini*, ready-made sliced white bread with mixed fillings – less appetizing than the average panino but still tasty and slightly cheaper at around L3000 a time. If you want hot takeaway food, it's possible to find slices of pizza (*pizza rustica* or *pizza al taglio*) pretty much everywhere, and you can get most things, plus spit-roast chicken, pasta, and hot meals, in a *rosticceria*. Italian **ice cream** (*gelato*) is justifiably famous; reckon on paying upwards of L2000 for a cone (*un cono*) depending on how many scoops you want. Most bars have a fairly good selection, but for real choice go to a *gelateria*, where the range is a tribute to the Italian imagination and flair for display; we've listed our favourites at the end of this chapter.

An **Italian meal** traditionally starts with **antipasto** (literally "before the meal"), consisting of various cold cuts of meat, seafood and various vegetable dishes. A plateful of various antipasti from a self-service buffet will set you back L8000–10,000 a head, an item chosen from the menu a few thousand less. Bear in mind that if you're moving onto pasta, let alone a main course, you may need quite an appetite to tackle this. The next course, **il primo**, consists of a soup or pasta dish, and it's fine to eat just this and nothing else; pasta dishes go for around L8000–10,000. This is followed by **il secondo** – the meat or fish course, usually served alone, except for perhaps a wedge of lemon or tomato. Watch out when ordering fish, which will either be served whole or by weight: 250g is usually plenty for one person, or ask to have a look at the fish before it's cooked; main fish or meat courses will normally be anything between L10,000 and L15,000. **Vegetables or salads** – *contorni* – are ordered and served separately, and sometimes there won't be much choice: potatoes will usually come as chips (*patatine fritte*); salads are either green (*verde*) or mixed (*mista*). Afterwards you nearly always get a choice of fresh fruit (*frutta*) and a selection of **desserts** (*dolci*) – sometimes just ice cream, but often more elaborate items, like *zuppa inglese* (spongecake or trifle).

Many Italians wouldn't dream of going out to eat and not ordering a full five-course **meal** — starter, first, second, vegetable, desert or fruit, plus wine, mineral water, coffee and a *digestivo*, such as an *amaro* (home-made herb liqueur) — but don't think you have to follow the pattern; you can order as little or as much as you want, and no one will raise an eyebrow. Roman restaurants keep pretty rigid **hours**, generally from noon to 3pm and from 7pm to midnight, although some stay open later, especially in summer. Early in the week tends to be quieter, and many places are closed in August. It's always a good idea to make a reservation, particularly towards the weekend. Getting **the bill** (*il conto*) can sometimes be a struggle – nothing moves fast in Rome when it comes to mealtimes – but, when you do, **service** of 10-15 percent will sometimes be included, and if so it will be clearly indicated. Otherwise a small tip is fine, rounding the bill up to the next thousand lire or so, as waiters in Italy are paid well. Almost everywhere they add a **cover charge** of around L3000 a head; on your bill it will normally be labelled as "pane", and is technically for the bread, which they bring automatically, So if you don't want it — and don't want to pay for what you don't eat — you can send it back.

Price Guide

The restaurants listed in this book are graded into one of five **price categories**; the prices given are for a three-course meal, including a starter, a first or second course, and a vegetable, but without drinks or dessert. Generally speaking, adding drinks will add around L5000–8000 a head. Going for the full monty and having both a first and a second plus dessert as well, making five courses in total, will add a further L15,000–25,000.

Inexpensive:	under L20,000
Moderate:	L20,000-50,000
Expensive:	L50,000-100,000
Very expensive:	100,000 and above

CENTRO STORICO

Acchiappafantasmi
Map 3, E6. Via dei Cappellari 66 ©06.687.3462. Bus #64 or #492. Daily 8pm–2am. Inexpensive.
Fine "ghost-shaped" pizzas — the name of the place is Italian for 'Ghostbusters' — appetizers, and a selection of Calabrian salamis. Plus a lively, over-the-top atmosphere.

Armando al Pantheon
Map 3, G4. Salita de' Crescenzi 30. ©06.6880.3034. Bus #63. Mon–Fri 12.30–3pm & 7–11pm, Sat 12.30–3pm. Closed Sat pm and all day Sun. Moderate.
Surprisingly unpretentious surroundings and hearty food in a spot so close to the Pantheon. Good prices, too.

Da Baffetto
Map 3, D5. Via del Governo Vecchio 114 ©06.686.1617. Bus #64.

Daily 7pm–midnight. Inexpensive.

A tiny, highly authentic pizzeria that has long been a Rome institution, though it now tends to be swamped by tourists. Amazingly it's still good value, and has tables outside in summer, though you'll always have to queue. Especially good *bruschette* (toasted hunks of bread with savoury toppings).

Baronato Quattro Bellezze

Map 3, B4. Via di Panico 23 ©06.687.2865. Bus #64.

Daily 8pm–2am. Moderate.

A one-of-a-kind place, serving great home-cooked couscous in a wonderfully camp environment. The owner-chef sings Piaf on Thursdays; see also p.299.

Dal Bolognese

Map 5, E5. Piazza del Popolo 1 ©06.361.1426. Metro A Flaminia.

Tues–Sun 12.45–3pm & 8.15–11pm. Expensive.

An elegant restaurant that is *the* place to go if you want to treat yourself to good Emilian cuisine; *tortellini in brodo* are a must if you like chicken soup. Reservations are recommended, especially if you'd rather eat outside and watch the passers-by in the piazza.

Caffé Capranica

Map 3, H4. Piazza Capranica 104 ©06.679.0860. Bus #64 or #492.

Daily noon–midnight. Moderate.

This restaurant, *enoteca*, taverna and pizzeria all in one is admirably located on a fairly quiet piazza near the Pantheon. Standard fare, well prepared, and average prices, plus no serious limits on when you can eat.

La Carbonara

Map 3, E6. Campo de' Fiori 23 ©06.686.4783. Bus #64 or #492.

Wed–Mon noon–3.30pm & 7pm–midnight. Moderate.

The most expensive of the square's restaurants, but always busy, with plenty of outdoor seating and an excellent selection of

RESTAURANTS AND PIZZERIAS: CENTRO STORICO

antipasti. Try their home-made ravioli, pappardelle in wild boar sauce, or their namesake, *spaghetti alla carbonara*.

Cartoccio d'Abruzzo

Map 3, E4. Largo Febo 12 ©06.6880.2427. Bus #64 or #492.
Tues–Sun noon–3.30pm & 7pm–midnight. Moderate.
In fine weather you can eat in a large, charming garden in the middle of this small square behind Piazza Navona and enjoy traditional Italian cooking. Frankly, it's a bit of a tourist joint, but on a beautiful summer evening the setting is unique: subdued amber lighting, vine-covered walls and arbours and the purply-blue Roman night.

Ciccia Bomba

Map 3, D5. Via del Governo Vecchio 76 ©06.6880.2108. Bus #64 or #492.
Thurs–Tues noon–3pm & 7pm–1am. Moderate.
Mirrors and antique furniture make this versatile pizzeria/trattoria look pricey, but it isn't at all bad considering the quality. Rather in at the moment with the young chic set.

La Focaccia

Map 3, D4. Via della Pace 11 ©06.6880.3312. Bus #64 or #492.
Daily noon–3.30pm & 7.30pm–1am. Moderate.
A great location, just off Piazza Navona, and hearty, unusual dishes – and, of course, a dozen different kinds of focaccia. Try the one with sesame. Twenty-four different pizza offerings and big salads, plus original pastas. The *paccheri* on a bed of shredded smoked ricotta is especially delicious. For dessert, the pear tart smothered in amarena sauce is memorable. The red house wine is good too. See also p.300.

Da Giggetto

Map 3, H8. Via del Portico d'Ottavia 21a-22 ©06.686.1105. Bus #H or #63 .

Tues–Sun noon–3.30pm & 7.30pm–midnight. Moderate.
Roman-Jewish fare in the Jewish Ghetto, featuring deep-fried artichokes, *baccalà*, and *rigatoni con pajata*, along with good non-offal pasta dishes, eaten outside in summer by the ruins of the Portico d'Ottavia. Not cheap, but worth the splurge. It's usually very crowded, but so huge you can normally get a table.

Grappolo d'Oro
Map 3, E6. Piazza della Cancelleria 80 ©06.686.4118. Bus #64 or #492.
Mon–Sat noon–3 & 8–11pm. Moderate.
Curiously untouched by the hordes in nearby Campo de' Fiori. Genuine Roman cuisine in traditional trattoria atmosphere. Try the risotto with *tartufi* and *funghi*. Closed all of August.

La Grotta
Map 3, E7. Via delle Grotte 27 ©06.686.4293. Bus #64 or #492.
Mon–Sat noon–3pm & 7pm–midnight. Inexpensive.
An out-of-the-way, cosy trattoria with a traditional, limited menu and the deeply authentic feel of old Rome. Outdoor seating in summer, towards the river from Campo de' Fiori.

'Gusto
Map 5, F6. Piazza Augusto Imperatore 9 ©06.322.6273. Metro A Flaminia.
Daily 12.30–3pm & 7.30pm–1am. Inexpensive–moderate.
A slick establishment that's more like something you might find in San Francisco or Sydney. However, the food is unique and often wonderful, and the atmosphere very chic. There's a reasonably priced Mediterranean buffet lunch every day that is very popular. Otherwise, the restaurant upstairs offers true gourmet dishes: try the marinated chopped sea bass and tuna with ginger rice for starters. The tagliolini with *mazzancolle* (a sort of Mediterranean crayfish), asparagus and star anise is sub-

lime, as is the roasted breast of duck. Unusual, well-executed desserts, too, and a very complete wine list.

L'Insalata Ricca

Map 3, F6. Largo dei Chiavari 85/86 ℂ06.6880.3656. Bus #64 or #492. Daily noon–3.30pm & 7pm–1am. Inexpensive.

An Anglo-American presence in a relaxed and slightly out-of-the-ordinary place, although it is just one of a Roman chain of six. Interesting, big salads, as the name suggests, wholefood options and reasonably priced Italian fare. A good choice for vegetarians. Nice setting, next to a church, between Piazza Navona and Campo de' Fiori.

Il Leoncino

Map 3, H1. Via del Leoncino 28 ℂ06.687.6306. Metro A Spagna or Flaminia. Mon–Fri 1–2.30pm & 7pm–midnight, Sat & Sun 7pm–midnight. Inexpensive.

Cheap, hectic and genuine pizzeria, little known to out-of-towners. Really one of the very best for lovers of crispy Roman-style pizza, baked in wood ovens. Just off Via del Corso. No credit cards.

Malastrana

Map 3, D6. Via Monserrato 32, ℂ06.686.5617. Bus #64 or #492. Wed–Mon 7pm–midnight. Moderate.

A new restaurant featuring some very original and delicious dishes, including such things as chickpea and hazelnut soup, quail en croûte with grapes and walnut flour *gnocchetti*, and warm fig and walnut pie with red wine sauce for dessert. The decor is striking, featuring powerful paintings by the artist Catalano, and yet romantic. Just off Piazza Farnese.

La Montecarlo

Map 3, D5. Vicolo Savelli 12 ℂ06.686.1877. Bus #64.

Daily noon–3pm & 6.30pm–1am. Inexpensive.

Hectic pizzeria owned by the daughter of Da Baffetto (see above) and serving similar crisp, blistered pizza, along with good pasta dishes. Tables outside in summer, but be prepared to queue. Tucked off Corso Vittorio, not far from Piazza Navona.

Myosotis

Map 3, F3. Via della Vaccarella 3/5 ©06.686.5554. Bus #64 or #492. Mon–Sat 12.30–2.45pm & 8–11pm. Moderate.

Excellent food, service and value at this slightly upscale restaurant a short walk from the Pantheon. Try the *maltagliati* or *stracci* if you like fresh pasta.

Der Pallaro

Map 3, F7. Largo del Pallaro 15 ©06.6880.1488. Bus #64 or #492. Tues–Sun noon–3pm & 7pm–midnight. Moderate.

An old-fashioned trattoria serving a set daily menu for L32,000, including wine. A good option when you're starving. Located in a quiet piazza between Campo de' Fiori and Largo Argentina. No credit cards.

Pizza Re

Map 5, F5. Via di Ripetta 14 ©06.321.1468. Metro A Flaminia. Daily, except Sun lunch, noon–3pm & 7pm–midnight. Moderate.

Authentic Neapolitan pizzeria (thicker than Roman) made in a wood-stoked oven. Just up from Piazza del Popolo. Busy, so book.

La Primavera

Map 3, G6. Via del Sudario 37 ©06.687.5417. Bus #64 or #492. Daily noon–3pm & 7pm–midnight. Inexpensive.

A rather elegant (by Roman standards) Chinese restaurant, just off Largo Argentina, which has a fixed lunch menu for L10,000. Dinner is around L25,000, but you can buy food to take away. Reservations are recommended.

RESTAURANTS AND PIZZERIAS: CENTRO STORICO

La Rosetta

Map 3, G4. Via della Rosetta 9 ©06.6830.8841. Bus #63 or #492.
Mon–Fri noon–3pm & 8–11.30pm, Sat 8–11.30pm. Very expensive.

Rome's premier fish restaurant, which all the others try to imitate. Set on a quiet side street a block from the Pantheon, it's an elegant dining experience, and well worth the price.

Sora Margherita

Map 3, G8. Piazza delle Cinque Scuole 30 ©06.686.4002. Bus #H or #63.
Mon–Fri noon–3.30pm. Moderate.

A tiny and famous trattoria in the heart of the Jewish quarter serving home-made pasta, gnocchi, and desserts. Great artichokes, Jewish-style, and stuffed squash blossoms. For something rare and delicious, try *aliciotti*, a casserole of fresh anchovies and curly endive. No sign outside — look for the doorway with red fuzzy plastic streamers.

Tapa Loca

Map 3, E4. Via di Tor Millina, 4a/5 ©06.683.2266. Bus #64 or #492.
Daily 8pm–2am (for meals). Moderate.

Something new and unusual for Rome, a Spanish restaurant, featuring four different paellas (including vegetarian), tapas of all sorts, gazpacho, meat, fish and fish soup, and Spanish tortilla. Just off Piazza Navona in a very busy area, so reservations are a good idea. During the day, it's a bar with snacks.

El Toulà

Map 3, G2. Via della Lupa 29b ©06.687.3498. Bus #63.
Mon–Fri noon–3pm & 8–11.30pm, Sat 8–11.30pm. Very expensive.

This is one of Rome's chicest and most beautiful restaurants, with a menu featuring some nostalgic Venetian recipes.

Da Vito

Map 3, G4. Via delle Colonnelle 5 ©06.679.3842. Bus #64 or #492.

Thurs–Tues, noon–3.30pm & 7.30pm–midnight. Moderate.

Hidden away, and very authentic, this trattoria has several set menus and an extensive à la carte selection. All the standards plus their own typically Roman specialities, including *cacio pepe* and *pennette arrabbiata*. Located near the Pantheon.

EAST OF VIA DEL CORSO

Beltramme

Map 5, G6. Via della Croce 39 No phone. Metro A Spagna.

Daily noon–3pm & 7–11pm. Moderate.

This very old-fashioned *fiaschetteria* (originally it sold only wine, by the *fiasco* or flask), two blocks from the Spanish Steps, is just about always packed and is fairly pricey, but if you want authentic Roman food, atmosphere and service the way it used to be, this is the place. No credit cards.

Colline Emiliane

Map 3, M2. Via degli Avignonesi 22 ©06.481.7538. Metro A Barberini.

Sat–Thurs noon–3pm & 8–11.30pm. Moderate.

Many Italians consider the cuisine of the Emilia Romagna region to be the country's best. Try it for yourself, lovingly prepared by a family, oddly enough, from Le Marche. Located just down from Piazza Barberini, on a quiet back street parallel to Via del Tritone.

The Cowboy

Map 3, L1. Via Francesco Crispi 68 ©06.488.3504. Metro A Spagna.

Tues–Sun 11.30am–3pm & 6.30pm–1.30am. Inexpensive.

This old-guard Roman establishment, just above the Spanish Steps,

Ethnic Restaurants

Chinese restaurants — most of them so-so — abound. Otherwise there's a slowly growing list of **international options** in and around the centre. See our listings for full reviews.

Africa (Eritrean)
Il Guru (Indian)
Akropolis (Greek-Snacks Section)
Hamasei (Japanese)
ATM Sushi Bar (Japanese)
Little India (Indian)
Baronato Quattro Bellezze (Tunisian)
Il Mondo in Tasca (Int'l-Snacks)
Charro Café (Tex-Mex)
La Primavera (Chinese)
The Cowboy (Tex-Mex)
Tapa Loca (Spanish)

offers Tex-Mex specialities, including various chilli dishes (including vegetarian), and hamburgers, and Mexican beer to go with it.

Doney
Map 5, J6. Via Veneto 145, ©06.4708.2805. Metro A Spagna or Barberini or Bus 63.
Mon–Sat noon–3.30pm & 7–11pm, Sun noon–3.30pm. Moderate.
An elegant dolce vita-era institution, serving buffet lunch and dinner and Sunday brunch, including salads, pasta dishes, meat and fish, and elaborate desserts. Eat inside or along the famous street, full of promenaders dressed to kill.

Hamasei
Map 3, J2. Via della Mercede 35/36 ©06.679.2134. Metro A Spagna.

Tues–Sun noon–2.30pm & 7pm–10.30pm. Moderate.
An elegant Japanese restaurant right in the centre of town.
Tranquil, refined atmosphere and a full range of Japanese dishes, including a sushi bar. A la carte prices are high, but there
are economical luncheon specials.

Caffé Leonardo

Map 3, K1. Piazza Mignanelli 21a ℂ06.679.7310. Metro A
Spagna.
Daily noon–11pm. Moderate.
In an ideal location just around from the Spanish Steps, this
bistro offers sandwiches and dozens of big, satisfying salads at
amazing prices for the chic zone it's in. Beautifully decorated
inside, with comfortable tables outside on one of Rome's finest
piazzas.

Margutta

Map 5, F5. Via Margutta 118 ℂ06.3265.0577. Metro A Flaminia or
Spagna.
Daily 12.30–3pm & 7.30–11.30pm. Moderate.
Good taste is not only about art and antiques on this famous
street. There's also this upmarket, vegetarian restaurant that
serves generous helpings – albeit at rather high prices. Try the
Sunday brunch. They've also recently opened another branch
near the Pantheon — *Margutta Vegetariano alle Cornacchie*, Piazza
Rondanini 53, ℂ06.6813.4544.

Naturist Club – L'Isola

Map 3, I2. Via della Vite 14 ℂ06.679.2509. Metro A Spagna or bus
#53.
Mon-Sat 12.30–2.45pm & 7.30–10.30pm. Moderate.
A friendly vegetarian, semi-self-service restaurant at lunchtime,
Naturist Club features wholegrain risottos, vegetable pies and

Vegetarian Restaurants

Rome doesn't have many specifically **vegetarian** restaurants — since most traditional Italian places offer plenty of meatless options — but the few that exist are excellent. As always, see the listings for full reviews.

Acqua e Farina?   *Margutta* (2 locations)
L'Insalatiera 2   *Naturist Club*

fresh juices. In the evenings it becomes *L'Isola*, a unique, but still affordable, restaurant, specializing in fish dishes. Aloma, the beautiful proprietor and accomplished chef, also offers wonderful organic wines, home-made ice creams and other delicious desserts. Just off Via del Corso, a block away from Piazza San Silvestro, up on the fourth floor.

Otello alla Concordia

Map 5, G6. Via della Croce 81 ©06.678.1454. Metro A Spagna.
Mon–Sat 11.30–3pm & 7.30–11pm. Moderate.
This place used to be one of Fellini's favourites — he lived just a few blocks away on Via Margutta — and remains an elegant, yet affordable choice in the heart of Rome. A complete offering of Roman and Italian dishes, but ask for "spaghetti Otello" (never on the menu) for a taste of pure tradition — fresh tomatoes and basil with garlic.

Pizza Cir

Map 3, J2. Via della Mercede 43/45 ©06.678.6015. Metro A Spagna or bus #63.
Daily noon–3pm & 7pm–midnight. Moderate.
A big, friendly pizza place that also has first courses, main courses, and desserts. Try the *linguine al cir* which comes with seafood. Just up from Piazza San Silvestro.

Africa

Map 4, F5. Via Gaeta 26 ©06.494.1077. Metro A Repubblica.
Tues–Sun noon–3.30pm & 7.30–11pm. Moderate.
Arguably the city's most interesting Eritrean food, and the first culinary sign of Rome's mostly recently arrived Ethiopian and Somalian population.

Baia Chia

Map 4, F11. Via Machiavelli 5 ©06.7045.3452. Metro A Vittorio.
Mon–Sat noon–3pm & 7.30pm–midnight. Moderate.
Near Santa Maria Maggiore, this Sardinian restaurant has lots of good fish starters and tasty first courses. The fish baked in salt is spectacular. For dessert don't fail to try the *sebadas*, hot pastries stuffed with cheese and topped with Sardinian honey. Closed Sun.

Alle Carrette

Map 4, B10. Via Madonna dei Monti 95 ©06.679.2770. Metro B Cavour or bus #75.
Daily 8pm–midnight. Inexpensive.
A simple, large pizzeria just up Via Cavour from the Imperial Forums. Expect to wait for the exceptional pizza here. Home-made desserts.

Il Dito e la Luna

Map 4, I9. Via dei Sabelli 49/51 ©06.494.0726. Bus #492.
Mon–Sat 7.45–11pm. Moderate.
Creative Sicilian cuisine in a bistro-like San Lorenzo restaurant popular with thirty-something-ish Romans. Go early, as they tend to run out of dishes.

Formula 1

Map 4, I9. Via degli Equi 13 ©06.445.3866. Bus #492.
Mon–Sat 7.30–midnight. Inexpensive.

RESTAURANTS AND PIZZERIAS: TERMINI AND AROUND

Justifiably popular San Lorenzo pizzeria, with tables outside in summer. Delicious pizza all'Ortolana (with courgettes, aubergines and peppers) and good courgette flower fritters.

Il Guru

Map 4, B9. Via Cimarra 4/6. ℂ06.474.4110. Metro B Cavour or bus #75.
Daily 7pm–1am. Moderate.
An elegant, inviting atmosphere and good northern Indian cuisine. The vegetarian menu costs L27,000. Great location in an evocative, little-frequented neighbourhood, just above the Imperial Forums.

Da Lisa

Map 4, F11. Via Foscolo 15 ℂ06.7049.5456. Matero A Vittorio.
Sun–Thurs noon–3pm & 7–11pm. Fri noon–3pm. Moderate.
Kosher Israeli cuisine, including hummus, fish soup and kebabs, and also kosher home-made fettuccine prepared by Lisa herself. Reasonable prices, simple atmosphere. No credit cards.

Little India

Map 4, G10. Via Principe Amedeo 303/305 ℂ06.446.4980. Metro A Vittorio.
Daily noon–3pm & 7.30–midnight. Moderate.
Wonderful Indian food in a medieval Italian setting. Delicious chicken tikka, courgette curry and palak paneer. Non-vegetarian menu for L30,000. Lunchtime it's Indian fast food. Located between Termini and Piazza Vittorio.

Il Podista

Map 4, I8. Via Tiburtina 224 ℂ06.4470.0967. Bus #492.
Mon-Sat 7.30–midnight. Moderate.
Literally owned and run by marathon-runners — hence, perhaps, the quickly served pizzas and fried food, along with typically Roman fare. Family atmosphere.

Pommidoro

Map 4, I8. Piazza dei Sanniti 44 ©06.445.2692. Bus #492.
Mon–Sat noon–3pm & 7.30–midnight. Moderate.

A typical, family-run Roman trattoria, with a breezy open verandah in summer and a fireplace in winter. Try the tasty *pappardelle al cinghiale* (large fettuccine with a wild-boar sauce), *cicoria ripassata* if you like vegetables, and *abbacchio* (lamb) *scotta-dito*, always perfectly grilled.

Tram Tram

Map 4, I8. Via dei Reti 44–46 ©06.490.416. Bus #492.
Tues–Sun noon–3pm & 7.30–midnight. Moderate.

Trendy, animated and smoky San Lorenzo restaurant, serving some fine Pugliese pasta dishes, notably seafood lasagne, and unusual salads. Reservations are recommended. There's also a bar if you want to carry on drinking after dinner.

TRASTEVERE AND TESTACCIO

Acqua e Farina?

Map 2, D14. Piazza O. Giustiniani 2 ©06.574.1382. Bus #75.
Daily noon–3pm & 8pm–midnight. Moderate.

Testaccio restaurant serving dishes that are unique: everything, from starters to desserts, is a variation on the theme of pastry creations – hence the name, "Water & Flour?". Ideal for a light meal, lunch or dinner, for as little as L15,000 a head. A very busy place in the middle of an area bustling with streetlife, especially in summer.

Ai Marmi

Map 7, D4. Viale Trastevere 53/59 ©06.580.0919. Bus #H, #63 or #75.
Thurs–Tues 6.30pm–2.30am. Inexpensive.

Nicknamed "the mortuary" because of its stark interior and marble tables, this place serves unique *"supplì al telefono"* (so

Italian Regional Cuisine

Not all Rome's restaurants just serve Roman specialities; in fact Rome offers a good sampling of the varied *cucina* of Italy's many distinct **regions**. See the listings for the full run-down on these places.

Acchiappafantasmi (Calabrian)   *El Toulà* (Venetian)
Baia Chia (Sardinian)   *Ferrara* (Multiregional)
Colline Emiliane (Emilian)   *Il Dito e La Luna* (Sicilian)
Dal Bolognese (Emilian)   *Monzù Vladi* (Neapolitan)
Dal Toscano (Tuscan)   *Tram Tram* (Pugliese)

named because of the string of mozzarella it forms when you take a bite), fresh *baccalà* and the best pizza in Trastevere. Nice house red wine too. Rapid service, despite the crowds. A lively feel of the real Rome.

ATM Sushi Bar

Map 7, B1. Via della Penitenza 7 ©06.6830.7053. Bus #H, #75 or #63. Tues–Sun 7pm–midnight. Moderate.

Tucked away in Trastevere, this cool yet cosy place comes as a real surprise, serving delicious sushi and sashimi, as well as lacy-perfect tempura. The sashimi salad is very special. Start off with a flawless miso soup and finish with home-made green tea ice cream, and a lime cocktail. There's a great wine list, too.

Augustarello

Map 2, D13. Via G. Branca 98 ©06.574.6585. Bus #75. Mon–Sat noon–3.30pm & 7.30–11.30pm. Moderate.

Testaccio standard serving genuine Roman cuisine in an old-fashioned atmosphere. A good place to come if you appreciate oxtail and sweetbreads, although, as with all Italian restaurants, even strict vegetarians can find good choices.

Bibli

Map 7, D4. Via dei Fienaroli 28 ©06.588.4097. Bus #H, #75 or #63.

Tues–Sun open 11am–midnight; Mon 5.30pm–midnight. Moderate.
After a morning of shopping at Porta Portese flea market, try
this Trastevere multipurpose American-style destination for
Sunday brunch – everything the homesick American might
want, including real American-style pancakes fresh from the
griddle, for L28,000, between noon and 4pm. There's also a
mini-brunch served on Saturday and a buffet starting at 8.30pm
daily, both for L20,000. *Bibli* is also a huge bookstore, art centre and Internet access provider. See p.269 for more.

Casetta de' Trastevere

Map 7, D2. Piazza de' Renzi 31a/32 ©06.580.0158. Bus #H, #75 or
#63.

Tues–Sun noon–3.30pm & 7pm–1am. Inexpensive.
A traditional Trastevere eatery in every way. Beautiful setting,
good food, low prices. Delicious *spaghetti alle vongole*.

Charro Café

Map 2, D14. Via Monte Testaccio 73 ©06.578.3064. Bus #75.

Tues–Sun 8.30–2am. Moderate.
Right in Testaccio's busiest stretch (look for the red-pepper-
coloured lights in the tree to find it), this has a Tex-Mex menu
with everything on it. Prices are higher that average, as with all
establishments along this side of Monte Testaccio. But the lively, party atmosphere more than compensates, as does the salsa
music.

Checchino dal 1887

Map 2, D14. Via Monte Testaccio 30 ©06.574.6318. Bus #75.

Tues–Sat noon–3pm & 8–11.30pm. Expensive.
A historic symbol of Testaccio cookery, with an excellent wine
cellar, too. Go the end of Via Galvani to find the road that circles Monte Testaccio, lined with restaurants and nightspots.

Felice

Map 2, D13. Via Mastro Giorgio 29 ℂ06.574.6800. Bus #75.
Mon–Sat 12.30–2.45pm & 8–10.30pm. Moderate.

Don't be put off by the "riservato" signs on the tables — the owner likes to "select" his customers. Smile and make Felice understand that you're hungry and fond of Roman cooking. Try *bucatini cacio e pepe*, or lamb, and, in winter, artichokes.

Ferrara

Map 7, D2. Via del Moro 1/A ℂ06.580.3769. Bus #H, #75 or #63.
Daily 7.30–1am. Expensive.

Trastevere's most original spot, with an exciting regional menu, a *sommelier* who really knows how to choose the perfect wine for every course, and an inviting series of rooms elegantly stripped back to their medieval walls. The vegetarian antipasto selection is a great choice, and different every time, depending on the season and the chef's inspiration. The Sardinian *ravioloni* are napkin-sized creations using such ingredients as cinnamon, saffron and red peppercorns. Reservations are a must. Expect to spend about L60,000 a head, including wine.

Ivo

Map 7, D4. Via di San Francesco a Ripa 158 ℂ06.581.7082. Bus #H, #75 or #63.
Wed–Mon 7.30pm–1am. Inexpensive.

The Trastevere pizzeria, almost in danger of becoming a caricature, but still good. A nice assortment of desserts, too — try the *monte bianco* for the ultimate chestnut cream and meringue confection. Arrive early to avoid a chaotic queue.

La Maison Rose

Map 7, B3. Via Garibaldi 8/9 ℂ06.581.4521. Bus #H, #75 or #63.
Tues–Sun noon–3pm & 7pm–midnight. Moderate.

Candlelit dining, inside or out, year-round. A full range of Italian dishes, plus crepes, in keeping with its name. Delicious home-made bread. Try the *fusilli* with mussels and porcini mushrooms or *bocconcini* of "chicken al curry". The chocolate mousse is unforgettable. A set fish menu costs L40,000, including wine.

Monzù Vladl

Map 7, C2. Piazza San Giovanni della Malva 2 ©06.589.5640 Bus #H, #75 or #63.
Mon–Sat noon–3pm & 7.30–midnight. Expensive.
A welcome newcomer to Trastevere, this great restaurant specializes in fine Neapolitan cuisine. The word "Monzù" is the Neapolitan version of "Monsieur", and in this case refers to the fabulous owner/chef, Vladimiro. Go on Monday, Wednesday, or Friday, when the cheeses arrive fresh from Campania, and try the smoked *provolone* and *mozzarella di buffala* — tastes and textures you'll never forget. The *Falanghina* wine is Campanian, made from a grape brought from Greece by the ancient Romans.

Da Paris

Map 7, D4. Piazza San Callisto 7a ©06.581.5378. Bus #75 or #H.
Tues–Sat noon–3pm & 8–11.30pm, Sun noon–3pm. Moderate.
Fine Roman Jewish cookery in one of Trastevere's most atmospheric piazzas. Also other traditional dishes.

Pizzeria da Remo

Map 2, D13. Piazza Santa Maria Liberatrice 44 ©06.574.6270. Bus #75.
Mon–Sat 7.30–1am. Inexpensive.
Typical Testaccio neighbourhood pizzeria: raucous and cheap, serving excellent, rustic food.

Pizzeria San Callisto

Map 7, D4. Piazza di San Callisto 9/a ©06.581.8256. Bus #H, #63 or #75.
Tues–Sun 7.30–1am. Inexpensive.

RESTAURANTS AND PIZZERIAS: TRASTEVERE AND TESTACCIO

Large pizzas at small prices. Friendly, fast service and a vibrant, welcoming atmosphere.

Dar Poeta
Map 7, C2. Vicolo del Bologna 45 ©06.588.0516. Bus #H, #63 or #75.
Tues–Sun 7.30–1am. Inexpensive.
Without any doubts, one of the top-ten pizzerias in Rome. Don't expect the typical crusty Roman pizza here; the margherita (ask for it *con basilico* — with basil) comes out of the oven soft and with plenty of good mozzarella on top. They have good imported *birra rossa* — a rarity outside a pub — and there's even a non-smoking room.

Romolo
Map 7, D2. Via Porta Settimiana 8 ©06581.3873. Bus #H, #63 or #75.
Tues-Sun noon-3pm & 7-11pm. Moderate.
A Trastevere institution, apparently located in the very building where Raphael's lover, "La Fornarina", lived. Great garden setting in fine weather. Traditional Roman menu and nice house wines. Try the *bombolotto al carciofo*. The kiwi ice cream with *Vecchia Romagna* liqueur is great too. Menus are decorated with sketches by famous artists who have dined here.

Saperi e Sapori
Map 2, D14. Via di Monte Testaccio 34b ©06.574.3167. Bus #75.
Tues–Sun 8.30–1am. Moderate.
Big pizzas, big salads, all in an area rich with nightlife, especially in the warm months.

La Scala
Map 7, C2. Piazza della Scala 60 ©06.580.3763. Bus #H, #63 or #75.
Daily 7pm–2am. Moderate.

This place was originally just a *birreria* and gradually expanded its offerings, at reasonable prices, including – usually indigestible – live music. It now has a very broad menu, including really good vegetarian chilli. Almost always packed, so go early or you'll have to wait. See also p.272.

Roman Jewish Restaurants

Most, but not all, of the places specializing in traditional **Roman Jewish** cookery are in the Ghetto. Here are our favourites; full reviews can be found among the listings.

Da Giggetto	*Sora Margherita*
Da Lisa	*Zi Fenizia* (Snacks Section)
Da Paris	

VATICAN AREA

La Grotta Azzurra

Map 6, H2. Via Cicerone 62a ©06.323.4490. Metro A Lepanto or bus #280.
Fri–Wed noon–3.30pm & 7.30–midnight. Moderate.
Quiet, relaxing refuge after a day at the Vatican. Fish specialities and impeccable service at moderate prices.

Les Étoiles

Map 6, F3. Via dei Bastioni 1 ©06.687.3233. Metro A Ottaviano or bus #23.
Daily noon–3.30pm & 7.30–midnight. Very expensive.
A ravishing roof-garden restaurant with magnificent views of Rome, perfect if you have something to celebrate. Truly sublime food and very friendly and courteous staff make this an unforgettable experience.

L'Insalatiera 2

Map 2, A6. Via Trionfale 94 ℂ06.3974.2975. Metro A Ottaviano or bus #70.

Mon–Sat 1-4pm & 8pm–midnight. Moderate.

A vegetarian restaurant specializing in regional Italian cuisine, located right across from Rome's flower market. Try their *tagliolini alle noci* or *gnocchi al radicchio e gorgonzola*. For seconds go for the *rotolo di verdura al cartoccio*, the *focaccia napoletano* (with olives, pine nuts and raisins) or the *involtini di radicchio*. Everything is home-made, including the wonderful desserts, such as chocolate and ricotta pie. No smoking.

Osteria dell'Angelo

Map 2, A6. Via G. Bettolo 24 ℂ06.372.9470. Metro A Ottaviano.

Mon–Sat 8–11.15pm; plus Tues & Fri 12.45–2.30pm. Moderate.

Above-average traditional Roman food, in a highly popular restaurant run by an ex-rugby player. Booking advisable.

Dal Toscano

Map 6, D2. Via Germanico 58/60 ℂ06.3972.5717. Metro A Ottaviano.

Tues–Sun 12.30-3pm & 8–11pm. Moderate.

Don't come here for a salad. This restaurant specializes in *fiorentine* (the famous thick Tuscan T-bone steaks), perfectly grilled on charcoal, and delicious *pici* (thick home-made spaghetti) or *ribollita* (veg & bread soup) – all at honest prices. Tremendously popular with Roman families, so reservations recommended for dinner. Near the Piazza del Risorgimento end of Via Germanico.

GELATERIE AND PASTICCERRIE

Cinque Lune

Map 3, F4. Corso Rinascimento 89 ℂ06.6880.1005. Bus #492 or #64.

Tues–Sun 9am–1pm & 4–7pm.

Traditional Roman pastries, including *baba* with whipped cream, and, at Christmas, perfect soft torrone. Just outside Piazza Navona. All takeaway.

La Dolceroma

Map 3, H8. Via Portico d'Ottavia 20b ©06.689.2196. Bus #63. Tues–Sun 9am–1pm & 4–7.30pm.

First-class Austrian (quark cake, plum crumble) and American classics – brownies, blueberry muffins and, best of all, white chocolate chip cookies.

Dolci & Doni

Map 5, G7. Via delle Carrozze 85 ©06.678.2913. Metro A Spagna. Daily 8am–8pm.

A truly sumptuous array of pastries right in the heart of the city, just a few steps away from Piazza di Spagna. Don't miss the lemon cheesecake. Tea and other snacks, too.

Doppia Coppia

Map 7, C2. Via della Scala 51 ©06.581.3174. Bus #H or #75. Daily 1pm–midnight, later in summer.

This Sicilian-owned Trastevere joint has some of the very best ice cream in town. Sublime consistency and unusual flavours like cinnamon and cassata. The amarena and coconut are also great.

Il Forno del Ghetto

Map 3, G8. Via del Portico d'Ottavia 1 ©06.687.8637. Bus #63. Sun–Fri 8am–8pm.

Marvellous kosher Jewish bakery whose unforgettable ricotta pies and *pizza giudia* (a hard cake, crammed with dried and candied fruit) draw quite a crowd.

Il Gelato di San Crispino

Map 3, K3. Via della Panetteria 42 ©06.7045.0412. Bus #63. Wed–Mon noon–midnight.

GELATERIE AND PASTICCERIE

Considered by many to be the best ice cream in Rome, and certainly the most genuine. Wonderful flavours – all natural – will make the other *gelato* you've known pale by comparison. Worth paying a few extra lire for. Not far from Trevi Fountain.

Giolitti

Map 3, H3. Via Uffici del Vicario 40 ©06.699.1243. Bus #63.
Tues–Sun 7am–2am.
An Italian institution that once had a reputation — now lost — for the country's top ice cream. Still pretty good, however, with a choice of seventy flavours.

Innocenti

Map 7, E4. Via della Luce 21 ©06.580.3926. Bus #63 or #H.
Mon–Sat 9am–1pm & 4–7.30pm, Sun 9am–1pm.
Trastevere's – and maybe Rome's – best *biscottificio*, a family operation for 100 years. Wonderful, chewy *croccantini* — half chocolate, half vanilla. Plus *amarettii* (almond biscuits), *brutti ma buoni* (hazelnut biscuits), *straccetti* (almond and hazelnut biscuits) and dozens more varieties. Closed from 15 Aug to 15 Sept.

Palazzo del Freddo di Giovanni Fassi

Map 4, G10. Via Principe Eugenio 65/7 ©06.446.4740. Metro A Vittorio.
Tues–Sun midday–midnight.
A wonderful, airy 1920s ice cream parlour (not far from Termini). Brilliant fruit ice creams and good milk shakes.

Pascucci

Map 3, G6. Via di Torre Argentina 20 ©06.686.4816. Bus #64 or #492.
Daily 6.30am–midnight.
Frullati central for the centro storico. Your choice of fresh fruit whipped up with ice and milk — the ultimate Roman refreshment on a hot day.

Tre Scalini

Map 3, E4. Piazza Navona 30 ©06.6880.1996. Bus #64 or #492.
Open Thurs–Tues, 8am–1.30am.

Piazza Navona institution that is renowned for its famous *tartufo* – death by dark chocolate.

Valzani

Map 7, D3. Via del Moro 37 ©06.580.3792. Bus #H, #63 or #75
Wed–Sun 10–8.30pm.

One of the oldest of the city's pastry shops, still keeping up tradition with marvellous *mostaccioli* and *pangiallo* (both are traditional dried fruit and nut honey bars, the former chocolate covered), amazing *sachertorte* (classic Viennese double-chocolate cake with apricot filling), and, at Easter time, huge, gift-filled chocolate eggs which you can have your name etched on. Extended hours at Christmas and Easter. Closed June–15 Sept.

Drinking

Drinking is not something Romans do a lot of, at least not in public. Despite that, you'll find plenty of **bars** in Rome, and, although, as with the rest of Italy, most are functional daytime haunts and not at all the kinds of places you'd want to spend an evening, due to the considerable presence of Anglo-Americans, there are plenty of more conducive bars and pubs – there's now an Irish pub practically on every corner in central Rome. Many drinking spots are slick and expensive excuses for people to sit and pose, but most have the advantage of having late opening hours – sometimes until 4am in summer, and almost always until around 1am. Prices start from about L6000 for a medium (40cl) beer (ask for a *media*, pronounced "maydia"), but anywhere really fancy won't charge any less than L10,000; sitting at a table will usually cost more, often as much as twice the price. The only slightly cheaper places you'll find are the odd *birreria*.

A recent phenomenon is the upsurge of **wine bars** (*enoteche* or *vinerie*). The old ones have gained new cachet and newer ones, with wine lists the size of unabridged dictionaries, are weighing in too, often with gourmet menus to go with the superb wines they offer. There's also been a recent proliferation of wine-tastings (*degustazioni*), a chance to sample some interesting vintages, often at no cost. Those *enoteche* that also feature great food have been listed in Chapter 13. Those that still concentrate on the fruit of the vine, however, are many in number and we've listed the best here.

Bear in mind also that there is sometimes considerable **crossover** between Rome's bars, restaurants and clubs. For the most part, the places listed in this chapter are drinking spots, but you can eat, sometimes quite substantially, at many of them, and several could be classed just as easily as nightclubs, with loud music and occasionally even an entrance charge.

Although we've, again, divided these listings into the usual **neighbourhoods**, the truth is that there are plenty of drinking establishments all over Rome. However, the areas around Campo de' Fiori and the Pantheon, plus, of course, Trastevere and Testaccio, are the densest and most happening.

Opening hours have been given for all bars and cafés; note, however, that many places are closed during August.

CENTRO STORICO

Bar del Fico
Map 3, D4. Piazza del Fico 26/28 ©06.686.5205. Bus #64 or #492. Daily 8am–2am.

Currently one of several hotspots in the area — just around the corner from *Bar della Pace*, and slightly cheaper. Outdoor heating in winter.

Bar della Pace
Map 3, D4. Via della Pace 5 ©06.686.1216. Bus #64 or #492. Daily 10am–2am.

Just off Piazza Navona, this is *the* summer bar, with outside tables full of Rome's self-consciously beautiful people. Quietest during the day, when you can enjoy the nineteenth-century interior — marble, mirrors, mahogany and plants — in peace, although the prices and rather snooty staff may put you off altogether.

Bevitoria Navona

Map 3, F4. Piazza Navona 72 ℭ06.6880.1022. Bus #64 or #492.
Daily 11am–midnight, till 1am in summer.
Right by the Fountain of Neptune, a wine-tasters' tradition. Regulars swear it's the only place in Rome to *really* drink Italian wine, and that wonderful things can happen here – charmed trysts, serendipitous encounters, that sort of thing.

La Curia di Bacco

Map 3, E7. Via dei Biscione 79 ℭ06.689.3893. Bus #64 or #492.
Daily 4pm–2am.
This lively place looks like it was hollowed out of the ruins of the ancient Teatro di Pompeii, near Campo de' Fiori – and, in fact, it was. A very young crowd, some good wines and interesting snacks.

The Drunken Ship

Map 3, E6. Campo de' Fiori 20–21 ℭ06.6830.0535. Bus #64 or #492.
Daily 6pm–2am, opens early in summer.
A lively meeting-point, with great music, tremendously popular with young Romans and foreign students. Happy hour 7–9pm, brunch at weekends.

Il Goccetto

Map 3, B5. Via dei Banchi Vecchi 14 ℭ06.686.4268. Bus #64 or #492.
Mon-Sat 11am–2pm & 4pm–10pm. Aug closed.

CENTRO STORICO

Probably the most complete wine list in Rome – the proprietor Sergio Ceccarelli is a thoroughgoing expert. You can try some of his over 500 labels "*alla mescita*" (by the glass).

Jonathan's Angels

Map 3, D4. Via della Fossa 18 ©06.689.3426. Bus #64 or #492. Daily 1pm–2am.

This quirky bar, just behind Piazza Navona, certainly wins the "most decorated" award. Every inch (even the toilet, which is worth a visit on its own) is plastered, painted or tricked out in outlandish style by the artist/proprietor.

Miscellanea

Map 3, H4. Via delle Paste 110a. No phone. Bus #63 or #492. Daily 12.30pm–3am.

Located halfway between Via del Corso and the Pantheon, this place was the first American-style bar in Rome, a boozy hangout of US students, and inevitably packed at night. Reasonable prices and the best-value sandwiches in town — jaw-breaking doorsteps for L5000. Also open Christmas Eve and other holidays for lonesome expats.

O'Conner's

Map 3, C5. Via dei Cartari 7 ©06.6830.7161. Bus #64. Daily 9pm–2.30am, later at weekends.

Irish pub with live music, cosy atmosphere — and Guinness. Situated off Corso Vittorio Emanuele, just across from Chiesa Nuova.

Pasticceria Farnese

Map 3, E7. Via de' Baullari 106 ©06.6880.2125. Bus #64 or #492. Daily 7am–2am.

Popular with business types and beautiful young things, but actually not expensive, and a pleasant place to come for breakfast or lunch as well as evening drinks. Good cappuccino and

Bar Essentials

It's important to be aware of the procedure when you enter an Italian **bar**. It's cheapest to drink standing at the counter (there's often nowhere to sit anyway), in which case you pay first at the cash desk (*la cassa*), present your receipt (*scontrino*) to the barperson and give your order. It's customary to leave an extra L50 or L100 on the counter for the barperson, although no one will object if you don't. If there's waiter service, just sit where you like, though bear in mind that this will cost perhaps twice as much, especially if you sit outside (*fuori*) – the difference is shown on the price list as *tavola* (table) or *terrazzo* (any outside seating area).

Coffee is always excellent, drunk small and black (espresso, or just *caffè*), which costs around L1000 a cup, or as a cappuccino (about L2000). If you want your espresso watered down ask for a *caffè lungo*; coffee with a shot of alcohol is *caffè corretto*; with a drop of milk it's *caffè macchiato*. Many places also now sell decaffeinated coffee (ask for "Hag", even when it isn't); while in summer you might want to have your coffee cold (*caffè freddo*). For a real treat ask for *caffè granita* – cold coffee with crushed ice, usually topped with cream. In summer you can drink iced **tea** (*tè freddo*) – excellent for taking the heat off; hot tea (*tè caldo*) comes with lemon (*con limone*) unless you ask for milk (*con latte*). **Milk** itself is drunk hot as often as cold, or you can get it with a dash of coffee (*latte macchiato*) and sometimes as milk shakes – *frappe* or *frullati*.

Among **soft drinks**, a *spremuta* is a fresh fruit juice, squeezed at the bar, usually orange, lemon or grapefruit. There are also crushed-ice granitas, offered in several flavours, and available with or without whipped cream (*panna*) on top. Otherwise there's the usual range of fizzy drinks and concentrated juices: Coke is as prevalent as it is everywhere; the home-grown Italian version, *Chinotto*, is less sweet – good with a slice of lemon. Tap water (*acqua normale*) is quite drinkable, and you won't pay for it in a bar. Mineral water (*acqua minerale*) is a more common choice, either still (*senza gas* or *naturale*) or sparkling (*con gas* or *frizzante*) – about L1000 a glass.

Beer (*birra*) is always a lager-type brew which usually comes in one-third or two-third litre bottles, or on draught (*alla spina*), measure for measure more expensive than the bottled variety. A small beer is a *piccola*, (20cl or 25cl), a larger one (usually 40cl) a *media*. If you want Italian beer, ask for *birra chiara*. You may also come across darker beers (*birra nera* or *birra rossa*).

All the usual **spirits** are on sale and known mostly by their generic names. There are also Italian brands of the main varieties: the best Italian brandies are *Stock* and *Vecchia Romagna*. A generous shot of these costs about L2500, imported stuff much more. The home-grown Italian firewater is *grappa*, available just about everywhere. It's made from the leftovers from the winemaking process (skins, stalks and the like) and is something of an acquired taste; should you acquire it, it's probably the cheapest way of getting plastered.

You'll also find **fortified wines** like Campari; ask for a Campari-soda and you'll get a ready-mixed version from a bottle; a slice of lemon is a *spicchio di limone*, ice is *ghiaccio*. You might also try *Cynar* – believe it or not, an artichoke-based sherry often drunk as an aperitif. There's also a daunting selection of **liqueurs**. *Amaro* is a bitter after-dinner drink, *Amaretto* much sweeter with a strong taste of almond, *Sambuca* a sticky-sweet aniseed concoction, traditionally served with a coffee bean in it and set on fire (though, increasingly, this is something put on to impress tourists), *Strega* – yellow, herb-and-saffron-based stuff in tall, elongated bottles, about as sweet as it looks but not unpleasant.

cornetti, and excellent pizza and sandwiches. Free seating at the window bar, but you might want to pay to sit outside on a warm evening for the view of the graceful, recently restored Palazzo Farnese.

Rock Castle Café

Map 3, G8. Via B. Cenci 8 ℰ06.6880.7999. Bus #H or #63.
Daily 9pm–3am.
In the Jewish Ghetto, just across from Trastevere, a student hangout consisting of six medieval-style rooms, all for dancing and mingling. See also p.284.

Simposio di Piero Costantini

Map 5, C7. Piazza Cavour 16 ℰ06.321.1502. Bus #492.
Mon-Fri 11.30-3pm & 6.30-1am, Sat 6.30-1am.
Not actually in the centro storico, but close enough, just across the Tiber, a few minutes' walk from Piazza Navona, this place has a fine and authentic art nouveau feel. Look for the wrought-iron grapes on the doors and windows. Good food, too.

Taverna del Campo

Map 3, E6. Campo de' Fiori 16 ℰ06.687.4402. Bus #64 or #492.
Tues–Sun 8am–2am.
Trendy new wine bar with a wide range of fancy foods, too. Quite in vogue at the moment, so you may have to contend for an outside table.

Trinity College

Map 3, J4. Via del Collegio Romano 6 ℰ06.678.6472. Bus #63 or #492.
Daily 11am–3am.
A warm and inviting establishment offering international beers and food. It can get quite loud and crowded. Food includes complete meals (vegetarian tacos, Greek salad, chicken supreme and much more) until 1am, and a special brunch menu for L20,000.

Vineria

Map 3, E6. Campo de' Fiori 15 ©06.6880.3268. Bus #64 or #492.
Mon-Sat 9am–1am, Sun 5pm–1am.
Long-established bar/wine shop right on the Campo, patronized by devoted regulars, although it's recently been refurbished for comfort, and now also offers light meals.

EAST OF VIA DEL CORSO

L'Enoteca Antica di Via della Croce

Map 5, G6. Via della Croce 76b ©06.679.0896. Metro A Spagna.
Daily 11am–1am.
An old Spanish Steps-area wine bar with a selection of hot and cold dishes, including soups and attractive desserts. Intriguing trompe-l'oeil decorations inside, majolica-topped tables outside.

Lowenhaus

Map 5, F5. Via della Fontanella 16d ©06.323.0410. Metro A Spagna.
Tues-Sun noon–2am, Mon 6pm–2am.
Just off Piazza del Popolo, a Bavarian-style drinking establishment with beer and snacks to match. Live jazz from 10pm onwards on Fridays.

Victoria House

Map 5, F6. Via Gesù e Maria 18 ©06.320.1698. Metro A Spagna.
Daily 6pm–12.30am, Fri & Sat 5.30pm–1am, Sun 5pm–12.30am.
Decor imported from Sheffield, along with the beer and the food, just a stone's throw from Piazza di Spagna. There's a non-smoking room, and a happy hour from 6pm to 9pm.

TERMINI AND AROUND

Druid's Den

Map 4, D9. Via San Martino ai Monti 28 ©06.488.0258. Metro A Vittorio.

Tues–Sun 8pm–1am.

Appealing Irish pub near Santa Maria Maggiore with a genuine Celtic feel (and owners). It has a mixed ex-pat/Italian clientele, and is not just for the homesick. Cheap and lively, with occasional impromptu Celtic music.

Fiddler's Elbow

Map 4, D9. Via dell'Olmata 43 ℂ06.487.2110. Metro A Vittorio.

Daily 4.30pm–1am, weekends later.

One of the two original Irish bars in Rome, one block closer to Santa Maria Maggiore than its rival the *Druid's*, and roomier, with a decidedly more Latin feel.

Monti D.O.C.

Map 4, D10. Via G. Lanza 93 ℂ06.487.2696. Metro A Vittorio.

Mon–Sat 9am–3.30pm & 6.30pm–1am.

Comfortable Santa Maria Maggiore neighbourhood wine bar, with a good wine list and some nice food: quiches, salads and pastas.

Rive Gauche 2

Map 4, I9. Via dei Sabelli 43 ℂ06.445.6722. Bus #492.

Daily 6pm–2am.

The San Lorenzo district's mythic dive, a smoky, noisy, cavernous evocation of intellectual Left Bank Paris – more or less. Lots of Irish beer choices and snacks to sustain your night of drinking. Happy hour till 9pm.

TRASTEVERE AND TESTACCIO

Aldebaran

Map 2, D14. Via Galvani 54. ℂ06.574.6013. Bus #75.

Mon–Sat 10pm–2.30am.

Laid-back Testaccio cocktail bar with 250 wines to choose from, around the corner from the nightspots of Via di Monte

Testaccio. Red earth-coloured ethnic decor in two large, inviting rooms. Occasional live music.

Internet Cafés

The following places offer **access to the Internet**, although by the time you read this the number is almost certain to have grown. See also p.332.

Art Café Friends; Map 7, D2. Piazza Trilussa 34 ✆06.581.6111. Bus #H, #75 or #63. Mon–Sat 6am-2am, Sun 5pm–2am. Fashionable Trastevere bar with Internet access for L7500 for half an hour.

Bibli; Map 7, D4. Via dei Fienaroli 28 ✆06.588.4097. Bus #H or #75. Tues–Sun 11am-midnight, Mon 5.30pm–midnight. A large, multipurpose bookstore, offering snacks, concerts, presentations, performances and Internet access. Half an hour costs L8000, an hour L12,000. See also p.251.

Internet Café; Map 4, B10. Via Cavour 213 ✆06.4782.3051. Metro B Cavour or Bus #75. Daily 9am–1am. Efficiently run, this spacious, pleasant environment offers Internet access, scanning and printing. Ten minutes on-line goes for L2000, or, with the "Internet Café Card", you get an hour for L6000. Soft drinks and coffee and tea.

Raccolta Multimedia; Map 7, C3. Vicolo del Cinque 58 ✆06.5833.2474. Bus #H, #75 or #63. Mon-Sat 6pm–midnight. Another "polifunzionale" multimedia space, featuring books, art and photography exhibitions, workshops, snacks and a suitably Bohemian atmosphere to go with the hi-tech environment. Internet access costs L10,000 an hour.

Splashnet; Map X, YZ. Via Varese 33 ✆06.493.80450. Mon-Sun 9am-10pm. This place also has laundry facilities so you can surf the Web while you get your washing done.

Il Cantiniere di Santadorotea

Map 7, C2. Via di Santa Dorotea 9 ℰ06.581.9025. Bus #75 or #H.
Wed–Mon 7pm–2am.

In the heart of Trastevere, near Piazza Trilussa, this place has
some great wines and a range of delicious snacks – don't miss
the cheesecake. The cosy decor is part Parisian, part Roman,
with tables outside, too. The proprietor, Alberto Costantini,
really knows his wines and will be delighted to help you
choose the perfect one.

Clamur

Map 7, E6. Piazza del'Emporio 1 ℰ06.575.4532. Bus #75.
Daily 8.30pm–2am.

A large yet cosy Irish pub, on the Testaccio side of the Porta
Portese (Trastevere) bridge, offering the usual beers plus snacks.

Fidelio

Map 7, E3. Via degli Stefaneschi 3/7 ℰNone. Bus #H, #75 or #63.
Daily noon–2am.

Just behind Piazza Sonino in Trastevere, a *vineria* that does
good food too. See also p.231.

Fiestaloca

Map 2, C14. Via degli Orti di Cesare 7 ℰ06.5833.3494. Bus #H, #75
or #63.
Tues–Sun 8.30pm–3am.

Mexico-by-the-Tiber-in-Trastevere with very mixed music
and very Tex-Mex menu. You have to pay to get in at weekends – L10,000, drink included, on Friday, L15,000, drink
included, on Saturday.

Four XXXX Pub

Map 2, D13. Via Galvani 29/29a ℰ06.575.7296. Bus #75.
Tues–Sun 7pm–2am.

English-style Testaccio pub spread over two floors, with South

American-inspired food and snacks. Video, live music, art and photographic exhibitions are frequently arranged.

Enoteca Malafemmina

Map 7, E4. Via San Crisogono 31 ℂ06.580.6941. Bus #75 or #H. Thurs–Tues 5.30pm–1.30am.

This Trastevere wine bar is one of the friendliest places in town. Some amazing wines and delicious light snacks ordered fresh from the first-class restaurant next door.

Il Giardino dei Ciliegi

Map 7, D3. Via dei Fienaroli 4 ℂ06.580.3423. Bus #H, #75 or #63. Daily 6pm–2am, Sat & Sun 5pm–2am. Closed in July & Aug.

A cosy, if rather expensive, tearoom in an out-of-the-way corner of Trastevere. Open late, with a selection of 140 teas, BIG salads and other light choices.

Mr Brown

Map 7, C2. Vicolo del Cinque 29 ℂ06.581.2913. Bus #H, #75 or #63. Mon–Sat 8pm 3am.

This popular night-time hangout is on one of Trastevere's most charming detours. A young, fun-loving crowd, happy hour from 9pm to 10pm daily, with beers going for L5000 instead of the usual L7500, and an assortment of salads, sandwiches and crepes, plus chilli and fondue.

Picasso

Map 2, D14. Via di Monte Testaccio 63 ℂ06.574.2975. Bus #75. Tues–Sat 10.30pm–3am.

A cool, but not too pretentious, Testaccio bar hosting the occasional art exhibition and performance arts event, as well as playing an interesting and eclectic mix of music. Perch on a bar-stool rather than taking a table to avoid paying extra for service. It's also a pizzeria.

San Callisto

Map 7, D4. Piazza San Callisto 4 ©06.583.5869. Bus #H, #75 or #63.

Mon–Sat 6am–1.30am.

An old-guard Trastevere dive bar with a smoky side-room full of card-playing old men and their dogs, which attracts a huge crowd of just about everybody on late summer nights. It's a great place to drink: the booze is cheap, and you can sit at out-side tables for no extra cost. Things are slightly less demimon-deish during the day, when it's simply a great spot to sip a cappuccino, read and take the sun; and it's perfectly OK to bring your own sandwich or pizza slice.

La Scala

Map 7, C2. Piazza della Scala 60 ©06.580.3763. Bus #H, #75 or #63.

Daily noon–2am, later Sat.

Perhaps the most popular Trastevere *birreria* — big, bustling and crowded, with a Texan ranch-meets-McDonald's decor. Food too and occasional (dire) music. See also p.254.

Stardust

Map 7, D3. Vicolo de' Renzi 4 ©06.5832.0875. Bus #H, #75 or #63.

Irregular opening hours.

One of Trastevere's most authentic haunts, and just the place for all-night partying. See also p.281.

Nightlife

Roman **nightlife** retains some of the smart ethos satirized in Fellini's film *La Dolce Vita*, and designer-dressing-up is still very much a part of the mainstream scene. Entrance prices to the big **clubs** tend to be high (as much as L40,000, including a drink), but there are a few smaller, more alternative nightspots, where your travel-crumpled clothes will be perfectly acceptable. To get around the licensing laws, some of Rome's night haunts are run as private clubs – usually known as "centri culturali" – a device that means you may be stung for a membership fee, particularly where there's music, though as a one-off visitor some places will let you in without formalities; and some places charge no fee at all to be a member. In recent years these sorts of places have sprung up all over the city, particularly in the suburbs, and these are becoming the focus of political activity and the more avant-garde elements of the music and arts scene.

On the **live music scene**, summer offerings are plentiful, with several venues all over town, featuring concerts of every sort, including practically free events in Testaccio. However, the chances of catching major rock and pop acts are virtually nonexistent, and getting worse. Rome has been all but abandoned by most big UK and US acts because of its almost complete lack of organization and a suitable venue. Big promoters book the cities up north, especially Milan and Bologna, and leave Rome entirely out of the loop. However, there is a chance you can catch up-and-coming US and UK indie bands playing some of the city's more alternative venues.

Rome's **clubs** run the gamut. There are vast glitter palaces with stunning lights and sound systems, predictable dance music and an over-dressed, over-made-up clientele — good if you can afford it and just want to dance (and observe a good proportion of Romans in their natural Saturday-night element). But there are also places that are not much more than ritzy **bars** with music, and other, more down-to-earth places to dance, playing a more interesting selection of music to a younger, more cautious-spending crowd (we've listed some of these in Chapter 14, "Drinking", as well). There is also a small group of clubs catering specifically to **gay or lesbian** customers (see Chapter 17 for details of these). Whichever you prefer, all tend to open and close late, and some charge a heavy entrance fee – as much as L25,000, which usually includes a drink. During the hot summer months, many clubs close down or move to outdoor locations.

As for **location**, Roman nightlife can be found all over the city, including neighbourhoods on the very edge of town. However, in the central zone the best areas tend to be Testaccio (especially in summer), Trastevere, and the centro storico from the Jewish Ghetto to the Pantheon.

For what's on information, there's *Romac'è* (L2000, Thursdays), with its helpful section in English, and, if you understand Italian, *Time Out Roma* (L4500, Thursdays). Otherwise the main Rome **newspaper**, *Il Messaggero*, lists major musical events, and "**Trova Roma**" in the Thursday edition of *La Repubblica* is another handy guide to current offerings.

See the next chapter, "Culture and Entertainment",
for details of Rome's ticket services.

LIVE MUSIC

Rome's **rock scene** is a relatively limp affair, especially compared to the cities of the North, focusing mainly on imported product and the big venues. Summer sees local bands giving occasional free concerts in the piazzas, but the city is much more in its element with **jazz**, with lots of venues and a wide choice of styles performed by a healthy array of local talent. In October and November each year you'll also find the **Roma Jazz Festival**, with an international cast of fairly big names. There's a big Latin music scene, too, particularly Brazilian, including a **Festival Latino Americano** in summer, from the end of July to the end of August, held out at the *Ippodromo delle Capannelle* on the Via Appia Nuova; tickets are available only on site.

Other summer live-music offerings include **Testaccio Village**, and the **Festa dell'Unità**, both held in and around the old slaughterhouse in Testaccio. The annual **Festa dell'Unità** charges no admission and includes live music, dancing and an array of other entertainments, as well as ethnic eateries. **Testaccio Village** offers a different group every night during the warm months, followed by three outdoor **discos**, all for free on production of a very low-priced weekly pass – available at the ticket booth near the entrance. Again, check *Romac'è* or *Time Out* for details.

ROME'S LARGE PERFORMANCE VENUES

For information about concerts at either of these **two venues** – really the city's only options for big, internationally renowned visiting bands and solo acts – call the Orbis agency (details in Chapter 16).

Palacisalfa

Map 2, EUR inset. Viale del Oceano Atlantico No phone. Metro B EUR Palasport.

A giant tent-like structure 400 metres from Palaeur, one of two sports arenas where major acts tend to end up. It's inadequate, but Rome doesn't have much else.

Palaeur

Map 2, EUR inset. Piazzale dello Sport No phone. Metro B EUR Palasport.

Immense sports arena out in EUR that's one of the two automatic choices for visiting megastars. Appalling acoustics and usually packed.

ROCK & POP

Accademia

Map 7, D3. Vicolo della Renella 90 ©06.589.6321. Bus #H, #75 or #63.

Daily noon–3pm & 6pm–2am.

Live rock Mon & Wed evenings, otherwise there's a DJ. A popular Trastevere eatery and party spot for a youngish crowd. It's huge — on four floors — but this joint jumps, so it's a good idea to make a reservation if you want a table.

Alpheus

Map 2, E14. Via del Commercio 36 ©06.574.7826. Metro B Piramide or bus #75.

Tues–Sun 10pm–4.30am.

Housed in an ex-factory off Via Ostiense, a little way beyond Testaccio, the Alpheus has space for three simultaneous events — usually a disco, concert and exhibition or piece of theatre.

Entrance L10,000–15,000, free on Wednesdays for students. Currently Friday night is gay night – see p.297.

Blue Knight

Map 6, D6. Via delle Fornaci 8–10 ℗06.630.011. Metro A Ottaviano. Daily 7am–3am.

Right near St Peter's, the main floor here is a bar and gelateria, while downstairs there are concerts, almost always acoustic music ranging from rock to blues to pop, featuring some of Rome's best musicians and occasional imports. Concerts take place Thurs–Sat, usually starting at 10.30pm. No admission charge.

Caffè Latino

Map 2, D14. Via Monte Testaccio 96 ℗06.5728.8384. Bus #75. Tues–Sun 10pm–3am.

Multi-event Testaccio club with varied live music almost every night, as well as cartoons, films, and cabaret. There's also a disco playing a selection of funky, acid jazz and black music. Best at weekends when it gets more crowded. L15,000–20,000.

Circolo degli Artisti

Map 2, I12. Via Casilina Vecchia 42 ℗06.7030.5684. Bus #105 or Metro A Re di Roma or San Giovanni. Tues–Sun 9.30pm–3am.

A very large venue – 800 square metres inside plus 5000 out-side in the summer, located beyond Porta Maggiore. A good range of bands, with frequent discos and theme nights — Seventies, reggae, rock, etc. L7000 for a three-month member-ship.

Circolo Vizioso

Map 4, I8. Via dei Reti 25 ℗0347.814.6544. Bus #492. Tues–Sun 9pm–2am.

Multi-room multi-venue in the San Lorenzo district, featuring live rock, reggae and jazz, plus performance art, theatre and cabaret in the main hall. Elsewhere you can dine and chat. L10,000 with yearly membership.

I Giardini di Adone
Map 4, I8. Via dei Reti 38a ©06.445.4382. Bus #492.
Tues–Sun 8pm–3am.
A San Lorenzo venue with rock acts every night, plus theme nights from time to time. Also food, cocktails and beer. L10,000 entrance.

Il Locale
Map 3, D4. Vicolo del Fico 3 ©06.687.9075. Bus #64.
Tues–Sun 10.30pm–2.30am.
Centrally located close to Piazza Navona, this trendy joint enjoys a lively, not to say chaotic, atmosphere, and up-to-the-minute musical awareness, featuring English and American alternative bands and Italian folk-rock. L5000 to get in.

Radio Londra
Map 2, D14. Via di Monte Testaccio 67 ©06.575.0044. Bus #75.
Wed–Mon 9pm–3am, till 4am on Sat.
Air force theme rock and new wave live music venue (with food) in Testaccio. Entrance L10,000–20,000.

RipArte Café
Map 7, D7. Via Orti di Trastevere 7 ©06.586.1852. Bus #H, #63 or #75.
Mon–Sat 8pm-1am.
Live music at 11pm every evening in an elegantly modern environment, where you can also eat. A current favourite with a lot of people, so reserve ahead. L30,000.

Villaggio Globale
Map 2, D14. Lungotevere Testaccio ©06.5730.0329. Bus #170.

ROCK & POP

Variable opening and closing times.

Situated in the old slaughterhouse along the river, the "global village" is an alternative, left-wing meeting space with a multi-ethnic, campus feel. Lectures, concerts, disco, performances and exhibitions make up its busy schedule; there's something on almost every night. Winter months only. Opening hours depend on events. Entrance is L5000.

JAZZ & LATIN

Alexanderplatz
Map 6, C1. Via Ostia 9 ℂ06.3974.2171. Metro A Ottaviano.
Mon–Sat 9pm–2.30am.
Rome's top live jazz club/restaurant with reasonable membership and free entry, except when there's star-billing.
Reservations recommended.

Berimbau
Map 7, D4. Via dei Fienaroli 30b ℂ06.581.3249. Bus #H or #75.
Wed–Sun 10.30pm–3am.
Plenty of live samba and strong Brazilian drinks and food in the heart of Trastevere. L15,000–20,000, drink included.

Big Mama
Map 7, D5. Vicolo San Francesco a Ripa 18 ℂ06.581.2551. Bus #H or #75.
Opening hours depend on concerts; closed July–Oct.
Trastevere-based jazz/blues club of long standing, hosting nightly acts. Membership L10,000 a month, L20,000 a year. Fri & Sat concerts only for those with yearly memberships. Get tickets ahead of time for important names.

Caruso
Map 2, D14. Via di Monte Testaccio 36 ℂ06.574.5019. Bus #75.
Tues–Sun 8pm–late.

Tropical rhythms in Testaccio. Live concerts about twice a week. Brazilian bands shake up the cocktail bar, while varied music – hip hop, Latin, rock – pumps you up in the disco. L15,000 monthly membership.

Escopazzo

Map 3, I7. Via d'Aracoeli 41 ©06.6920.0422. Bus #63 or #64.
Daily 8.30pm–2.30am.
Halfway between Piazza Venezia and Largo Argentina, this friendly bar attracts a crowd of thirty-somethings and offers food and wine along with live concerts or jam sessions most nights. Free entrance.

Fonclea

Map 6, E2. Via Crescenzio 82a ©06.689.6302. Metro A Ottaviano.
Daily 7pm–2am.
Located near the Vatican, this twenty-year-old jazz/soul, funk and rock venue is fitted out like a British pub and has live music most nights. Free Mon–Fri and Sun, L10,000 on Sat. Happy Hour 7–8pm. Concerts begin at 9.30pm. Non-smoking section up near the stage.

Four Green Fields

Map 2, A6. Via C. Morin 42 ©06.372.5091. Metro A Ottaviano.
Daily 7.30pm–2am.
Mixed crowds visit this long-running, versatile Vatican area pub, which also has a cocktail bar. They call their happy hour "Power Hour" and it happens every Tues from 10–11pm. Live music in the basement every night starting at 9.30pm. Free admission.

Four XXXX Pub

Map 2, D13. Via Galvani 29 ©06.575.7296. Bus #75.
Tues–Sun 7.30pm–2.30am.
Testaccio pub spread over two floors, with South American-

inspired food and snacks, live jazz and Latin music. Entrance L5000–10,000 when there's a gig on. See also p.270.

Gregory's

Map 5, H7. Via Gregoriana 54d ⓒ06.679.6386. Metro A Spagna. Tues–Sun 5.30pm–3am.

Just up the Spanish Steps and to the right, an elegant nightspot featuring live jazz improvised by Roman and international musicians. Always crowded. Snacks on offer, too.

New Mississippi Jazz Club

Map 6, E3. Borgo Angelico 18a ⓒ06.6880.6348. Metro A Ottaviano. Wed–Sat 9pm–3am. Sun noon–4pm.

Historical Vatican area jazz venue which also runs a music school. They serve cold buffet dinners, and concerts start at 10pm. Annual membership L15,000. Look out, too, for their Sunday live "Jazz Brunch".

Stardust

Map 7, D3. Vicolo de' Renzi 4 ⓒ06.5832.0875. Bus #H or #75. Irregular opening times.

One of Trastevere's most authentic haunts, this tiny jazz venue stays open as long as there's somebody there and organizes all-night jam sessions in the basement whenever the mood strikes – or the regulars demand.

CLUBS

Agonium

Map 3, C5. Corso Vittorio Emanuele II 205 ⓒ0360.805.192. Bus #64 or #492.

Daily 7pm–4am.

Irish-style disco-pub that plays rave music: house, techno, drum'n'bass – a different category every night. Right next to

CLUBS

the Augustus Cinema (near Piazza Navona). No admission charge.

Alien

Map 5, M4. Via Velletri 13/19 ℂ06.841.2212. Bus #63.
Tues–Sun 10.30pm–4am.

Currently one of the hippest clubs in Rome, located near Piazza Fiume, a few blocks beyond Via Veneto. Art shows, fashion shows, performance art and exhibitions as well as lots and lots of house music. There are two separate spaces, one of which sometimes plays 1970s & 1980s disco hits. Entrance L35,000, though women are sometimes let in free. It also has a summer venue, Alien 2 Mare, in Fregene at Piazzale Fregene 5, ℂ06.6656.4761.

Black Out

Map 2, I13. Via Saturnia 18, ℂ06.7049.6791. Metro A San Giovanni or Re di Roma or Bus #85.
Thurs–Sat 10.30pm–4am.

Punk, trash and indie music, with occasional gigs by US and UK bands. Located out by San Giovanni in Laterano. L10,000–15,000 to get in. Closed in summer.

Bush

Map 2, D13. Via Galvani 46 ℂ06.5728.8691. Bus #75.
Tues–Sun 11pm–4am.

A Testaccio disco with international multimedia events, installations and performances and alternative music spread over three floors. Entrance is L15,000–30,000, depending on what's happening.

Gilda

Map 3, J2. Via Mario de' Fiori 97 ℂ06.678.4838. Metro A Spagna.
Mon–Sun 10pm–4am.

A few blocks from the Spanish Steps, this slick, stylish and expensive club (L40,000 entry), is the focus for the city's minor (and would-be) celebs. Jacket required. Their summer venue, Gilda-on-the-Beach, is in Fregene, at Lungomare di Ponente 11 (Tues–Sun 10.30pm–4am; ℂ06.6656.0649).

Goa

Map 1, D6. Via Libetta 13 ℂ06.574.8277. Metro B Garbatella.
Tues & Thurs–Sat 11pm–3am.

Opened by famous local DJ Giancarlino, Goa, as you might expect from the name, has an ethnic feel – a shop sells hand-made items, there's incense burning – and the music is techno, house, and trance. There are couches to help you recover after high-energy dancing; the decor changes every few weeks. Located near St Paul's Fuori le Mure. Entrance L15,000–30,000.

Jam Session

Map 4, C10. Via del Cardello 13/a ℂ06.6994.2419. Metro B Cavour.
Thurs–Sun 11pm–4am.

Just off Via Cavour, this place hosts a young crowd bopping to 1970s & 1980s disco tunes they couldn't possibly have heard first-time around. The L10,000 entrance fee includes a drink. Wednesday is gay night; see p.299.

Le Bain Art Gallery

Map 3, H7. Via delle Botteghe Oscure 32a/33. Bus #64 or #492.
Tues–Sun 8pm–2am.

Perhaps the current favourite of the radical chic set – three spaces, just off Largo Argentina, featuring art exhibitions, a cocktail bar and cool music. A minimalist but not oppressive decor. No entrance fee.

Piper

Map 2, H5. Via Tagliamento 9 ℂ06.855.5398. Bus #63.
Tues–Sun 11pm–4am, Sat & Sun also 4–8pm for youngsters.

CLUBS

Established in the Seventies by singer Patty Pravo, Piper has survived by undergoing a reincarnation every season. There are different nightly events (fashion shows, screenings, parties, gigs and the like), a smart-but-casual mixed-aged crowd, and a heavy pick-up scene. It's hard to predict the kind of music you'll hear; it varies hugely, depending on the night. Entrance is L15,000–35,000, also depending on the night. Saturday nights are gay nights. Its summer venue, from the end of May to the beginning of September, is by the sea at the AcquaPiper di Guidonia, Via Maremmana, before the 23.9km marker, ℂ0774.326.538.

Rock Castle Café

Map 3, G8. Via B. Cenci 8 ℂ06.6880.7999. Bus #63.
Daily 9pm–3am.

A fun foreign students' hangout playing rock and nothing but. Entrance is L10,000 Saturdays, including a drink, otherwise free. See also p.266.

Culture and entertainment

L et's face it: Rome is a bit of a backwater for the **performing arts**. Northern Italy is where creativity in theatre and dance – and, of course, opera – flourishes, and very few international performers of renown in any of the arts regularly put in an appearance here. Nevertheless, there is cultural entertainment available, and the quality is sometimes better than you might expect. In any case, what the arts here may lack in professionalism, they often make up for in the charm of the setting. Rome's **summer festival**, for example, organized by "Estate Romana", means that there's a good range of classical music, opera, theatre and cinema running throughout the warm months, often in picturesque locations – amidst ancient ruins with soaring columns, or perched on hills with brilliant panoramas of Rome by night – although obviously some of what's on is of little interest if you don't speak Italian. During the winter season, you'll find a regular programme of **classical music** at the Accademia Santa Cecilia, and other sporadic musical offerings of mixed quality, sometimes in beautiful

Tickets

Rome has no comprehensive **ticket service**; you usually have to go to the venue in person some time before the event. However, you can first try **Orbis**, near Santa Maria Maggiore, at Piazza Esquilino 37 (Mon–Sat 9.30am–1pm & 4–7.30pm; ✆06.474.4776), or, not far from the Vatican, **Box Office**, Viale Giulio Cesare 88 (Mon 3.30–7pm, Tues–Sat 10am–1.30pm & 2.30–7pm; ✆06.372.0216), but these two provide only information by phone. If you have a credit card you may be able to save time by calling the Italian-language **Prenoticket** (Mon 3.30–5pm, Tues–Fri 10am–1pm & 2.30–5pm, Sat 10am–1pm; ✆06.520.721); let the recorded voice speak for about a minute, then dial ✆1 to select the reservation service.

churches or palatial halls, and on occasions free. **Opera** is well established in Rome and on occasion approaches world-class levels, but not often enough. Good **dance** is a rarity in Rome, although international companies do show up from time to time, usually at the Teatro Olimpico and the Teatro Argentina (see below). Finally, **cinema**-lovers will find an increasing number of films in the original language, as Italy gradually breaks away from its nationalistic dubbing mania.

For current **information** about what's on where in English, consult the English section at the back of **Romac'è** (L2000, Thursdays) or **Wanted in Rome**, the English language bi-weekly (every other Wednesday), which you can pick up at almost any newsstand in the centre. Otherwise, in Italian, **Time Out Roma** (L4500, Thursdays) is your best bet. There's also the "**Trova Roma**" insert in *La Repubblica*'s Thursday edition.

CLASSICAL MUSIC

Rome's own **orchestras** are not of an international standard, and the city attracts far fewer prestigious orchestras and artists than you might expect of a capital, although there are plenty of music-lovers and students from around the world. Check the listings and keep a look-out for posters advertising little-known **concerts** — a wide range of choral, chamber and organ recitals — in churches or other often spectacular venues, sometimes including the private halls in Renaissance or Baroque palaces. The city's main classical venue is the *Accademia Santa Cecilia* (see below), and we've listed a number of other places where the city's other orchestras and musical associations perform. Otherwise, the many national academies and cultural institutes (Belgian, Austrian, Hungarian, British, American, French, et al) frequently offer free concerts as well, along with the *Auditorium Cavour* (©06.721.9771). In the summer, concerts are staged in cloisters, in the Villa Giulia and Teatro di Marcello, just off Piazza Venezia, and in the ancient Roman theatre at Ostia Antica. In addition there are sponsored Sunday-morning concert cycles, such as the *Telecom Italia* one at the *Teatro Sistina*, Via Sistina 129 (©06.482.6841), between November and April. It may be that you'll just stumble across a concert-in-progress while out on an evening stroll, passing by some ancient church with all its lights on (a rarity not to be missed); Rome is a city where such magical musical moments can still happen.

Accademia Filarmonica Romana

Map 2, B3. Teatro Olimpico, Piazza Gentile da Fabriano 17 ©06.326.5991. Tram from Piazzale Flaminia.
A programme of classical standards, with occasional contemporary works. Performances are on Thursdays and run from October to early May. Tickets range from L30,000 to L60,000.

Accademia di Santa Cecilia

Map 6, F4. Via della Conciliazione 4. Bus #64.

Box Office ©06.6880.1044; Information ©06.361.1064.

Year-round, the focus of the Rome classical music scene is here. Santa Cecilia stages concerts by its own orchestra (Rome's best) and by visiting orchestras and artists. Orchestral concerts are held at the auditorium, just down the road from St Peter's. Most of the tickets are pre-sold by season pass, but for certain special events tickets can go for as little as L15,000.

Gonfalone

Map 3, B5. Oratorio del Gonfalone, Via del Gonfalone 32a ©06.687.5952. Bus #64.

The season here runs from November to early June, offering performances of chamber music, with an emphasis on the Baroque, every Thursday at 9pm. Tickets cost L25,000 and you can reserve by phone. Reservations are strongly recommended. For those wishing to visit the Oratorio, or to pick up tickets in advance, the entrance is at Vicolo della Scimia 1b, during office hours.

Istituzione Universitaria dei Concerti

Map 4, H7. Aula Magna of the Sapienza University, Piazzale Aldo Moro 5 ©06.361.0051. Bus #492 or Metro B Policlinico.

Musical offerings which range from Mozart to Miles Davis, and from Ravel to Kurt Weill. Tickets cost L15,000–50,000. The season runs from October to April, and performances are usually held on Tuesday evenings and weekends.

OPERA

Rome's **opera** scene has long been overshadowed by that of Milan but is improving. The **Teatro dell'Opera** is located near Termini Station and Piazza della Repubblica, at Via Firenze 72 (box office daily 9am–4.30pm; English spoken; ✆06.4816.0255; metro A Repubblica). Rome's opera season runs from November to May. Nobody compares it to *La Scala*, but cheap tickets are a lot easier to come by, and important singers do sometimes perform here. Expect to pay at least L30,000. If you buy the very cheapest tickets, bring some high-powered binoculars, as you'll need them in order to see anything at all.

In summer, the opera moves **outdoors** and ticket prices come down. Summer performances used to be held in a stunning setting at the ancient Baths of Caracalla, but that practice was terminated a few years ago due to excessive damage to the monument. At press time, the 2000 summer programme had not yet been set. The last few years the venue has been the Stadio Olimpico (bring a cushion and some mosquito repellent), where first-rate productions have been staged at one end of the football stadium. However, since the Teatro dell'Opera is now air-conditioned, the entire summer programme may be held there. Tickets start at L20,000 for Stadio Olimpico productions and are available through the Opera box office.

THEATRE AND DANCE

There is a good bit of **theatre** in Rome, but it's virtually all in Italian. Very occasional English-language **musicals**, usually put together by some travelling American company, come to town during the winter season, as well as the odd **dance** troupe. The venue for such rare events is almost always either the Teatro Olimpico or the Teatro Sistina.

Local efforts are generally very missable, although there is one **English language theatre group**, who perform current American one-acts, mostly comedies, on Friday evenings from October to June. However, they tend to change their venue, and even the day of the week, from year to year. At

THEATRE AND DANCE

time of writing they were performing at the L'Arte del Teatro, at Via Urbana 107 – take Metro B to Cavour. Call impresario **Gaby Ford** on ©06.444.1375 for current information, or keep an eye out for posters in some of the Anglo-American hangouts — bookstores, movie houses, pubs, etc.

Incidentally, virtually all Roman stages are **dark on Mondays**. Again, check the usual sources for your options.

ENGLISH-LANGUAGE THEATRES

Teatro Olimpico

Map 2, B3. Piazza Gentile da Fabriano 17 ©06.326.5991. Tram from Piazzale Flaminio.

Located well beyond Piazza del Popolo, this theatre tends to get Rome's best international dance and sometimes some important alternative performers of various stripes. Tickets generally cost L40,000 and up. There's a decent snack bar, where you can sometimes spy the performers taking a break during the interval.

Teatro Sistina

Map 5, I7. Via Sistina 129 ©06.482.6841. Metro A Spagna or Barberini.

Every now and then an English-language (American, very off-Broadway) musical revue blows into town and it generally ends up here, just up from Piazza di Spagna. Expect to pay about L40,000 for a decent seat. Gershwin seems to be a perennial favourite, along with other jazzy-bluesy musical confections.

OTHER THEATRES

Teatro Agorà

Map 7, B1. Via della Penitenza 33 ©06.687.4167. Bus #H or #75.

Once upon a time this Trastevere theatre sometimes produced English-language plays and other entertainments, and it could always happen again. Tickets start at L15,000.

Teatro Argentina

Map 3, G6. Largo Argentina 52 ✆06.6880.4601. Bus #64 or #492.
One of the city's most important theatres for dramatic works in
Italian, and for dance. Quality varies widely. Tickets go for
L20,000 and up.

Teatro Colosseo

Map 4, D13. Via Capo d'Africa 7 ✆06.700.4932. Metro B Colosseo
or bus #75.
Just up from the Colosseum, this theatre presents new, usually
vaguely underground plays by contemporary Italian playwrights
or translations. Themes often centre around alternative sexuality.
They have also been known to offer English-language one-acts
in their small theatre downstairs. Tickets start at L12,000.

Teatro Eliseo

Map 4, B8. Via Nazionale 183e ✆06.4880.8311. Metro A
Repubblica.
One of Rome's main theatres, hosting plays by Italian playwrights, and adaptations into Italian of foreign works, and featuring some of the top dramatic talent Italy has to offer. Tickets
start at L15,000.

Teatro Flaiano

Map 3, I6. Via San Stefano del Cacco 15 ✆06.679.6496. Bus #64 or
#492.
Located between the Pantheon and Piazza Venezia, this is a
small theatre presenting experimental plays in Italian that often
deal with what are – for relatively conservative Rome – con-
troversial topics. Tickets start at L15,000.

Teatro Greco

Map 1, D5. Via Ruggero Leoncavallo 12 ✆06.860.7513. Bus #310,
#63, #92 or #235.
Located well out of the centre, on the far side of Villa Ada, this

OTHER THEATRES

theatre generally offers some of the best Italian dance, with tickets starting at L15,000. In October the Italian National Dance competition is often held here.

Teatro Prati

Map 6, E1. Via degli Scipione 98 ©06.3974.0503. Metro A Ottaviano.

A few blocks away from St Peter's, another small space that often features Italian comic classics, such as works by Edoardo De Filippo. Tickets start at L20,000.

Teatro Romano di Ostia Antica

Map 1, A8. Ostia Antica. Information ©06.6880.4601; box office daily 10am-2pm & 3-6pm. Ostia train from Piramide. Metro B Piramide, Tram #30 or bus #75.

In July and August specially scheduled performances of all kinds are offered in the restored ancient Roman theatre – a spectacular, unforgettable setting, even if you don't speak Italian. Performances begin at 8.45pm. Go early for a chance to visit the ruins. Tickets cost L15,000–20,000. It's a twenty-minute train ride to Ostia Antica, then a short walk over the footbridge into the ruins.

Teatro Valle

Map 3, F5. Via del Teatro Valle 23a ©06.6880.3794. Bus #64 or #492.

Between Piazza Navona and the Pantheon, this theatre some-times offers special works in English by visiting actors and companies. Tickets start at L15,000.

Teatro Vittoria

Map 2, D13. Piazza Santa Maria Liberatrice 8 ©06.574.0598. Bus #75.

In Testaccio's main square, this large theatre sometimes books cabaret-like acts or dance-theatre companies that need no translation. Tickets start at about L20,000.

OTHER THEATRES

FILM

There tends to be more and **more English-language cinema** on offer in Rome these days, partly due to foreign demand, but also because Italians are finally beginning to realize that they've been at a disadvantage culturally, linguistically and economically by being spoon-fed a steady diet of dubbed travesties. If you can manage with Italian, you'll naturally also find current Italian productions available all over town. There is really no Roman film festival as such, although each year, June 11–18, there's a rather halfhearted attempt to put together an event called the **Fantafestival** – nothing to do with the orange-flavoured soda pop, but a series of science fiction and fantasy films shown in various centrally located cinemas. And each year some of the new films — though rarely the most significant ones — from **Cannes and Venice** are frequently given special viewings at Trastevere theatres a week or two after the festivals.

You'll find usually accurate **listings** in the English language section of *Romac'è* and in all the newspapers, which also include a section on "film clubs" or "cinema d'essai", a euphemism for stifling rooms where two or three aficionados sit on hard wooden chairs in front of a tiny, blurred screen watching films in their original language. Also, the "Italy Daily" supplement to the International Herald Tribune lists current English-language films; and if you speak Italian there's also *Time Out Roma*.

Alcazar

Map 7, D4. Via Merry del Val 14 ©06.588.0099.
Trastevere cinema featuring mainstream American and English films, with the occasional weird one slipping in. You'll pay L8000 afternoons and L13,000 evenings.

Nuovo Olimpia

Map 3, H2. Via in Lucina 16 ©06.686.1068. Bus #63 or #492.
Very central, just off Via del Corso, with two screens; tickets
here cost L8000 afternoons and all day Wednesday, L12,000
evenings and weekends. They nowadays always feature at least
one foreign film in the original language.

Nuovo Sacher

Map 7, D6. Largo Ascianghi 1 ©06.581.8116. Bus #H or #75.
Again in Trastevere, this film theatre shows their current film in
its original version, often in French, on Mondays. Tickets are
L8000 afternoons, L10,000 evenings. Their choices tend
toward independent, left-leaning works from Eastern Europe,
France and Asia.

Pasquino

Map 7, C3. Piazza Sant'Egidio 10 ©06.580.3622. Bus #H or #75.
Long-established in Trastevere as Rome's premier English-language cinema, with three screens showing recent general
releases and the odd indie from Sundance, etc. The programme
changes every Friday. Tickets for weekday evening and weekend showings cost L10,000, while afternoons from Monday to
Friday cost L8000. For the two "Pasquino Club" screens you
have to buy a L2000 pass first, valid for two months. A word of
warning: expect problems with the projector, and avoid screen
3 unless you're really dying to see the film. The screen is terrible, the sound worse.

Quirinetta

Map 3, J4. Via. M. Minghetti 4 ©06.679.0012. Bus #63 or #64.
Centrally located, just off Via del Corso, near the Trevi
Fountain, tickets here go for L8000 afternoons, L13,000
evenings and weekends. They always have films in the original
language, 90 percent of the time first-run mainstream American
fare. A huge screen and great Dolby surround-sound.

FILM

—

Gay and lesbian Rome

The Year 2000 promises to be a breakthrough year for **gay and lesbian Rome**. In direct competition with the pope's officially homophobic policies, the Eternal City has been declared the official site of "World Pride 2000". The first week of July should see an inundation of the Rainbow Coalition from all over, come to celebrate their love among the ruins – which should be interesting, considering that the city will also be hosting hundreds of thousands of Catholic pilgrims.

Intriguingly, Italy has never had anti-same-sex laws; it was presumably always enough simply to create an aura of massive disapproval around same-sex love. Consequently, gay and lesbian life in Rome is still conducted a bit on the sly, with gay venues hidden away and blacked-out from the street. There isn't any danger – Rome is a remarkably safe city – just a pervasive feeling of original sin. Perhaps this will change with the millennial festivities.

There's a full range of same-sex offerings in Rome, although the city is certainly no Barcelona or Amsterdam

Contacts and information

ARCI-Gay Caravaggio, Via Lariana 8, ✆06.855.5522. Rome branch of the nationwide Italian gay organization. Political gatherings every Wed 8.30–10.30pm. Social gatherings every Sun 5–8pm.

ARCI-Lesbica Roma, Via dei Monti di Pietralata 16, ✆06.418.0369; Web site: *www.women.it/~arciles/roma*. Again, the local branch of the national gay activist group. Social-political gatherings every Thurs 8.30–10.30pm.

Gay Information in English ✆06.541.3985, Mon evenings, 8.30am–10.30pm.

Gay Information in Italian ✆167.162.966, Mon–Fri 2–4pm.

Mario Mieli Cultural Association, Via Efeso 5, ✆06.541.3985; email: *info@mariomieli.it*. Web site: *www.mariomieli.it*. Rome's gay activist organization, offering a broad range of social and health services. Welcome group Sat 3–6pm. Political group Mon 6.30pm. Volunteer group Wed 6.30pm.

The number of clubs, bars, saunas and suchlike, is relatively limited, and you have to be on guard for the considerable presence of trade, usually recent arrivals from Eastern Europe, who cater largely to Vatican officials and other closet cases. However, you can certainly find a good time; there are also outdoor cruising/sex areas and some clubs have dark rooms, too, for those who prefer their encounters to be anonymous. There is no particularly gay part of town; clubs and bars are spread far and wide. Also, choices exclusively for women remain very few, although most places welcome both gay men and lesbians.

BARS AND CLUBS

Alcatraz

Map 4, D5. Via Aureliana 38 ℂ06.4201.3286. Metro Termini.
Thurs–Sat 10pm–3am, Sun 5pm–2am.

Very near Termini Station, this video bar on three floors features music, big screens, "video hard", a discotheque and a dark room. It has special theme evenings, too, such as "Army Night" on Thursdays, and there's a Sunday Tea Dance starting at 5pm.

L'Alibi

Map 2, D14. Via Monte Testaccio 44 ℂ06.574.3448. Bus #75.
Wed–Sun 11pm–4.30am.

Predominantly – but by no means exclusively – male venue that's one of Rome's oldest and best gay clubs. Downstairs there's a multi-room cellar disco and upstairs an open-air bar. There's a big terrace to enjoy in the warm months. Situated in the middle of the lively Testaccio neighbourhood, with lots of fun restaurants and a plethora of activities in the summer. Free admission Wed & Thurs. Other nights L20,000.

Alpheus

Map 2, E14. Via del Commercio 271/b ℂ06.541.3985. Bus #75 or Metro B Piramide.
Fri only 10.30pm–4am.

Every Friday here at 10.30pm it's the "Muccassassina", a thoroughly gay, lesbian, bisexual and transgender event sponsored by the Mario Mieli Cultural Association. It's a great night, with three different discos pounding away, a garden open in the warm months, and special events, such as drag shows and amateur male strippers. It costs L18,000 to get in, which includes one drink.

Apeiron

Map 4, D9. Via dei Quattro Cantoni 5 ©06.482.8820. Metro Termini.
Most nights 10.30pm–2am, later on Fri and Sat.

A big-screen video bar upstairs, erotic videos and dark room downstairs. Located in the Termini area, near the Basilica of Santa Maria Maggiore. One-drink minimum for L6000.

Edoardo II

Map 3, J7. Vicolo Margana 14 ©06.6994.2419. Bus #63 or #64.
Tues–Sat 10pm–2am.

Right in the middle of the old Jewish Ghetto, just off Piazza Venezia, this medieval torture chamber theme bar, named after the infamously gay English king, is actually pretty tame. Quite a young crowd and conveniently cruisy if you're having a wander through the centre of town. Membership is required, but it's free.

Garbo

Map 7, D3. Vicolo di Santa Margherita 1/A ©06.5832.0782. Bus #H or #75.
Wed–Mon 10pm–2am.

A friendly Trastevere bar, with a relaxed atmosphere and a nice setting, just behind the main piazza. A nice mix of Italians and foreigners, presided over by Tom, the Irish proprietor. No admission charge. Drinks start at L5000.

Gender

Map 1, D6. Via Faleria 9 ©06.7049.7638. Metro A Re di Roma.
Tues–Sat 11pm–4am.

A bit of a step from the city centre, this multi-gender club specializes in theme nights, covering everything from erotic cartoons to drag lessons to sexy couple contests… and more. L15,000 entrance.

L'Hangar

Map 4, D10. Via in Selci 29 ℅06.488.1397. Metro B Cavour or Metro A Vittorio.

Tues–Sun 10.30pm–2am.

About halfway between Termini and the Roman Forum, just off Via Cavour, this is one of Rome's oldest and least expensive gay spots, always crammed with young people. Monday night features gay videos, and Saturday night it's almost impossible to get in the door it's so jammed. There's no charge to get in, you just take a ticket and pay when you leave for whatever you've had to drink.

Jam Session

Map 4, B10. Via del Cardello 13/a ℅06.6994.2419. Metro B Cavour.

Wed only midnight–4am.

Wednesday night here is "gay party" night, with Seventies and Eighties disco music and loads of buff young Italians – a somewhat posey affair. The L10,000 entrance fee includes a drink.

Joli Coeur

Map 1, D5. Via Sirte 5 ℅06.8621.5827. Bus #010 or #63.

Sat only 11pm–4am.

Pretty far from the centre, in the Villa Ada area, but this club features Rome's only lesbian night every Saturday.

Piper

Map 2, H5. Via Tagliamento 9 ℅06.855.5398. Bus #63.

Tues–Sun 11pm–4am, Sat & Sun also 4–8pm for youngsters.

Saturday nights are gay nights at this eclectic club. See p.283 for more details.

RESTAURANTS

Baronato Quattro Bellezze

Map 3, B4. Via di Panico 23 ℅06.687.2865. Bus #64.

Daily 8pm–2am. Moderate.

Definitely one-of-a-kind, this place is owned and run by the inimitable Dominot, life-long drag chanteuse, formerly of Paris, who performs Piaf here on Thursday evenings. There's nothing else like it, at least not in Rome. Dominot is Tunisian by birth and the fare here is accordingly couscous, made by himself, including one for vegetarians. The decor is a charming hodge-podge of memorabilia from his glittering career, including a gaily-lit carousel pony that floats above the bar.

La Focaccia

Map 3, D4. Via della Pace 11 ℂ06.6880.3312. Bus #64 or #492.
Daily noon–3.30pm & 7pm–1am. Moderate.

Just off Piazza Navona, this place serves hearty, unusual dishes, a dozen different kinds of focaccia, pizzas and salads. Good desserts, too, and excellent red house wine. See p.238 for more.

Le Sorellastre

Map 7, B1. Via San Francesco di Sales 1b ℂ06.718.5288. Bus #H or #75.
Tues–Sat 7pm–2am.

This Trastevere bar and restaurant, serving Italian and international cuisine, is the only *exclusively* lesbian place in town.

SHOPS AND SERVICES

Energie

Map 3, I2. Via del Corso 486, ℂ06.687.1258. Metro A Spagna.
Mon–Sat 10am–8pm, Sun 10am–1.30pm & 3.30–8pm.

Clothing store with trendy young styles and friendly young assistants, plus a 15 percent discount if you flash your ARCI-Gay membership card (available for L20,000 through ARCI-Gay or at our sauna listings).

Libreria Babele

Map 3, B5. Via dei Banchi Vecchi 116, ✆06.687.6628. Bus #64.
Mon–Sat 9.30am–7.30pm.

Rome's gay and lesbian bookshop, with lots of gay-themed books, some in English, plus gadgets, posters, videos, guides and postcards. Towards the river from Campo de' Fiori, just off Corso Vittorio Emanuele.

Zipper

Map 4, D5. Via Castelfidardo 18 ✆06.488.2730; fax: 06.488.2729; email: *zipper.travel@flashnet.it*. Web site: *www.adv.it/zipper*. Metro A Repubblica.
Mon–Sat 9am–8pm.

Gay travel agent, located near Termini, brokering round-the-world or round-Italy travel for gay and lesbian groups and individuals.

SAUNAS

Europa Multiclub

Map 4, D5. Via Aureliana 40 ✆06.482.3650. Metro Termini.
Sun 1pm–midnight, Mon–Thurs 3pm–midnight, Fri & Sat 1pm–6am.

Near Termini, this has pleasant, clean facilities, and a snack bar. L20,000 per visit, plus L20,000 for ARCI-Gay annual membership (good for discounts at gay venues throughout Italy).

Mediterraneo

Map 4, E12. Via Pasquale Villari 3 ✆06.7720.5934. Metro A Vittorio.
Daily 2pm–midnight.

Also in the Termini area, near Piazza Vittorio, this is a sauna on three levels, with all the usual choices, including a snack bar. L20,000 per visit, plus ARCI-Gay yearly membership of L20,000.

SAUNAS

ACCOMMODATION

Scalinata di Spagna Hotel

Map 5, H7. Piazza Trinità dei Monti 17 ℂ06.679.3006, fax 06.6994.0598. Metro A Spagna.

Gays and lesbians are welcome at this centrally located hotel, just up from the Spanish Steps. Doubles for L450,000–500,000, singles L350,000–380,000. Everything you would expect at this price, plus a terrace for breakfast. See p.212 for more.

Seiler Hotel

Map 4, C7. Via Firenze 48 ℂ06.485.550 or 06.488.0204, fax 06.488.0688. Metro A Repubblica.

Another gay-friendly accommodation option, a little cheaper than the *Scalinata di Spagna*, just down from Piazza della Repubblica, across Via Nazionale from the Teatro del'Opera. Singles here go for L180,000, doubles for L250,000, triples for L300,000. Breakfast included.

Michela Leone Rooms

Map 1, D6.

Lesbian-friendly accommodation, both in Rome and at the seaside, for L40,000 per person. Contact Michela on ℂ06.718.5288, or write to Via Lucciano 30, 00178 Rome. Strictly women only.

Shops and Markets

At first glance, you may wonder where to start when it comes to **shopping** in a big, chaotic city like Rome. In fact the city is a more appealing shopping experience than you might think, abounding with pleasant shopping streets and colourful markets, most of which are in the city centre. Many shopping areas have been pedestrianized, and, perhaps best of all, the city hasn't yet been entirely overrun by department stores and shopping malls, or by the international chain stores that characterize most European city centres. One-stop shopping opportunities are rare, but you will find corners of the city that have been colonized by stores featuring the same sort of merchandise – fashion, antiques, food – making it easy for you to check out the competition's products and prices. You will also find true artisans in Rome, who take great pride in their crafts.

You can find the best of Italy in Rome. **Fashion** straight from the catwalk is well represented on the fashionable streets close to the Spanish Steps – **Via Condotti, Via Borgognona,** and **Via Frattina** – where you'll find chic boutiques like Gucci, Prada and Valentino. If you want to do more than window–shop, head to **Via del Tritone**, **Via Nazionale,** below piazza della Repubblica, or **Via Cola di Rienzo**, near the Vatican, for more middle-range and affordable fashion. The stores on and around **Via del Corso** are a mixture, selling mainstream, and fairly youth-orientated, fashions, while **Via Veneto**, off Piazza Barberini, caters to those who were youthful when Fellini's *La Dolce Vita* opened, and are now the fashionably well-off patrons of the street's expensive leather shops and boutiques.

Antiques shops – a huge selection – line **Via dei Coronari** and neighbouring **Via dell'Orso** and **Via dei Soldati**, just north of Piazza Navona; **Via Giulia**, south-west of Campo dei Fiori, and **Via del Babuino** and **Via Margutta,** between Piazza del Popolo and the Spanish Steps, are also good sources of art and antiques. As for **food,** if you want to take home a bottle of extra virgin olive oil or some vacuum-packed porcini mushrooms, end your day visiting the food shops and markets around **Campo de' Fiori** or **Via Cola di Rienzo** across the river.

The city's many **markets** offer a change of pace from Rome's busy shopping streets. Many of these are bustling local food markets, and, even in the centre, are still very much part of Roman life. The **Campo de' Fiori** market is probably the most central of these. Otherwise there's Trastevere's **Porta Portese** flea market, a venue for antiques, clothing, books, and indeed virtually anything else, every Sunday morning.

These days some shops in the centre of Rome stay open all day. However, many still observe the city's traditional **hours** – Monday 3.30–7.30pm, Tuesday–Saturday 9.30am–1.30pm & 3.30–7.30pm, and closed on Sunday. Food shops are also often closed on Thursday afternoon in the winter and Saturday afternoon during the summer; and most shops close for at least two weeks in summer, usually in August. Most places accept all major **credit cards**.

ANTIQUES

Antichità
Map 5, F5. Via del Babuino 83 ©06.320.7585.
Mon 3.30–7pm, Tues–Sat 9am–1pm & 3.30–7.30pm.
One of the several fine antique stores in the area, with a large collection of stunning Italian furnishings from the 1700s. There is also an entrance on Via Margutta.

La Bottega del Principino
Map 5, F5. Via Margutta 59B ©06.320.7979.
Mon 3.30pm–7.30pm, Tues–Sat 3.30pm–7.30pm.
An interesting little shop quite different from the fancy antique shops that surround it, offering quite an eclectic array of bric-a-brac – everything from eighteenth-century farm equipment to crystal chandeliers from the 1940s.

Hendy
Map 3, I4. Piazza di Pietra 42 ©06.678.5804.
www.hendy-gioieantiche.com.
Monday 3.30pm–7pm, Tues–Sat 10am–7pm.
Located in a peaceful piazza near the Pantheon, this place specializes in *gioie antiche* or antique jewellery. You will find a unique selection of Italian rings, necklaces, bracelets, mostly from 1900-40, although there are some pieces that date back as far as 1870.

Libreria Giuliana di Cave
Map 3, H4. Via dei Pastini 23 ©06.6780.297.
Mon–Sat 2.30pm–8pm.
Antique book and print shop run by a friendly mother and son. All the material here is Italian, with books dating from the sixteenth century and prints from the late-seventeenth century. They also sell inexpensive print reproductions.

ANTIQUES

Papadato Antichità Roma
Map 3, I4. Piazza di Pietra 41 ℭ06.679.6931.
Mon 3.30pm–7pm, Tues–Sat 10.30am–7pm.
Friendly antique store that has both Italian and English antiques. The store is mostly known for its large selection of European fans from the sixteenth and seventeenth centuries.

Valerio Turchi
Map 5, F5. Via Margutta, 91A ℭ06.323.5047, fax 06.323.3209.
Mon 3.30pm–7pm, Tues–Sat 10.30am–7pm.
A bit different from the other antique shops on Via Margutta, with exquisite pieces from Rome's past – various pieces of Roman statues and sarcophaguses dating from as early as 300 AD.

BOOKS

Anglo–American Bookstore
Map 3, J1. Via delle Vite 102 ℭ06.679.5222.
Mon 3.30–7.30pm, Tues–Sat 9am–1pm & 3.30–7.30pm.
Large selection of new English books on every subject, including textbooks for university students.

Bibli
Map 7, D4. Via dei Fienaroli 28 ℭ06.588.4097. *www.bibli.it*.
Mon 5.30pm–midnight, Tues–Sun 11am–midnight.
Bookstore, cultural centre and café that only has a small selection of English books, but they do have Internet access, and a helpful bulletin board with many ads in English for those looking for work, apartments, etc.

The Corner Bookshop
Map 7, D2. Via del Moro 48 ℭ06.583.6942.
Mon–Sat 10am–1.30pm & 3.30pm–8pm, Sun 11am–1.30pm &

3.30pm–8pm. Closed Sun in Aug.

The always friendly Claire Hammond runs this bookshop, which is entirely dedicated to new English books. If you can't find what you are looking for, she will order it for you.

Economy Bookstore and Video Centre

Map 4, D7. Via Torino 136 ©06.474.6877.

Mon–Sat 9am–8pm.

This bookstore has been supplying Rome with both new and used English titles for the past thirty years. They also rent and sell videos in English.

Feltrinelli International

Map 4, C6. Via Emanuele Orlando 84 ©06.482.7878.

Mon–Sat 9am–8pm, Sun 10am–1pm & 4–7.30pm.

This branch of the Italian chain stocks books in German, French, Spanish, Portuguese – and, downstairs, in English.

Italica Books

Map 3, E7. Via dei Giubbonari, 30/9 ©06.6880.5285.

Thurs 3–7pm.

If you can't find the old editions you're searching for, then drop by *Italica Books* – not actually a bookstore but the home of Louise McDermott, who has a large collection of out-of-print books in English about Italy, and encourages visitors to stop by for a browse once a week. Just off Campo de' Fiori.

Libreria la Strada

Map 5, J7. Via V. Veneto 42 ©06.482.4151.

Daily 9.30–12.30am.

Excellent Italian-language bookshop that boasts a fine stock of books about Rome – in English and Italian – in the pavilion outside: everything from tourist guides to well-selected fiction in English.

BOOKS

Lion Bookshop

Map 5, F6. Via dei Greci 33 ©06.3265.4007.

Mon 4.30–7.30pm, Tues–Sat 10am–7.30pm.

The comfortable new location of this all-purpose English bookshop has a lounge area where you can take a break from browsing and enjoy a coffee or tea. One of Rome's longest-established outlets for books in English.

Open Door Bookshop

Map 7, E3. Via della Lungaretta 25 ©06.589.6478.
www.books-in-italy.com.

Mon 4.30–8.30pm,Tues–Fri 10.30am–8.30pm, Sat 10.30am–midnight, Sun noon–6pm.

Although they do have some new titles, used books dominate the shelves at this friendly Trastevere bookshop. They also have a selection of books in Italian, German, French and Spanish.

Rizzoli International

Map 3, J3. Largo Chigi 15 ©06.679.6641.

Mon–Sat 9am–7.25pm, Sun 10.30am–7.55pm.

Central branch of the Italian chain, with a great stock of books on Italy, and a reasonable stock of books in English.

CLOTHING AND ACCESSORIES

Davide Cenci

Map 3, H3. Via di Campo Marzio 1/7 ©06.699.0681.

Mon 4–7.30pm, Tues–Fri 9.30am–1.30pm & 3.30pm–7.30pm, Sat 10am–7.30pm.

An exclusive clothing shop that has been offering conservative high-quality fashion to men, women and children for the past .75 years.

Donèl

Map 6, F2. Piazza Cola di Rienzo 75 ©06.321.4744.
Mon 3.30–7.30pm, Tues–Sat 9.30am–7.30pm.
All the current trendy shoe styles for men and women at below average prices.

Dress Agency Donna

Map 5, F5. Via del Vantaggio 1B ©06.321.0898.
Mon 4–7.30pm, Tues–Sat 10am–1pm & 4pm–7.30pm.
Used women's clothing and accessories from Chanel, Versace, Armani and other big-name designers. Not as cheap as you might expect, but still worth a rummage.

Esse Tre Group

Map 3, H4. Via del Seminario 111 ©06.678.7661.
Daily 10am–7.30pm.
New and used clothing piled high, in this huge, eclectic shop just steps away from the Pantheon. Used leather jackets, American T-shirts, and fake Levis mingled with new business suits and casual wear.

Energie

Map 5, F6. Via del Corso 486 ©06.322.7046, *energie@iol.it*
Mon–Sun 10am–8pm.
One of the city's most popular clothing stores, mainly aimed at teenagers, with expensive trendy clothes, loud music and an omnipresent group of kids hanging out around the entrance. Definitely the place to be seen if you're loaded and under 21.

Giorgio Sermonata Gloves

Map 5, G7. Via Frattina 58 ©06.679.6924.
Mon 3.30–7.30pm, Tues–Sat 10am–7.30pm.
A glove specialist, with a large collection of Italian gloves in every price range, that has for the past 35 years catered to celebrities, politicians and tourists.

CLOTHING AND ACCESSORIES

Designer Stores

Dolce & Gabbana Piazza di Spagna 82–83 ✆06.679.2294.

Fendi Via Borgognona 36–40 ✆06.679.7641.

Ferre Via Borgognona 6 ✆06.679.7445.

Gianni Versace Via Borgognona 24–26 ✆06.670.5037.

Giorgio Armani Via Condotti 77 ✆06.699.1460.

Gucci Via Condotti 8 ✆06.678.9340.

Krizia Piazza di Spagna 87 ✆06.679.3772.

Missoni Piazza di Spagna 78 ✆06.679.2555.

Moschino Via Belsiana 53–57 ✆06.6920.0415.

Prada Via Condotti 92–95 ✆06.679.0897.

Salvatore Ferragamo Via Condotti 63 ✆06.679.1565.

Valentino Via Condotti 13 ✆06.678.3656.

La Cravatta su Misura

Map 3, H4. Via Seminario 93 ✆06.6994.2199.

Mon 3.30–7.30pm, Tues–Sat 10am–7.30pm.

Ezio Pellicano only sells one thing: ties, made by Ezio himself or his daughter. You can buy any of the hundreds of ties you see on display, or you can choose from one of the hundreds of rolls of material and have your own made up in about a week.

Leo Calzature

Map 3, H8. Via del Portico d'Ottavia 57.

Mon–Fri & Sun 9am–7.30pm.

A bargain hunter's delight, hidden away in the Jewish Ghetto, and selling a large variety of new shoes and occasional leftovers from past fashion shows at a price you can't beat: all shoes are L25,000.

Ugo Celli

Map 3, G7. Via Arenula 86 ✆06.880.355.

Mon–Sat 9am–8pm.

Popular shop, filled with high-quality, high-priced shoes from all over Italy.

DEPARTMENT STORES

COIN
Map 6, G1. Via Cola do Rienzo 173 ©06.324.3319; Piazza Appio 7 ©06.708.0020; Via Mantova 1B ©06.841.6279.

Mon 3.30–8pm, Tues–Sat 9.30am–1.30pm & 3.30–8pm.

Inexpensive clothes, accessories, and a great place to find cheap kitchenware.

La Rinascente
Map 3, I2. Largo Chigi 20 ©06.679 7691.

Mon–Sat 9am–9pm, Sun 10.30am–8pm.

Part of a national chain, this is the closest Rome gets to an upscale department store like a Harrod's or a Macy's, with several floors of high-quality merchandise.

Standa
Map 7, E4. Viale di Trastevere 62 ©06.589.8229; Via Cola di Rienzo 173 ©06.324.319.

Mon 3.30–8pm, Tues–Sat 9am–8pm.

Reasonably priced clothing for men and women, linens, but most convenient for their grocery store in the basement.

Upim
Map 4, C7. Via Nazionale 211 ©06.484.502; Piazza Santa Maria Maggiore ©06.446.5579; Via Tritone 172 ©06.678.3336.

Mon noon–8pm, Tues–Sat 9am–8pm.

The most inexpensive of the chain stores, good for cheap clothes and household goods.

DEPARTMENT STORES

FOOD AND WINE

Buccone
Map 5, E7. Via di Ripetta 19 ✆06.361.2154.
Mon–Tues 9am–8.30pm, Wed–Sat 9am–midnight, Sun
10am–7.30pm.
Every alcoholic beverage you could dream of, with a large
selection of wines from all over the world, spirits, even ten-litre
bottles of grappa.

Castroni
Map 6, F2. Via Cola di Rienzo 196 ✆06.687.4383.
Mon–Sat 8am–8pm.
Huge international food store with a large selection of Italian
treats including chocolates, pastas, sauces, and olive oils, as well
as hard to find international favourites like plum pudding and
Mexican specialities.

Del Frate
Map 6, F1. Via degli Scipioni 118/128a ✆06.321.1612.
Mon–Sat 8am–8pm.
This large wine and spirits shop is located on a quiet street
near the Vatican, and has all the Barolos and Chiantis you
could want, alongside shelves full of grappa in all shapes and
sizes.

Gusto
Map 5, F6. Piazza Augusto Imperatore 9 ✆06.322.6273.
Mon–Sun 10.30am–2am.
Everything for the aspirant gourmet: bottled olive oils and
sauces, spices, chocolate, jams, wine, decanters, glasses, kitchen
appliances – and even a large selection of cookbooks in
English.

FOOD AND WINE

Panella

Map 4, E10. Via Merulana 54 ℂ06.487.2435, fax 06.487.2344.
Mon–Fri 8am–1.30pm & 5–8pm, Sat 8am–1.30pm and 4.30–8pm,
Sun 8.30am–1.30pm.

The art of bread making is the speciality here, as well as
pasta, like colourful *sombrerini* (hats), packaged to take
home.

Rome's food markets are detailed on p.318.

GIFTS, CRAFTS, HOUSEHOLD GOODS

Art'e

Map 3, G4. Piazza Rondanini 32 ℂ06.683.3907.
Mon 1–7.30pm, Tues–Sat 9.30am–7.30pm.

Ultramodern kitchenware and home furnishings, including
lamps, clocks and kitchen utensils and appliances in flashy neon
colours and shiny stainless steel. The perfect stylish gift to
yourself from Italy.

Artigianato in Cuoio

Map 3, F7. Via dei Chiavari 39 ℂ06.6830.7297.
Mon 3.30–7.30pm, Tues–Sat 9.30am–1.30pm & 3.30–7.30pm.

On a quiet street near Campo dei Fiori, this leather shop is
filled with beautifully hand-crafted products – belts, luggage,
handbags, etc – all made in their workshop a few doors down.

La Bottega del Marmoraro

Map X5, G6. Via Margutta 53B ℂ06.320.7660.
Mon–Sat 9am–1pm and 3.30–7.30pm.

Enrico and Sandro Fiorentini, a father-and-son team, are true
artisans, creating personalized marble plaques for every
occasion.

GIFTS, CRAFTS, HOUSEHOLD GOODS

Campo Marzio Penne

Map 3, H3. Via Campo Marzio 41 ©06.6880.7877.
Mon 3.30–7.30pm, Tues–Sat 9.30am–1pm & 3.30pm–7.30pm.
Small shop dedicated to exquisite pens and writing accessories.

Canova

Map 6, F4. Via della Conciliazione 4F ©06.6880.6373, fax 06.689.3507.
Daily 9am–7pm.
One of the nicer gift shops leading up to St Peter's, with its fair
share of religious souvenirs, and some delicately hand-crafted
chess sets.

Carmignani

Map 3, H3. Via della Colonna Antonina 42–43 ©06.679.5449.
Tues–Sat 10am–2pm and 3pm–7.30pm.
Even if you don't smoke, you will appreciate the beauty of the
handmade pipes, shiny silver cigar holders and cutters, and
poker sets, in this small shop a few minutes from the Pantheon.

Cesare Diomedi

Map 4, C6. Piazza San Bernardo 99 ©06.488.4822.
Mon–Sat 9am–7.30pm.
A few minutes' walk from Piazza della Repubblica, two floors
filled with Versace clocks, Cartier wallets, and all sorts of other
fancy gifts for every occasion.

C.U.C.I.N.A.

Map 5, G6. Via del Babuino 118A ©06.679.1275.
Mon 3.30–7.30pm, Tues–Fri 9.30am–7.30pm, Sun 10.30am–7.30pm.
A basement shop filled with modern kitchen appliances,
including a large selection of Italian *cafeterie*.

Fratelli Alinari

Map 5, G6 Via Alibert 16A ©06.679.2923, fax 06.6994.1998.
Mon–Sat 3.30–7.30pm

If you want to know what Rome's piazzas looked like before
McDonald's, come here for their selection of black and white
photographs of Rome from at least 100 years ago.

Frette
Map 5, G6. Piazza Spagna 10 ✆06.679.0673, fax 06.6994.1843
nromad@frette.it
Mon 3.30–7.30pm, Tues–Sat 9.30am–1.30pm & 3.30–7.30pm.
A luxurious linen shop, located among all the designer shops in
Piazza Spagna. They are happy to fill custom orders and will
ship their product anywhere.

Il Gancio
Map 3, H4. Via del Seminario 82/83 ✆06.679.6646.
Mon 3.30–7.30pm, Tues–Sat 10am–1pm and 3.30–7.30pm.
High-quality leather bags, purses, shoes all made right here, in
the workshop on the premises.

Guaytamelli
Map 7, D3. Via del Moro 59 ✆06.588.0704
Mon 3.00–8pm, Tues–Sat 10am–1pm & 3.30–8pm.
A unique little shop in the heart of Trastevere dedicated to
ancient ways of telling the time. Especially popular are finger-
sized sundial rings, available in silver or gold.

Horvath
Map 4, D6. Via V.E. Orlando 91 ✆06.474.1607.
Mon–Sat 9am–9pm, Sun 11am–9pm.
Unusual collection of replica ancient Roman armour, swords
and daggers.

Pineider
Map 5, H7. Via Due Macelli 68 ✆06.239.344, fax 06.239.447.
Mon 3.30–7.30pm, Tues–Sat 10am–1.30pm & 3.30–7.30pm.
An exclusive store that has been selling beautiful handmade

GIFTS, CRAFTS, HOUSEHOLD GOODS

paper, invitations, and writing materials for Roman society since 1774.

Vacanze Romane

Map 3, H4. Via dei Pastini 18a ©06.6992.5056.
Mon 3.30–7pm, Tues–Sat 10.30am–7pm.

Upscale gift shop with fun and often tacky "art" souvenirs – suitcases decorated with Raphael's angels, Michelangelo lampshades and suchlike.

MUSIC

Metropoli Rock

Map 4, D9. Via Cavour 72 ©06.488.0443.
Mon–Sat 9am–1pm & 4–8pm.

The place to come if you are looking for old and out-of-print recordings – whether it's classical, rock, or jazz. Two floors stocked floor-to-ceiling with vinyl, 33rpm and 45rpm, as well as new and used CDs.

Ricordi

Map 3, K6. Via Cesare Battisti 120 ©06.679.8022.
Mon–Sat 9am–7.30pm, Sun 3.30pm–8pm.

Rome's largest and most complete music store, with a good array of CDs, plus also books on music, scores, musical instruments, videos in their original language, sound equipment – and concert tickets.

Disfunzioni Music

Map 4, I9. Via degli Etruschi 4–14 ©06.446.1984.
Mon–Sat 10.30am–7.30pm.

Supplying nearby college students with a huge collection of both new and used music. A large selection of underground, rare and bootlegged recordings.

MARKETS

Borghetto Flaminio
Map 5, E3. Piazza della Marina 32.
Sept–June Sún 10am–7pm; entrance L3000.
A partly covered flea market with plenty of knick-knacks,
designer clothing and antiques. Rummage alongside Rome's
upper classes and celebrities – Cher was a recent sighting
here.

Fontanella Borghese
Map 5, F7. Piazza Fontanella Borghese.
Mon–Sat 8am–sunset.
A small print market off Via del Corso, where you can find
expensive antique prints and etchings along with inexpensive
reproductions.

Galleria delle Stimmate
Map 3, H6. Largo delle Stimante 1.
Sept–April last Sun of the month 10am–7.30pm.
Mostly household goods, and some jewellery, with some great
finds like antique lace, silver serving dishes, and old cutlery.

L'Antico in Terrazza Peroni
Map 5, N4. Via Mantova 24.
Third Sun of every month 10am–8pm; entrance L2500.
Located in the underground parking garage of the former
Peroni brewery, this is basically a regular carboot sale.

Porta Portese
Map 7, C7. Viale Trastevere.
Sun 5am–2pm.
By far, Rome's most famous and largest market, with hundreds
of stalls selling a myriad of goods, including antiques, clothing,

MARKETS

carpets, art, tools, appliances, fake brand-name jeans, linens, and even puppies.

Sotto I Portici
Map 5, F6. Piazza Augusto Imperatore.
Sept–June third Sun of every month 10am–sunset.
Flea market selling a diverse mix of clothing, household items and antiques.

Underground
Map 5, I7. Via Francesco Crispi 96.
Oct–June first Sun of each month and the Sat before; Sat 10am–8pm, Sun 10.30am–7.30pm.
Located in an underground parking garage near Piazza Spagna, and selling all the usual flea market finds, but with a special section for children's goods.

Via Sannio
Map 4, G14. Via Sannio.
Mon–Sat 8am–1pm.
Centrally located market selling mostly new and used clothing.

Food Markets

Rome's **food markets** are a perfect place to stop to pick up a snack or picnic provisions. The one on **Piazza di Campo de' Fiori** (map 3, E7) is the city's most famous and picturesque, and has been around for the last four hundred years. Other central options include the **Quattro Coronati** market, near the Colosseum (map 4, D13), the one on **Piazza Vittorio Emanuele**, not far from near Termini (map 4, F10), and **Piazza San Cosimato**, in Trastevere (map 7, C4). Most are open Mon–Sat 6am–2pm.

FOOD MARKETS

Sports and outdoor activities

Spectator sports are popular in Italy, although the hallowed *calcio*, or football, is far and away the most popular, and tends to overshadow everything else – a rule to which Rome, with two clubs in the top flight, is no exception. As for **participation in sport**, there isn't the same compulsion to hit the hell out of a squash ball or sweat your way through an aerobics class after work as there is, say, in Britain or the US. However, Mussolini placed a special emphasis on fitness, and the notion of keeping fit and being active is as fashionable a notion here nowadays as it is in most European countries – especially when it offers the opportunity to wear the latest designer gear.

FOOTBALL

Rome's two **football** teams, **Roma** and **Lazio**, play at the Stadio Olimpico, on Via del Foro Italico, on alternate Sundays from September to May, reachable by way of metro line A to Ottaviano, then bus #32, or by taking bus #910 from Termini.

Unsurprisingly, feelings run high between the two teams, and derby games are big – and sometimes violent – occasions. **Roma**, traditionally the team of the inner-city urban working-class, was until recently the better of the two sides, but have in recent years ceded ground to **Lazio**, aided by the drive and money of their president Sergio Cragnotti, who has built a dynamic squad full of international stars. At time of writing, both teams were challenging for the *scudetto,* or Italian championship, making local derbies even more of needle matches. We've given ticket details below, but bear in mind that the Stadio Olimpico is an enormous stadium, capacity 100,000, and at most games, except perhaps Roma-Lazio clashes, you should be able to get a ticket for all but the cheapest seats on the night.

Lazio supporters traditionally occupy the Curva Nord end of the ground, where you can get seats for around L28,000; seats in the *distinti*, or corners of the ground, or the *tribuna*, along the sides, are more expensive; reckon on paying around L100,000 for a reasonable *tribuna* ticket. To book ahead, try Lazio Point, Via Farini 34 (Mon–Sat 9am–7pm; ©06.482.6768), the Lazio ticket office (©06.323.7333), or the stadium itself. More information on *www.sslazio.it*

Roma fans occupy the Curva Sud, which is usually completely sold out to season ticket holders, making a visit to a Roma game a slightly more expensive business, since the cheapest seat you'll find will be in the *distinti*, at about L38,000. The Roma team office has information about ticket outlets and availability (©06.506.0200), or go directly to Orbis at Piazza Esquilino 37 (Mon–Sat 9.30am–1pm © 4–7.30pm; ©06.482.7403, no credit cards). Again, there's more information on *www.asromacalcio.it*

If you want more information about the Italian
football season in general, the Federazione Italiana
Giuoco Calcio (©06.84.911) can give you information
(in Italian) about all the season's games. Or, if you
speak good enough Italian, get hold of one of the
Italian sports newspapers, which are published daily.
The Rome paper is the Corriere dello Sport and will
have details of any upcoming games – as will Time
Out Roma.

GOLF

If you simply can't go a week or two without hitting a ball,
it's worth knowing that **golf** is slowly becoming a popular
sport in Italy. Most clubs welcome non-members but you
must be able to produce a membership card from your
home-town club. For more information call the Federazione
Italiana Golf, Via le Tiziano 74 (©06.323.1825). Among a
number of the better-known and more easily accessible golf
courses, there's Circolo del Golf di Roma, Via Appia Nuova
716A (©06.780.3407, fax 06.7834.6219; closed Mon); Golf
Club Parco de'Medici, Viale Parco de'Medici 22
(©06.655.3477, fax 06.655.3344; closed Tues); and Country
Club Castel Gandolfo, Via Santo Spirito 13, Castel Gandolfo
(©06.931.2301, fax 06.931.2244; closed Mon). All of the
above offer an eighteen-hole course and a driving range.

JOGGING

Except for one day in March during the Rome Marathon,
which circles around Rome's most famous monuments,
crazy drivers and crowds of people make it impossible, and
sometimes even dangerous, to **jog** in the city. Luckily,

though, there are plenty of green parks where you can escape the traffic. The most popular is **Villa Borghese**, where there are plenty of places to jog, including the Piazza di Siena, a grass horsetrack in the centre of the park. Other good options include the **Villa Ada**, a lush and vast green space just outside the city centre, which has a running track, and the **Villa Doria Pamphili** above Trastevere, which offers nice paths with exercise stations along the way. For more central – and public – jogging, the Circo Massimo is the perfect size, and shape, although it gets crowded with tourists early on. For more information about the **Rome Marathon** call the Italia Marathon Club (℮06.406.5064)

RIDING

There are not very many options for those who are looking to go **horse riding** in Rome. Il Galoppatoio, Via de Galoppatoio (℮06.322.6797), is a posh riding club that offers expensive lessons in an idyllic atmosphere deep in the heart of Villa Borghese.

SWIMMING

If you feel like cooling off from a hot summer day, a dip in a **pool** may be the perfect cure. Unfortunately, most of Rome's pools are privately run and can be quite expensive, although La Piscina delle Rose, Viale America 20 (℮06.592.6717), and Oasi della Pace, Via degli Eugenii 2 (℮06.718.4550), will only set you back around L15,000 a time. Of course, you could also either check into a hotel with a pool, or go to one of the hotels that let the public use their facilities. The *Cavalieri Hilton*, Via Cadloro 101 (℮06.3509.2950), and *Parco dei Principi*, Via Frescobaldi 5 (℮06.854.421), are two such places, and you can swim in a luxurious setting, but it will cost up to L50,000 for the day.

RIDING, SWIMMING

322

TENNIS

The massive Foro Italico sports complex hosts the **Italian Open**, one of Rome's major sporting events, each May. For more information contact the Federazione Italiana Tennis Via Eustachio 9 (&06.855.894), or the Foro Italico (&06.321.9064). If you want to **hire courts** to play, the Foro Italico also has public courts, or there's the Circolo della Stampa, Piazza Mancini (&06.323.2452) and Tennis Belle Arte, Via Flaminia 158 (&06.360.0602).

Kids' Rome

I talians love **children**. Don't be surprised by how much attention people pay yours here: peeking into buggies and cheek-pinching are quite normal, as is help lugging carriages up steps and giving up a seat for you and your child on public transport.

That said, Rome has a surprisingly limited amount of activities specifically geared towards children. Luckily, touring the sites of Rome is something of an educational experience, and one that children can enjoy – especially **Castel Sant'Angelo**, the **Colosseum**, and of course throwing coins into the **Trevi Fountain**. Pick up the English version of *Conosci Roma*, available free from any tourist kiosk; it's a **children's map** of the centre with interesting facts about sights, daily life of ancient Rome and stickers.

Of Rome's parks, the **Villa Borghese** is convenient, and has a lot to offer kids – pedalboats, a little train, pony rides, bikes, and a **zoo**. If all else fails, there's always **Luna Park**, a large amusement park in EUR, or if nothing strikes the right note, you can always head to the closest *gelato* stand. For more **information**, *Romacè*'s English section often has details of what's on for children that week, as does *Time Out Roma* – albeit in Italian.

PARKS AND OUTDOOR ACTIVITIES

Gianicolo
Map 2, B10–11.

This park, high up on Janiculum hill, is a good place to keep kids amused, with pony rides, bumper cars, puppet shows and other games, while adults enjoy a great view of the city below.

Luna Park
Map 2, EUR inset. Via delle Tre Fontane.

Mon–Fri 3–8pm, Sat 3pm–1am, Sun 10am–1pm & 3–10pm; free entrance, rides cost L2000–5000.

An amusement park in the EUR district, this is the only place in Rome that you'll find big-scale amusements, like a roller-coaster, haunted house, Ferris wheel, and the like. It's a bit dated, but is still a popular destination for families.

Villa Ada
Map 2, H1.

Beautiful grounds just north of the city with plenty to keep youngsters amused, including a roller-skating rink, bike paths, two playgrounds, and ponds.

Villa Borghese
Map 5.

A huge park offering plenty of entertainment for young ones. Enter at the Viale delle Belle Arti entrance to find pony rides, a children's train, swings and paddleboats. Kids might also be interested in the *Bioparco* on Via del Giardino Zooligico, (daily 9am–6pm; ✆06.360.8211), a once poorly kept zoo that has undergone many changes. It now also has a museum next door – see below – and often face-painting at weekends.

PARKS AND OUTDOOR ACTIVITIES

MUSEUMS

Museo dei Bambini
Map 5, E3. Via Flaminia 80 ©06.3600.5488.
Set to open sometime in the year 2000, Rome's long-antici-
pated children's museum is geared towards children under
twelve, and has a variety of hands-on activities, teaching
youngsters about all aspects of the world beyond. There is also
supposed to be a laboratory where kids can participate in
experiments.

Museo di Zoologia
Map 5, I2. Via Aldovrandi 18 ©06.321.6586.
Tues–Sun 9am–5pm; L5000, kids under 18 free.
Located next to the zoo, this museum is getting a facelift. A
new permanent exhibit, *Animals and their Habitats*, is on display
in a new wing, while a variety of stuffed animals fill the older
part of the museum.

Museo della Civiltà Romana
Map 2, EUR inset. Piazza Agnelli 10 ©06.592.6041.
Tues–Sat 9am–7pm, Sun 9am–1.30pm; L5000, kids under 12 free.
On your way to Luna Park, stop by the Roman Civilization
museum, where you can see replicas of Rome's famous statues
and buildings, as well as interesting models of Imperial and
Ancient Rome.

TOYS AND CLOTHING

Al Sogno
Map 3, E4. Piazza Navona 53 ©06.686.4198.
Mon 3.30–7.30pm, Tues–Sat 9.30am–1pm & 3.30–7.30pm.
Perfectly located at the north end of Piazza Navona, two floors

Rome's Puppet Theatres

Puppetry has been delighting Italian children for hundreds of years, and Rome has a few venues for viewing true puppeteers in action. Sometimes you can find a show in English, but the storyline is visually explanatory and kids don't seem to care whether they understand the words or not.

The outdoor theatres on the Janiculum Hill (see above), and in EUR on Largo K. Ataturk, are said to be the only places to view the true puppeteers left in Rome. Both are free, although a small donation is expected. You can also see shows near the Janiculum at *Teatro Verde*, Circonvallazione Gianicolense 10 (*©*06.588.2034), a children's theatre where they also put on musicals and marionette shows (L12,000). Most puppet shows go on from around 4pm till 7pm on weekdays and 10.30am until 1pm at weekends.

of stuffed animals, handmade dolls, board games, and replicas of Roman soldiers.

Benetton

Map X, YZ. Via Cesare Battisti 129 *©*06.6992.4010.
Mon 3.30–7.30pm, Tues–Sat 9.30am–1pm & 3.30–7.30pm.
Just one of the several locations of this famous Italian chain store that sells fairly expensive clothes for children and adults. This one conveniently has a children's hairdresser on the second floor.

Bertè

Map 3, F5. Piazza Navona 108 *©*06.687.5011.
Mon 3.30–7.30pm, Tues–Sat 9.30am–1pm & 3.30–7.30pm.
One of Rome's oldest toy stores at the other end of the Piazza from *Al Sogno,* that has a complete range of toys for children of all ages.

TOYS AND CLOTHING

La Bufana

There are many stories about **La Bufana**, always depicted as an ugly old woman who flies along on a broom draped in black. The most recognized version is that she was outside sweeping when the three kings walked by, she stopped them and asked where they were going. The kings responded that they were following a star, in search of a newborn baby. They invited her to come along, but she declined, saying she had too much sweeping and cleaning to do. When she found out who it was the kings were off to find, her regret for not having gone with them was so great that she has spent eternity rewarding good children with presents and sweets and bad children with pieces of coal on the day of Epiphany, January 6.

Each year, from early December until January 6, **Piazza Navona** sets up the **Bufana toy fair**, where endless stalls tempt children with every sort of sticky, gooey sweets and even chunks of black sugar made to look like coal. There are also toy stands and several manger scenes where children sometimes leave letters for La Bufana, asking her for specific presents and toys.

Città del Sole
Map 3, F4. Via della Scrofa 66 ✆06.6880.3805.
Mon 3.30–7.30pm, Tues–Sat 11am–1.30pm.
Toys, games and books for kids in a great central location.

IANA
Map 6, F2. Via Cola di Rienzo 182 ✆06.6889.2668.
Mon 3.30–7.30pm, Tues–Sat 10am–1.30pm & 3.30pm-7.30pm.
Popular Italian chain store selling moderately priced kids' clothes.

TOYS AND CLOTHING

La Bottega di Marinella
Map 5, G6Z. Via Margutta 34 ⓒ06.324.4793, fax 06.361.4143.
Mon 3.30–7.30pm, Tues–Sat 9.30am–7.30pm.
Adorable children's store on swanky Via Margutta, selling their own designs of infant and young children's clothes, plus fabrics to brighten up any child's bedroom.

Marina Menasci
Map 5, H8. Via del Lavatore 87 ⓒ06.678.1981.
Mon 3.30–7.30pm, Tues–Sat 9.30am–1pm & 3.30–7.30pm.
Toy store that sells exclusively wooden toys, in a great location a few steps from the Trevi Fountain.

TOYS AND CLOTHING |

Directory

AIRLINES Alitalia, Via Bissolati 11 (information ℃06.65.643; 24hr domestic flight information ℃06.65.641; international flights ℃06.65.642); British Airways, Via Bissolati 54 (℃06.485.480; Fiumicino airport ℃06.6501.1513); TWA, Via Barberini 67 (℃06.47.211; Fiumicino airport ℃06.6595.4921). Note that most other airlines are either in or very close by Via Bissolati and Via Barberini.

AIRPORT ENQUIRIES Fiumicino ℃06.6595.3640/06.6595.4455; Ciampino ℃06.794.941.

AMERICAN EXPRESS Travel office and exchange facilities at Piazza di Spagna 38 (Mon–Fri 9am–5.30pm, Sat 9am–12.30; longer hours in the summer; ℃06.67.641).

AUTO CLUB D'ITALIA (ACI) ℃06.49.981; 24hr recorded information ℃06.44.77. Italy's automobile club has an English-speaking staff that can help you with driving or repair information at little or no cost. If you belong to an autoclub in your home country you may be entitled to free services. Call their free recorded number for weather and road closure information.

BIKE AND SCOOTER RENTAL Collalti, Via del Pellegrino 82 (℃06.6880.1084; closed Mon) does bike rental and repairs; Rent-a-Scooter Motoservices, Via F. Turati 50 (℃06.446.9222) is the best deal for scooters and offers a 10 percent discount to Rough Guide readers; Romarent, Vicolo dei Bovari 7a (©06.689.6555) and Roma Solutions, Corso Vittorio Emanuele II 204 (©06.446.9222/06.687.6922) rent both scooters and bikes.

CAR RENTAL All the usual suspects have desks at Fiumicino, and well-posted signs lead you to a number of rental booths in the parcheggio multipiano at Termini. In the city centre itself, there are, among others, Avis, Via Sardegna 38a (©06.4282.4728), Hertz, Via Veneto 156 (©06.321.6831), and Maggiore, Via Po 8 (©06.854.8698).

CAR REPAIR Call ©116 for emergency breakdown service. Otherwise, consult the ACI (see above) or the Yellow Pages under Autoriparazioni for specialized repair shops.

CLUB ALPINO ITALIANO Corso Vittorio Emanuele 305 (©06.683.2684).

DENTIST The Ospedale di Odontoiatria G. Eastman, Viale Regina Elena 287b, has a 24-hour emergency service (©06.8448.3232). If you're an EU citizen be sure to take your E111 form, which entitles you to buy a "ticket" for a consultation – currently L26,400.

DISABLED TRAVELLERS Although changes are in the works, Rome can be quite a challenge for those with disabilities. Contact the Consorzio Cooperative Integrate-COIN, Via Enrico Giglioli 54a (©06.2326.7504, toll free in Italy ©800.271.027), who have English-speaking 24hr information on their phone line, and produce a guide, Roma Accessible, which contains information on accessibility to major sites, museums, hotels and restaurants. Also, their Web sites – *www.coin@inroma.roma.it* and *www.andi.casaccia.enea.it/hometur.htm* – have additional information.

ELECTRICITY 220 volts. If coming from the US buy an adaptor before you come as they are more expensive once you get here.

EMBASSIES Australia, Corso Trieste 25c (©06.852.721 or for emergencies toll free at ©800.877.790); Britain, Via XX Settembre

80a (©06.482.5441); Canada, Via Zara 30 (©06.445.981); Ireland, Piazza Campitelli 3 (©06.697.9121); New Zealand, Via Zara 28 (©06.441.7171); USA, Via Veneto 119 (©06.46.741).

EMERGENCIES ©113. Both the Police and the Carabinieri have offices in Termini. Otherwise the most central police office is off Via del Corso in Piazza del Collegio Romano 3 (©06.46.861), and there's a Carabinieri office in Piazza Venezia to the right of Via del Corso.

EXCHANGE American Express (see above); Thomas Cook, Piazza Barberini 21a (Mon–Sat 9am–8pm, Sun 9.30am-5pm), and Via della Conciliazione 23 (Mon–Sat 9am–8pm, Sun 9.30am-5pm). Post offices will exchange American Express traveller's cheques and cash commission free. The last resort should be any of the many Ufficio Cambio, almost always offering the worst rates (despite "no commission" signs).

HOSPITAL In case of emergency ©113 or ©118. Otherwise the most central hospitals are the Policlinico Umberto I, Viale del Policlinico 155 (©06.49.971), and the Santo Spirito, Lungotevere in Sassia 1 (©06.68.351), near the Vatican. The Rome American Hospital, Via E. Longoni 81 (©06.22.551) is a private multi-speciality hospital with bilingual staff.

INTERNET We've listed Internet cafés on p.269. Otherwise try one of the following: Museo del Corso, Via del Corso 320 (Tues–Fri 10am–8pm, Sat 10am–10pm, Sun 10am–8pm, closed Mon; ©06.678.6209); Netgate, Piazza Firenze 25 (Mon–Sat 10.30am-10.30pm; ©06.689.3445); Internet Point, Via Gaeta 25, Mon-Sun 9am-12am; ©06.4782.3862). All offer Internet access for around L10,000 an hour.

LAUNDRY Onda Blu, at Via Principe Amedeo 70b and Via Lamarmora 12 (both daily 8am–10pm); Wash and Dry, Via Della Pelliccia 35 and Via Della Chiesa Nuova 15/16 (both daily 8am-10pm). All offer a wash including soap and tumble-drying for about L15,000 for a 6kg (15lb) load.

LIBRARIES The British Council, Via delle Quattro Fontane 20 (Mon–Tues & Thu–Fri 10am–1pm, Wed 2–5pm; closed Aug & Christmas; ©06.478.141), has a lending library, for which yearly membership costs L100,000. Non-members are, however, allowed to use it for reference purposes for free.. There's also a library at the American church of Santa Susanna, Via XX Settembre 14 (©06.482.7510), which also has a good noticeboard for finding work, accommodation and so on, and at the American Studies Center, Via M. Caetani 32 (©06.6880.1613), though this last is for reference only.

LOST PROPERTY For property lost on a train call ©06.4730.6682 (daily 7am–11pm); on a bus ©06.581.6040 (Mon and Fri 8.30am–1pm, Tues-Thurs 2.30-6pm); on the metro ©06.487.4309.

MODEM If you want to use your laptop's modem, bring a plug adapter and check with your Internet service provider to be sure you can access your account from Italy.

NEWSPAPERS English newspapers are available the same day of publication later in the afternoon at newsstands in Tormini, Piazza Colonna and Via Veneto. The International Herald Tribune, available at most newsstands, is printed in Italy and includes an Italian news supplement.

PHARMACIES Piram, Via Nazionale 228 (©06.488.0754) and Farmicia della Stazione, Piazza dei Cinquecento (©06.488.0019) are both open 24hr, year-round.

POST OFFICES Rome's main post office is at Piazza San Silvestro 18/20 (Mon–Fri 9am–6pm, Sat 9am–2pm; closes midday last Sat of each month). Other post offices are usually open Mon–Sat 8.30am–1.30pm. The Vatican Post Office, located on each side of St Peter's Square and in the Vatican Museums (Mon-Fri 8.30-7pm, Sat 8.30-6), is run by the Swiss postal service and is more reliable, faster and a bit more expensive than the often unreliable Italian post.

RADIO Radio Centro Suono (101.3 FM), plays more interesting music than most of the local radio stations; for regular rock, try Radio Rock (106.6). Radio Citta' Futura (97.7) plays a variety of alternative sounds, and at 10.30am daily has information on what's on in Rome.

TELEPHONES All phones take phone cards available at most *tabacchi*, bars, and newsstands for denominations of L5000, L10,000 and L15,000. Very few Italian phones take coins, but those that do can be found around Termini.

TIME Rome is one hour ahead of GMT, six hours ahead of Eastern Standard Time, and nine hours ahead of Pacific Standard Time in North America.

TRAIN ENQUIRIES For general enquires about schedules and prices, ℂ1478.88.088 (daily 7am–9pm).

TRAVEL AGENTS For discount tickets try the CTS offices at Via Genova 16 (ℂ06.462.0431) and Corso Vittorio Emanuele II 297 (ℂ06.687.2672), both open on Saturday mornings, when all the other travel agents are closed. Other good places to try are Viaggiare, Via San Nicola da Tolentino 15 (ℂ06.421.171), who have some English-speaking staff, and Elsy Viaggi, Via di Torre Argentina 80 (ℂ06.689.6460).

CONTEXTS

A brief history of Rome

No one knows precisely when Rome was founded. Excavations on the Palatine Hill have revealed the traces of an **Iron Age** village, which date back to the ninth or eighth century BC, but the **legends** relating to Rome's earliest history tell it slightly differently. Rea Silvia, a vestal virgin and daughter of a local king, Numitor, had twin sons – the product, she alleged, of a rape by Mars. They were supposed to be sacrificed to the god but the ritual wasn't carried out, and the two boys were abandoned and found by a wolf, who nursed them until their adoption by a shepherd, who named them **Romulus and Remus**. Later they laid out the boundaries of the city on the Palatine Hill, but it soon became apparent that there was only room for one ruler, and, unable to agree on the signs given to them by the gods, they quarrelled, Romulus killing Remus and becoming in 753 BC the city's first **monarch**, to be followed by six further kings. Whatever the truth of this, there's no doubt that Rome was an obvious spot to build a city: the Palatine and Capitoline hills provided security, and there was, of course, the river Tiber, which could be easily crossed here by way of the Isola Tiberina, making this a key location on the trade routes between Etruria and Campania.

The Roman Republic

Rome as a kingdom lasted until about 507 BC, when the people rose up against the tyrannical King Tarquinius and established a **Republic**, appointing the first two consuls and instituting a more democratic form of government. The city prospered under the Republic, growing greatly in size and subduing the various tribes of the surrounding areas – the **Etruscans** to the north, the **Sabines** to the east, the **Samnites** to the south. The Etruscans were subdued in

474 BC, the Samnites a little later, and despite a heavy defeat by the **Gauls** in 390 BC, by the following century the city had begun to extend its influence beyond the boundaries of what is now mainland Italy, pushing south into Sicily and across the ocean to Africa and Carthage. By the time it had fought and won the **third Punic War** against its principal rival, **Carthage**, in 146 BC, it had become the dominant power in the Mediterranean, subsequently taking control of present-day Greece and the Middle East, and expanding north also, into what is now France, Germany and Britain.

Domestically, the Romans built roads – notably the Via Appia, which dates back to 312 BC – and developed their civic structure, with new laws and far-sighted political reforms, one of which cannily brought all of the Republic's vanquished enemies into the fold as Roman citizens. However, the history of the Republic was also one of **internal strife**, marked by factional fighting among the patrician ruling classes, as everyone tried to grab a slice of the riches that were pouring into the city from its plundering expeditions abroad – and the ordinary people, or plebeians, enjoying little more justice than they had under the Roman monarchs. This all came to a head in 44 BC, when **Julius Caesar**, having proclaimed himself dictator, was murdered in the Theatre of Pompey on 15 March, by conspirators concerned at the growing concentration of power into one man's hands.

After his murder, Julius Caesar's deputy, **Mark Antony**, briefly took control, joining forces with Lepidus and Caesar's adopted son, Octavian, in a **triumvirate** that marshalled armies that fought and won against those controlled by Caesar's assassins, Brutus and Cassius, in a famous battle at Philippi, in modern-day Greece, in 42 BC. Their alliance was further cemented by Antony's marriage to Octavians's sister, Octavia, in 40 AD, but in spite of this a brief period of turmoil followed, in which Antony, unable to put his political ambitions before his emotional alliance with the queen of Egypt, Cleopatra, was defeated by Octavian at the battle of Actium in 31 BC – escaping to Alexandria, where he committed suicide, with his lover, the queen.

The Roman Empire

A triumph for the new democrats over the old guard, **Augustus** (27 BC–14 AD) – as Octavian became known – was the first true Roman emperor, in firm control of Rome and its dominions. Responsible more than anyone for heaving Rome into the Imperial era, he was determined to turn the city – as he claimed – from one of stone to one of marble, building arches, theatres and monuments of a magnificence suited to the capital of an expanding empire. Perhaps the best and certainly the most politically canny of Rome's many emperors, Augustus reigned for forty years. He was succeeeded by **Tiberius** (14–37), who ruled from the island of Capri for the last years of his reign, and he in turn by **Caligula** (37–41), who was assassinated after just four years in power. **Claudius** (41–54), his uncle, followed, at first reluctantly, and proved to be a wise ruler, only to be succeeded by his stepson, **Nero** (54–68), whose reign became more notorious for its excess than its prudence, and led to a brief period of warring and infighting after his murder in 68 AD.

Rome's next rulers, the **Flavian emperors**, restored some stability, starting with **Vespasian** (69–79), who did his best to obliterate all traces of Nero, not least with an enormous ampitheatre in the grounds of Nero's palace, later know as the Colosseum, and ending with the emperor **Trajan** (98–117), under whose rule the empire reached its maximum limits. Trajan died in 117 AD, giving way to **Hadrian** (117–138), who continued the grand and expansionist agenda of his predecessor, and arguably provided the empire's greatest years. The city swelled to a population of a million or more, its people housed in cramped apartment blocks or insulae; crime in the city was rife, and the traffic problem apparently on a par with today's, leading one contemporary writer to complain that the din on the streets made it impossible to get a good night's sleep. But it was a time of peace and prosperity, the Roman upper classes living a life of indolent luxury, in sumptuous residences with proper plumbing and central heating, and the empire's borders being ever more extended.

The **decline of Rome** is hard to date precisely, but it could be said to have started with the emperor **Diocletian** (284–305), who assumed power in 284 and divided the empire into two parts, east and west, while becoming known for his relentless persecution of Christians. The first Christian emperor, **Constantine** (312–337), shifted the seat of power to Byzantium in 330, and Rome's heady period as capital of the world was over, the wealthier members of the population moving east and a series of invasions by Goths in 410 and Vandals about forty years later only serving to quicken the city's ruin. By the sixth century the city was a devastated and infection-ridden shadow of its former self, with a population of just 20,000.

The Christian era

It was the papacy, under Pope **Gregory I** ("the Great"; 590–604) in 590, that rescued Rome from its demise. In an eerie echo of the empire, Gregory sent missions all over Europe to spread the word of the Church and publicize its holy relics, so drawing pilgrims, and their money, back to the city, and in time making the papacy the natural authority in Rome. The pope took the name "Pontifex Maximus" after the title of the high priest of classical times (literally "the keeper of the bridges", which were vital to the city's well-being). Four of the city's great basilicas were built during this time, along with a great many other early Christian churches, underlining the city's phoenix-like resurrection under the popes, who as well as building their own new structures converted those Roman buildings that were still standing – for example fortifying the Castel Sant'Angelo to repel invaders. The crowning a couple of centuries later of Charlemagne as Holy Roman Emperor, with dominions spread Europe-wide but answerable to the pope, intensified the city's revival, and the pope and city became recognized as head of the Christian world.

There were times over the next few hundred years when the power of Rome and the papacy was weakened: Robert Guiscard, the Norman king, sacked the city in 1084; a century later, a dispute between the city and the papacy led to a series of popes relocating in Viterbo; and in 1308 the French-born Pope **Clemente V** (1305–16) transferred his court to Avignon. In the mid-fourteenth century, Cola di Rienzo seized power, setting himself up as the people's saviour from the decadent ways of the city's rulers and forming a new Roman republic. But the increasingly autocratic ways of the new ruler soon lost popularity; Cola di Rienzo was deposed, and in 1376 Pope **Gregory XI** (1370–78) returned to Rome.

The Renaissance and Counter-Reformation

As time went on, power gradually became concentrated in a handful of **families**, who swapped the top jobs, including the papacy itself, between them. Under the burgeoning power of the pope, the city began to take on a new aspect: churches were built, the city's pagan monuments rediscovered and preserved, and artists began to arrive in Rome to work on commissions for the latest pope, who would invariably try to outdo his predecessor's efforts with ever more glorious self-aggrandizing buildings and works of art.

This process reached a head during the **Renaissance**; Bramante, Raphael and Michelangelo all worked in the city,

THE RENAISSANCE AND COUNTER-REFORMATION

on and off, throughout their careers. The reigns of Pope **Julius II** (1503–13), and his successor the Medici pope, **Leo X** (1513–22), were something of a golden age: the city was at the centre of Italian cultural and artistic life and site of the creation of great works of art like Michelangelo's frescoes in the Sistine Chapel, Raphael's Stanze in the Vatican Palace and fine buildings like the Villa Farnesina, Palazzo Farnese and Palazzo Spada, not to mention the commissioning of a new St Peter's as well as any number of other churches. The city was once again at the centre of things, and its population had increased to 100,000. However, in 1527 all this was brought abruptly to an end, when the armies of the Habsburg monarch, Charles V, swept into the city, occupying it – and wreaking havoc – for a year, while Pope **Clement VII** (1523–34) cowered in the Castel Sant'Angelo.

The ensuing years were ones of yet more restoration, and perhaps because of this it's the **seventeenth century** that has left the most tangible impression on Rome today, the vigour of the **Counter-Reformation** throwing up huge sensational monuments like the Gesù church that were designed to confound the scepticism of the new Protestant thinking, and again using pagan artefacts (like obelisks), not to mention the ready supply of building materials provided by the city's ruins, in ever more extravagant displays of wealth. The Farnese pope, **Paul III** (1534–50), was perhaps the most efficient at quashing anti-Catholic feeling, while, later, Pope **Sixtus V** (1585–90) was perhaps the most determined to mould the city in his own image, ploughing roads through the centre and laying out bold new squares at their intersections. This period also saw the completion of St Peter's under **Paul V** (1605–1621), and the ascendancy of Gian Lorenzo Bernini as the city's principal architect and sculptor under the Barberini pope, **Urban VIII** (1623–44) – a patronage that was extended under the Pamphili pope, **Innocent X** (1644–55).

The eighteenth century to World War II

The **eighteenth century** saw the decline of the papacy as
a political force, a phenomenon marked by the occupation
of the city in 1798 by Napoleon; **Pius VI** (1775–1800) was
unceremoniously sent off to France as a prisoner, and
Napoleon declared another Roman republic, with himself
at its head, which lasted until 1815, when papal rule was
restored under **Pius VII** (1800–23).

Thirty-four years later a pro-Unification caucus under
Mazzini declared the city a republic but was soon chased
out, and Rome had to wait until **Garibaldi** stormed the
walls in 1870 to join the unified country – the last but symbolically most important part of the Italian peninsula to do
so. "Roma o morte", Garibaldi had cried, and he wasted
no time in declaring the city the capital of the new kingdom under Vittorio Emanuele I, and confining the by now
quite powerless pontiff, **Pius IX** (1846–78), in the Vatican
until agreement was reached on a way to coexist.

As **capital** of a modern European country, Rome was
(some would say still is) totally ill-equipped, and the
Piemontese rulers of the new kingdom set about building
a city fit to govern from, cutting new streets through
Rome's central core (Via Nazionale, Via del Tritone) and
constructing grandiose buildings like the Altar of the
Nation. **Mussolini** took up residence in Rome in 1922,
and in 1929 signed the **Lateran Pact** with Pope **Pius XI**
(1922–39), a compromise which forced the Vatican to
accept the new Italian state and in return recognized the
Vatican City as sovereign territory, independent of Italy,
together with the key basilicas and papal palaces in Rome,
which remain technically independent of Italy to this day.
Mussolini's motivations weren't dissimilar to the popes,
however, when he bulldozed his way through the Roman
Forum and began work on the futuristic, self-publicizing

planned extension to the city known as EUR. Rome was declared an "open city" during **World War II**, and as such emerged from the war relatively unscathed. However, after Mussolini's death, and the end of the war, the Italian king, Vittorio Emanuele III, was forced to abdicate and Italy was declared a republic – still, however, with its capital in Rome.

Modern times

Since the war, Italy has become renowned as a country which changes its government, if not its politicians, every few months, and for the rest of Italy Rome has come to symbolize the inertia of their nation's government – at odds with both the slick, efficient North, and the poor, corrupt South. Despite this, the city's growth has been phenomenal in the post-war years, its population soaring to close on four million and its centre becoming ever more choked by traffic. Though famous in the **Sixties** as the home of Fellini's *Dolce Vita* and Italy's bright young things, Rome is still, even by Italian standards, a relatively provincial place, and one which is in some ways still trying to lug itself into the twenty-first century. Great efforts were made to prepare the city for the arrival of the **Millennium** and the millions of visitors who will come to celebrate the Jubilee (Holy Year) declared by the pope, and the city is looking better than ever; museums and monuments that have been closed for decades have reopened to an eager public. Traffic congestion is still a major problem in the city centre, but by the time you read this, it's hoped that there will never have been a better time to visit Rome.

Books about Rome

There have been an enormous number of **books** published about Rome over the years, both in English, and of course in Italian, and so the list below is inevitably extremely selective, concentrating on the odd travelogue, key texts on history and art that go much further than this guide, and on works of fiction that might be instructive – or fun – to read while you're here. To help find the books, we've listed the publisher, with the British publisher first, and the US publisher second, except when the publisher is the same in both territories, when we've only mentioned it once; where a book is published in only one territory, we've said so.

History, art and architecture

Jerome Carcopino *Daily Life in Ancient Rome* (Penguin/Yale University Press). Originally published in 1941, and consistently in print since, Carcopino's book is a classic, bringing to life the beliefs, social life and customs of ordinary Romans during the first two centuries AD, at the height of the Roman Empire.

Amanda Claridge *Oxford Archeological Guides: Rome.* (OUP). A well-conceived and excellently written concise guide to the archeology of the ancient city – a good investment if this is your particular area of interest.

Edward Gibbon *The History of the Decline and Fall of the Roman Empire* (Penguin). If you can't manage all six volumes, this abridged version is your best chance to read this classic text, covering the period from the second century AD to the fall of Constantinople in 1453, that was conceived amidst the ruins of the Roman Forum in the latter part of the eighteenth century.

Michael Grant *History of Rome* (Faber/Prentice Hall). Perhaps the best concise history of ancient Rome. Grant's style is direct, dispassionate and ultra-readable, detailing everything from the early Etruscan monarchs to the division of the empire.

Christopher Hibbert *Rome: Biography of a City* (Penguin). Simply put, the most entertaining and accessible historical introduction to Rome that you can buy – which is perhaps no more than you would expect from this most prolific of popular historians.

Charles L. Stinger *The Renaissance in Rome* (Indiana UP). The best-value book to focus exclusively on the Renaissance period in Rome, documenting well the rehabilitation of the city under the papacy.

Ingrid D. Rowland *The Culture of the High Renaissance: Ancients and Moderns in Sixteenth-Century Rome* (CUP). An expensive buy, but generally regarded as the best scholarly evocation of the high Renaissance in Rome – looking not only at the art and architecture of the period, but also at its economics, culture and sociology.

Giorgio Vasari *The Lives of the Artists* (OUP). There is no better background work on the artists of the Renaissance, written by a contemporary and correspondent of his subjects, who include Raphael, Michelangelo, and others less relevant to Rome. Available in a very readable English translation.

Travel and Impressions

Alan Epstein *As Romans Do*. (Morrow, US). Subtitled "the delights, dramas and daily diversions of life in the Eternal City", this is a contemporary look at modern Roman society that goes far beyond the familiar tourist attractions. Obviously a labour of love.

William Murray *The Fatal Gift*. Out of print, but worth trying to get hold of for its perceptive essays on history and contemporary Italian life and culture, especially with regard to Rome, where Murray lived for many years – first as an aspiring opera singer and later as a writer and journalist, filing regular pieces for the *New Yorker*. He writes with flair and enthusiasm, and, best of all, knows the country intimately.

H.V. Morton *A Traveller in Rome*. Like all Morton's books, this is a marvellously personal stroll around the sights, reflecting on history, architecture and culture. Rather dated, and currently out of print, but it should be relatively easy to get hold of.

Literature

Lyndsey Davies *Shadows in Bronze* (Arrow/Ballantine). Davies's second novel is perhaps the best introduction to the ancient Roman thrillers in which she specializes, following the doings of her ancient Roman sleuth, Marcus Didius Falco, during the period of the emperor Vespasian. Like later volumes, it has pace and humour, and is creditably well researched and nicely written. In the UK, *Falco on his Metal* (Arrow), incorporates three Falco novels, and as such makes for a good sample of Davies's work.

Alberto Moravia *A Woman of Rome* (Steerforth Press, US). Probably the most pre-eminent post-war Roman novelist, Moravia uses the Rome of the Mussolini era as a delicate backdrop for this detached yet compassionate tale of a Roman model and prostitute. See also *Roman Tales* (OUP), a varied collection of short stories that has the lives of ordinary Romans of the 1950s as its thread.

Allan Massie *Augustus*; *Tiberius*; *Caesar* (Sceptre/Carroll & Graff). Massie's series of novels aspires to re-create the Roman empire at its height through the imagined memoirs of its key figures. Massie takes himself rather seriously, and sometimes his characters don't quite come to life; but his research is impeccable, and these novels constitute a wonderfully palatable way into the minutiae of the era.

LITERATURE

Iain Pears *The Raphael Affair* (HarperCollins; Berkeley). Pears is best-known for his recent bestseller, *An Instance of the Fingerpost*, but he also writes thrillers with an art historical bent, of which this is one, primarily Rome-based example. Plenty of local colour, not to mention art-world intrigue concerning robbery, forgery and general skullduggery, and as fast-paced – and perhaps as far-fetched – as the others.

Stephen Saylor *The House of the Vestals* (Robinson/St Martin's Press). Light, occasionally amusing detective yarns set in the days of the Roman republic, in which Saylor's fictional detective, Giordanius the Finder, solves mysteries with consummate ease. This collection of short stories, filling in the gaps between Saylor's previous six Giordanius novels, is a good introduction.

John Varriano (ed.) *A Literary Companion to Rome* (John Murray/St Martin's Press). Arranged as a series of walking tours, this picks out the best of the many observations made about the city over the years. Entertaining in itself, but also a taster for many other writers and books on Rome that you may not have yet come across.

William Weaver (ed.). *Open City: Seven Writers in Postwar Rome* (Steerforth Press, US). An anthology of pieces by some of the best modern Italian novelists – Bassani, Silone, Moravia, Ginzburg, among others – selected and with an introduction by one of the most eminent post-war Italian translators.

Marguerite Yourcenar *Memoirs of Hadrian* (Penguin/Noonday). Yourcenar's slow-moving, reflective narrative, most of it in the form of letters to his nephew, Marcus Aurelius, details the main events of the emperor Hadrian's rule, documenting at once the Roman Empire at its height, and the very human anxieties of perhaps its wisest and most accomplished leader. See also Yourcenar's conceptual Roman novel, *A Coin in Nine Hands* (Penguin/University of Chicago).

LITERATURE

A brief guide to Italian

The ability to speak English confers prestige in Italy, and there's often no shortage of people willing to show off their knowledge, especially in Rome. However, using at least some Italian, however tentatively, can mark you out from the masses in a city used to hordes of tourists, and having a little more can open up the city no end.

Italian is one of the easiest European languages to learn, especially if you already have a smattering of French or Spanish. Easiest of all is the **pronunciation**, since every word is spoken exactly as it's written, and usually enunciated with exaggerated, open-mouthed clarity. All Italian words are **stressed** on the penultimate syllable unless an **accent** (´ or `) denotes otherwise. The only difficulties you're likely to encounter are the few **consonants** that are different from English:

c before e or i is pronounced as in **ch**urch, while **ch** before the same vowels is hard, as in **c**at.

sci or **sce** are pronounced as in **sh**eet and **sh**elter respectively.

The same goes with **g** – soft before e or i, as in **g**eranium; hard before h, as in **g**arlic.

gn has the ni sound of our o**ni**on.

gl in Italian is softened to something like li in English, as in stal**li**on.

h is not aspirated, as in **h**onour.

When **speaking** to strangers, the third person is the polite form (ie lei instead of tu for "you"); using the second person is a mark of disrespect or stupidity. It's also worth remembering that Italians don't use "please" and "thank you" half as much as we do: it's all implied in the tone, though if in doubt, err on the polite side.

The most user-friendly **phrasebook** is the Rough Guides' own *Italian*. Among **dictionaries**, *Collins* publish a comprehensive series: their *Gem* or *Pocket* dictionaries are fine for travelling purposes.

The Basics

Good morning	*Buon giorno*
Good afternoon/evening	*Buona sera*
Good night	*Buona notte*
Hello/goodbye	*Ciao* (informal; to strangers use phrases above)
Goodbye	*Arrivederci*
Yes	*Sì*
No	*No*
Please	*Per favore*
Thank you (very much)	*Grázie* (*molte/mille grazie*)
You're welcome	*Prego*
All right/that's OK	*Va bene*
How are you?	*Come stai/sta?* (informal/formal)
I'm fine	*Bene*
Do you speak English?	*Parla inglese?*
I don't understand	*Non ho capito*
I don't know	*Non lo so*
Excuse me	*Mi scusi/Prego*
Excuse me	*Permesso* (in a crowd)
I'm sorry	*Mi dispiace*
I'm here on holiday	*Sono qui in vacanza*
I'm British/Irish/ American/ Australian/ New Zealander	*Sono britannico/irlandese/ americana, australiana/ neozelandese*
Today	*Oggi*
Tomorrow	*Domani*
Day after tomorrow	*Dopodomani*
Yesterday	*Ieri*

Now	*Adesso*
Later	*Più tardi*
Wait a minute!	*Aspetta!*
Let's go!	*Andiamo!*
In the morning	*Di mattina*
In the afternoon	*Nel pomeriggio*
In the evening	*Di sera*
Here/There	*Qui/Là*
Good/Bad	*Buono/Cattivo*
Big/Small	*Grande/Píccolo*
Cheap/Expensive	*Económico/Caro*
Early/Late	*Presto/Ritardo*
Hot/Cold	*Caldo/Freddo*
Near/Far	*Vicino/Lontano*
Quickly/Slowly	*Velocemente/Lentamente*
With/Without	*Con/Senza*
More/Less	*Più/Meno*
Enough, no more	*Basta*
Mr / Mrs / Miss	*Signor / Signora / Signorina*
Entrance/Exit	*Entrata/Uscita*
Free entrance	*Ingresso líbero*
Gentlemen/Ladies	*Signori/Signore*
No smoking	*Vietato fumare*
WC/Bathroom	*Gabinetto/il bagno*
Open/Closed	*Aperto/Chiuso*
Closed for restoration	*Chiuso per restauro*
Closed for holidays	*Chiuso per ferie*
Pull/Push	*Tirare/Spingere*
Cash desk	*Cassa*
Go, walk	*Avanti*
Stop, halt	*Alt*

THE BASICS |

Numbers, words and phrases

Numbers

1	*uno*	20	*venti*
2	*due*	21	*ventuno*
3	*tre*	22	*ventidue*
4	*quattro*	30	*trenta*
5	*cinque*	40	*quaranta*
6	*sei*	50	*cinquanta*
7	*sette*	60	*sessanta*
8	*otto*	70	*settanta*
9	*nove*	80	*ottanta*
10	*dieci*	90	*novanta*
11	*undici*	100	*cento*
12	*dodici*	101	*centuno*
13	*tredici*	110	*centodieci*
14	*quattordici*	200	*duecento*
15	*quindici*	500	*cinquecento*
16	*sedici*	1000	*mille*
17	*diciassette*	5000	*cinquemila*
18	*diciotto*	10,000	*diecimila*
19	*diciannove*	50,000	*cinquantamila*

Accommodation

Hotel	*Albergo*
Is there a hotel nearby?	*C'è un albergo qui vicino?*
Do you have a room . . .	*Ha una cámera . . .*
for one/two/three person/people	*per una/due/tre persona/e*
for one/two/three night/s	*per una/due/tre notte/i*
for one/two week/s	*per una/due settimana/e*
with a double bed	*con un letto matrimoniale*
with a shower/bath	*con una doccia/un bagno*
with a balcony	*con una terrazza*

hot/cold water	*acqua calda/freddo*
How much is it?	*Quanto costa?*
It's expensive	*È caro*
Is breakfast included?	*È compresa la prima colazione?*
Do you have anything cheaper?	*Ha niente che costa di meno?*
Full/half board	*Pensione completa/mezza pensione*
Can I see the room?	*Posso vedere la cámera?*
I'll take it	*La prendo*
I'd like to book a room	*Vorrei prenotare una cámera*
I have a booking	*Ho una prenotazione*

Questions and directions

Where?	*Dove?*
(where is/where are . . . ?)	*(Dov'è/Dove sono . . . ?)*
When?	*Quando?*
What? (what is it?)	*Cosa? (Cos'è?)*
How much/many?	*Quanto/Quanti?*
Why?	*Perché?*
It is/there is (is it/is there . . . ?)	*C'e . . . ?*
What time is it?	*Che ora è/Che ore sono?*
How do I get to . . . ?	*Come arrivo a . . . ?*
How far is it to . . . ?	*Cuant'è lontano a . . . ?*
Can you tell me when to get off?	*Mi può dire scendere alla fermata giusta?*
What time does it open?	*A che ora apre?*
What time does it close?	*A che ora chiude?*
How much does it cost (. . . do they cost?)	*Quanto costa? (. . . Quanto cóstano?)*
What's it called in Italian?	*Come si chiama in italiano?*

Food and drink

Basics and snacks

Aceto	Vinegar	*Olive*	Olives
Aglio	Garlic	*Pane*	Bread
Biscotti	Biscuits	*Pepe*	Pepper
Burro	Butter	*Riso*	Rice
Caramelle	Sweets	*Sale*	Salt
Cioccolato	Chocolate	*Uova*	Eggs
Formaggio	Cheese	*Yogurt*	Yoghurt
Frittata	Omelette	*Zúcchero*	Sugar
Marmellata	Jam	*Zuppa*	Soup
Olio	Oil		

The first course (*il primo*): soups, pasta . . .

Brodo	Clear broth
Farfalle	Butterfly-shaped pasta
Fettuccine	Narrow pasta ribbons
Gnocchi	Small potato and dough dumplings
Maccheroni	Macaroni (tubular pasta)
Minestrina	Clear broth with small pasta shapes
Minestrone	Thick vegetable soup
Pasta al forno	Pasta baked with minced meat, eggs, tomato and cheese
Pasta e fagioli	Pasta with beans
Pastina in brodo	Pasta pieces in clear broth
Penne	Smaller version of rigatoni
Rigatoni	Large, grooved tubular pasta
Risotto	Cooked rice dish, with sauce
Stracciatella	Broth with egg
Tagliatelle	Pasta ribbons, another word for fettucine
Tortellini	Rings of pasta, stuffed with meat or cheese
Vermicelli	Thin spaghetti ("little worms")

. . . and pasta sauce (*salsa*)

Amatriciana	Cubed bacon and tomato sauce
Arrabbiata	Spicy tomato sauce, with chillies ("Angry")
Bolognese	Meat sauce
Burro	Butter
Carbonara	Cream, ham and beaten egg
Funghi	Mushroom
Panna	Cream
Parmigiano	Parmesan cheese
Peperoncino	Olive oil, garlic and fresh chillies
Pesto	Sauce with ground basil, garlic and pine nuts
Pomodoro	Tomato sauce
Puttanesca	Tomato, anchovy, olive oil and oregano ("Whorish")
Ragù	Meat sauce
Vóngole	Sauce with clams

The second course (*il secondo*): meat (*carne*) . . .

Agnello	Lamb	*Salsiccia*	Sausage
Bistecca	Steak	*Saltimbocca*	Veal with ham
Carpaccio	Slices of raw beef	*Spezzatino*	Stew
Cervella	Brain, usually calves'	*Trippa*	Tripe
Cinghiale	Wild boar	*Vitello*	Veal
Coniglio	Rabbit		
Costolette	Cutlet, chop		
Fégato	Liver		
Maiale	Pork		
Manzo	Beef		
Ossobuco	Shin of veal		
Pancetta	Bacon		
Pollo	Chicken		
Polpette	Meatballs		
Rognoni	Kidneys		

continues . . .

FOOD AND DRINK

. . . fish (*pesce*) and shellfish (*crostacei*)

Acciughe	Anchovies
Anguilla	Eel
Aragosta	Lobster
Baccalà	Dried salted cod
Calamari	Squid
Céfalo	Grey mullet
Cozze	Mussels
Déntice	Sea Bream
Gamberetti	Shrimps
Gámberi	Prawns
Granchio	Crab
Merluzzo	Cod
Ostriche	Oysters
Pesce spada	Swordfish
Polpo	Octopus
Rospo	Monkfish
Sampiero	John Dory
Sarde	Sardines
Sógliola	Sole
Tonno	Tuna
Trota	Trout
Vóngole	Clams

Vegetables (*contorni*), herbs (*erbe aromatice*) and salad (*insalata*)

Asparagi	Asparagus
Carciofi	Artichokes
Carciofini	Artichoke hearts
Cavolfiori	Cauliflower
Cávolo	Cabbage
Cipolla	Onion
Fagioli	Beans

Fagiolini	Green beans
Finocchio	Fennel
Funghi	Mushrooms
Insalata verde/mista	Green salad/mixed salad
Lenticchie	Lentils
Melanzane	Aubergine
Patate	Potatoes
Peperoni	Peppers
Piselli	Peas
Pomodori	Tomatoes
Radicchio	Red salad leaves
Spinaci	Spinach

Some terms and useful words

Arrosto	Roast
Ben cotto	Well done
Bollito/lesso	Boiled
Alla braçe	Barbecued
Cotto	Cooked (not raw)
Crudo	Raw
Al dente	Firm, not overcooked
Al ferri	Grilled without oil
Al forno	Baked
Fritto	Fried
Alla griglia	Grilled
Alla milanese	Fried in egg and breadcrumbs
Pizzaiola	Cooked with tomato sauce
Ripieno	Stuffed
Al sangue	Rare
Allo spiedo	On the spit
Stracotto	Braised, stewed
In umido	Stewed

continues . . .

FOOD AND DRINK |

Sweets (*dolci*), fruit (*frutta*), cheeses (*formaggi*) and nuts (*noci*)

Amaretti	Macaroons
Ananas	Pineapple
Anguria/Coccómero	Watermelon
Arance	Oranges
Banane	Bananas
Cacchi	Persimmons
Ciliegie	Cherries
Dolcelatte	Creamy blue cheese
Fichi	Figs
Fichi d'India	Prickly pears
Fontina	Northern Italian cheese, often used in cooking
Frágole	Strawberries
Gelato	Ice cream
Gorgonzola	Soft, strong, blue-veined cheese
Limone	Lemon
Macedonia	Fruit salad
Mándorle	Almonds
Mele	Apples
Melone	Melon
Mozzarella	Soft white cheese, traditionally made from buffalo's milk
Pecorino	Strong, hard sheep's cheese
Pere	Pears
Pesche	Peaches
Pignoli	Pine nuts
Pistacchio	Pistachio nut
Provola/ Provolone	Smooth, round mild cheese, made from buffalo or sheep's milk. Sometimes smoked
Ricotta	Soft, white sheep's cheese
Torta	Cake, tart

Uva	Grapes
Zabaglione	Dessert made with eggs, sugar and marsala wine
Zuppa Inglese	Trifle

Drinks

Acqua minerale	Mineral water
Aranciata	Orangeade
Bicchiere	Glass
Birra	Beer
Bottiglia	Bottle
Caffè	Coffee
Cioccolata calda	Hot chocolate
Ghiaccio	Ice
Granita	Iced drink, with coffee or fruit
Latte	Milk
Limonata	Lemonade
Selz	Soda water
Spremuta	Fresh fruit juice
Spumante	Sparkling wine
Succo	Concentrated fruit juice with sugar
Tè	Tea
Tónica	Tonic water
Vino	Wine
Rosso	Red
Bianco	White
Rosato	Rosé
Secco	Dry
Dolce	Sweet
Litro	Litre
Mezzo	Half
Quarto	Quarter
Caraffa	Carafe
Salute!	Cheers!

FOOD AND DRINK |

INDEX

R

S

Stay in touch with us!

ROUGHNEWS** is Rough Guides' free newsletter.
In four issues a year we give you news, travel issues, music reviews, readers' letters and the latest dispatches from authors on the road.

ROUGH GUIDES: Travel

ROUGH GUIDES: Mini Guides, Travel Specials and Phrasebooks

MINI GUIDES

Antigua
Bangkok
Barbados
Big Island of Hawaii
Boston
Brussels
Budapest
Dublin
Edinburgh
Florence
Honolulu
Lisbon
London Restaurants
Madrid
Maui
Melbourne
New Orleans
St Lucia

Seattle
Sydney
Tokyo
Toronto

TRAVEL SPECIALS

First-Time Asia
First-Time Europe
More Women Travel

PHRASEBOOKS

Czech
Dutch
Egyptian Arabic
European
French

German
Greek
Hindi & Urdu
Hungarian
Indonesian
Italian
Japanese
Mandarin
  Chinese
Mexican
  Spanish
Polish
Portuguese
Russian
Spanish
Swahili
Thai
Turkish
Vietnamese

AVAILABLE AT ALL GOOD BOOKSHOPS

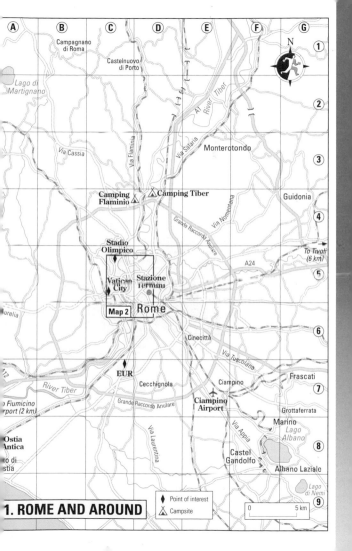

1. ROME AND AROUND

◆ Point of interest
△ Campsite

0 ——————— 5 km

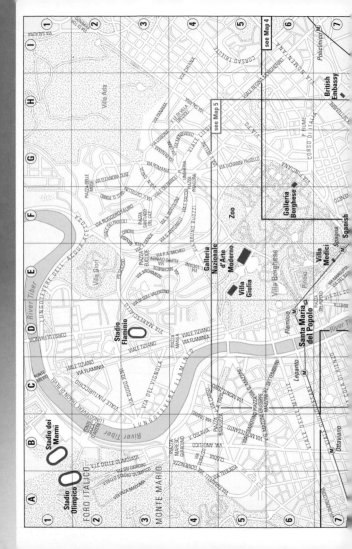

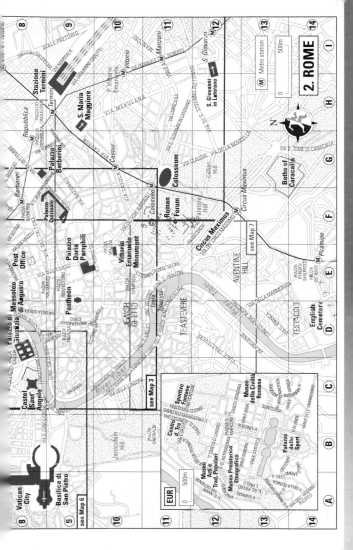

2. ROME

(M) Metro station

0   500m

VIALE PRETORIO

VALE CASTRENSE

Stazione Termini

S. Maria Maggiore

VIA MERULANA

S. Giovanni in Laterano

Repubblica

(M) Termini

VIA CAVOUR

Palazzo Barberini

(M) Barberini

Palazzo Quirinale

(M) Colosseo

Colosseum

Roman Forum

Palatine Hill

Celio Hill

VIA CLAUDIA

VIA DELLA NAVICELLA

VIA DI TERME DI CARACALLA

Baths of Caracalla

N

Palazzo Doria Pamphilii

Vittorio Emanuele Monument

Post Office

Pantheon

JEWISH GHETTO

Tiberina

Circus Maximus

(M) Circo Massimo

AVENTINE HILL

see Map 7

Castel Sant'Angelo

Palazzo di Giustizia

Mausoleo di Augusto

River Tiber

TRASTEVERE

see Map 3

TESTACCIO

English Cemetery

(M) Piramide

Vatican City

Basilica di San Pietro

see Map 6

Janiculum Hill

PIAZZA GARIBALDI

EUR

0   500m

Museo d'Arte e Trad. Popolari

Centro Sportivo d. Tre Fontane

Museo della Civiltà Romana

Museo Preistorico Etnografico

Palazzo dello Sport

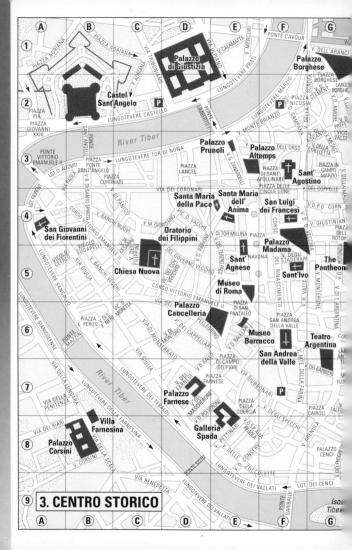

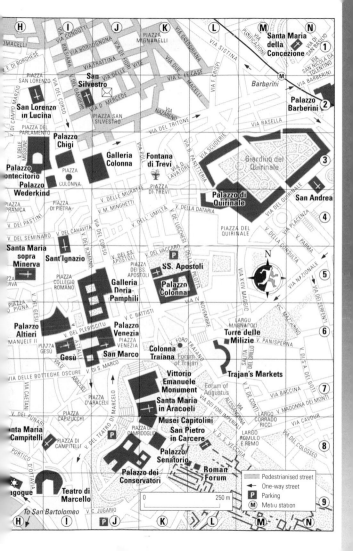

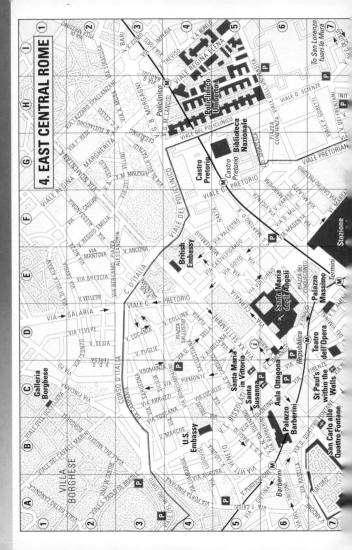

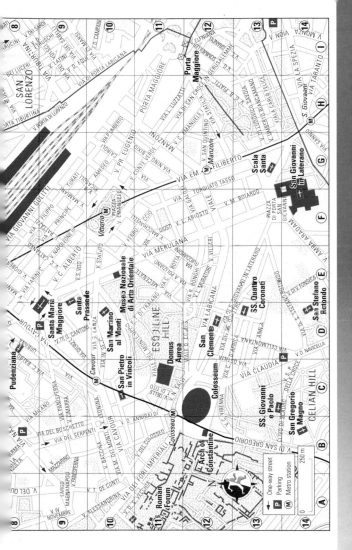

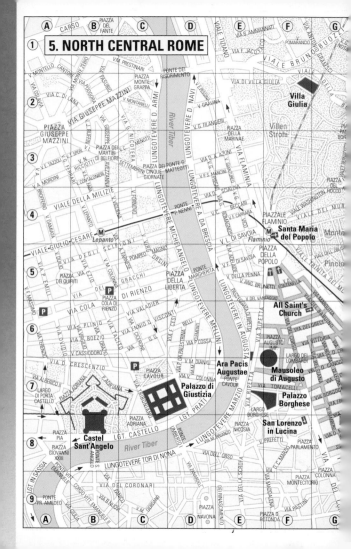

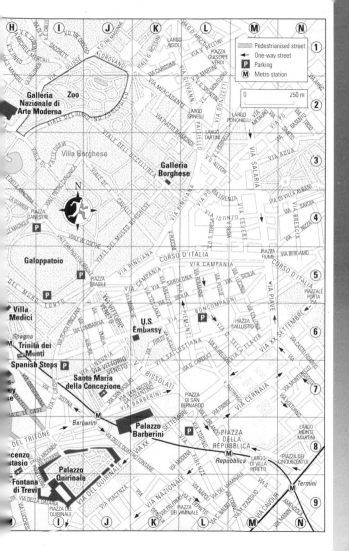

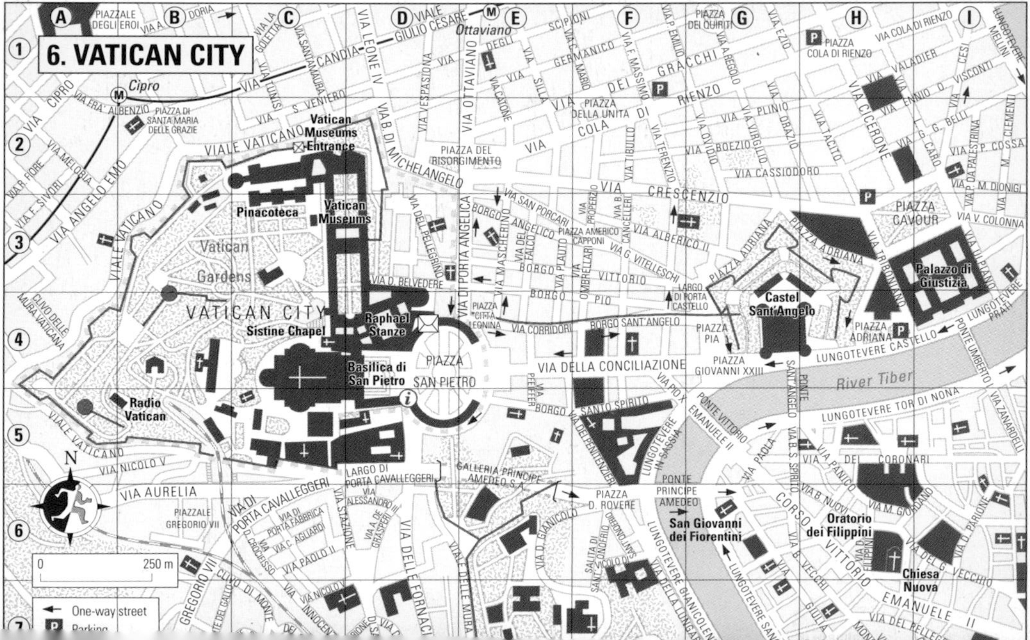
6. VATICAN CITY
Vatican Museums Entrance
Vatican Museums
Pinacoteca
Vatican Gardens
VATICAN CITY
Sistine Chapel
Raphael Stanze
Basilica di San Pietro
PIAZZA SAN PIETRO
Radio Vatican
Castel Sant'Angelo
Palazzo di Giustizia
River Tiber
San Giovanni dei Fiorentini
Oratorio dei Filippini
Chiesa Nuova
Ottaviano
Cipro
VIA DELLA CONCILIAZIONE
VIA CRESCENZIO
VIA COLA DI RIENZO
VIALE GIULIO CESARE
VIA OTTAVIANO
VIA DI PORTA ANGELICA
VIALE VATICANO
VIA AURELIA
CORSO VITTORIO EMANUELE II
LUNGOTEVERE CASTELLO
PIAZZA CAVOUR
PIAZZA DEL RISORGIMENTO
0 250 m
One-way street
Parking

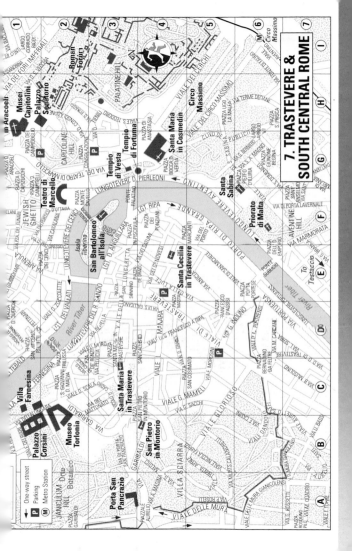

Map labels:

- VIA D. BACCINA
- VIA DEI FORI IMPERIALI
- LARGO CORRADO RICCI
- Musei Capitolini
- in Aracoeli
- Palazzo Senatorio
- Roman Forum
- PALATINE HILL
- VIALE DEI CERCHI
- Circo Massimo
- Circo Massimo Ⓜ
- VIA DEI FORI IMPERIALI
- PIAZZA D'ARACOELI
- PIAZZA DE CAMPIDOGLIO
- CAPITOLINE HILL
- VIA DEL TEATRO DI MARCELLO
- Teatro di Marcello
- Tempio di Vesta
- PIAZZA DI ANASTASIO
- Santa Maria in Cosmedin
- VIA DI S. TEODORO
- CLIVO DE' PUBLICII
- PIAZZA DELLA CONSOLAZIONE
- Tempio di Fortuna
- PIAZZA BOCCA DELLA VERITÀ
- LARGO G. MAGNANI
- PIAZZA DI PORTA CAPENA
- LA MALFA
- PIAZZA DELLE TERME DECIANE
- JEWISH GHETTO
- VIA CATALANA
- LUNGOTEVERE DE' CENCI
- PONTE FABRICIO
- Isola Tiberina
- LGT. D. ANGUILLARA
- LUNGOTEVERE DEI PIERLEONI
- Santa Sabina
- PIAZZA PIETRO D'ILLIRIA
- AVENTINE HILL
- VIA DI SANT'ALBERTO MAGNO
- San Bartolomeo all'Isola
- LGT RIPA
- PIAZZA DEI PONZIANI
- Priorato di Malta
- VIA DI PORTA LAVERNALE
- LUNGOTEVERE RIPA
- LUNGOTEVERE DI RIPA GRANDE
- PORTO DI RIPA GRANDE
- PIAZZA IN PISCINULA
- Santa Cecilia in Trastevere
- PIAZZA DEI MERCANTI
- VIA MARMORATA
- PIAZZA DELL'EMPORIO
- River Tiber
- Villa Farnesina
- Palazzo Corsini
- Museo Torlonia
- Santa Maria in Trastevere
- San Pietro in Montorio
- Porta San Pancrazio
- VIALE DI TRASTEVERE
- VIALE GLORIOSO
- VIALE G. MAMELI
- To Testaccio
- River Tiber
- JANICULUM HILL / Botanical Garden
- PIAZZA GARIBALDI
- VIALE DELLE MURA

Legend:

- → One-way street
- P Parking
- Ⓜ Metro Station

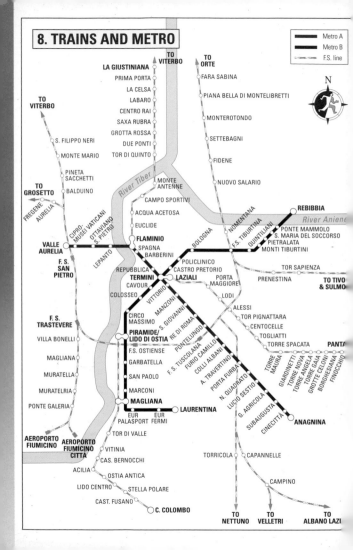